CHEAP MODERNISM

Edinburgh Critical Studies in Modernist Culture
Series Editors: Tim Armstrong and Rebecca Beasley

Available

Modernism and Magic: Experiments with Spiritualism, Theosophy and the Occult
Leigh Wilson

Sonic Modernity: Representing Sound in Literature, Culture and the Arts
Sam Halliday

Modernism and the Frankfurt School
Tyrus Miller

Lesbian Modernism: Censorship, Sexuality and Genre Fiction
Elizabeth English

Modern Print Artefacts: Textual Materiality and Literary Value in British Print Culture, 1890–1930s
Patrick Collier

Cheap Modernism: Expanding Markets, Publishers' Series and the Avant-Garde
Lise Jaillant

Forthcoming

Modernism, Space and the City
Andrew Thacker

Slow Modernism
Laura Salisbury

Primordial Modernism: Animals, Ideas, Transition (1927–1938)
Cathryn Setz

Modernism and the Idea of Everyday Life
Leena Kore-Schröder

Modernism Edited: Marianne Moore and The Dial *Magazine*
Victoria Bazin

Modernism and Mathematics: Modernist Interrelations in Fiction
Nina Engelhardt

Portable Modernisms: The Art of Travelling Light
Emily Ridge

Visit our website at: edinburghuniversitypress.com/series/ecsmc

CHEAP MODERNISM

Expanding Markets, Publishers' Series and the Avant-Garde

Lise Jaillant

EDINBURGH
University Press

Edinburgh University Press is one of the leading university presses in the UK. We publish academic books and journals in our selected subject areas across the humanities and social sciences, combining cutting-edge scholarship with high editorial and production values to produce academic works of lasting importance. For more information visit our website: edinburghuniversitypress.com

Edinburgh University Press Ltd
The Tun – Holyrood Road, 12(2f) Jackson's Entry, Edinburgh EH8 8PJ

Typeset in 10/12.5 Sabon by
Servis Filmsetting Ltd, Stockport, Cheshire,
and printed and bound in Great Britain by
CPI Group (UK) Ltd, Croydon CR0 4YY

A CIP record for this book is available from the British Library

ISBN 978 1 4744 1724 2 (hardback)
ISBN 978 1 4744 1725 9 (webready PDF)
ISBN 978 1 4744 1726 6 (epub)

Published with the support of the University of Edinburgh Scholarly Publishing Initiatives Fund.

CONTENTS

LIST OF FIGURES AND PLATES

The Plates can be found between pages 148 and 149.

ACKNOWLEDGEMENTS

The research for this book was made possible by two one-year fellowships: an IHR (Institute of Historical Research) fellowship funded by the Andrew W. Mellon Foundation in 2012–13; and a postdoctoral fellowship from the Alexander von Humboldt Foundation in 2014–15. In April 2014, a James Joyce Fellowship (funded by the UB Humanities Institute, in collaboration with the UB Libraries) allowed me to work in the Joyce collection at the University at Buffalo Library, New York State. In summer 2014, I was able to spend two months at the Harry Ransom Center in Austin, Texas, thanks to the Alfred A. and Blanche W. Knopf Fellowship and the Andrew W. Mellon Foundation. In London, I benefited from a Visiting Fellowship at the Institute of English Studies (2013–14 and 2014–15). I am very grateful for this support.

I also want to thank colleagues who have read and commented on sections of the typescript: William S. Brockman, Mary Hammond, Wim Van Mierlo, Nathan Waddell, Nicola Wilson and Claire Battershill. John Xiros Cooper, my former doctoral adviser, has also been very helpful.

Finally, I am grateful to the editors of the series Edinburgh Critical Studies in Modernist Culture, Rebecca Beasley and Tim Armstrong.

Earlier versions of two chapters have appeared in other publications: '"Introductions by eminent writers": T. S. Eliot and Virginia Woolf in the Oxford World's Classics Series', in *The Book World: Selling and Distributing Literature, 1900–1940* (Leiden: Brill, 2016), edited by Nicola Wilson; and

'Rewriting *Tarr* Ten Years Later: Wyndham Lewis, the Phoenix Library and the Domestication of Modernism', in *Journal of Wyndham Lewis Studies*, 5 (2014), 1–30. This article won the 2014 Wyndham Lewis Memorial Trust Essay Prize.

I am grateful to the editors for permission to reproduce these essays here.

SERIES EDITORS' PREFACE

This series of monographs on selected topics in modernism is designed to reflect and extend the range of new work in modernist studies. The studies in the series aim for a breadth of scope and for an expanded sense of the canon of modernism, rather than focusing on individual authors. Literary texts will be considered in terms of contexts including recent cultural histories (modernism and magic; sonic modernity; media studies) and topics of theoretical interest (the everyday; postmodernism; the Frankfurt School); but the series will also reconsider more familiar routes into modernism (modernism and gender; sexuality; politics). The works published will be attentive to the various cultural, intellectual and historical contexts of British, American and European modernisms, and to interdisciplinary possibilities within modernism, including performance and the visual and plastic arts.

LIST OF ABBREVIATIONS

CW Archives of Chatto & Windus, University of Reading
GR Archives of Grant Richards, 1897–1948 (Cambridge: Chadwyck-Healey, 1979), Microform
HP Archives of the Hogarth Press, University of Reading
HRC Harry Ransom Center, University of Texas at Austin
JC Archives of Jonathan Cape Ltd, University of Reading
JMD J. M. Dent & Sons Records, University of North Carolina at Chapel Hill
OUP Archives of the Oxford University Press, Oxford
UB University at Buffalo, NY

INTRODUCTION:
DISCOVERING MODERNISM – TRAVEL, PLEASURE AND PUBLISHERS' SERIES

Cheap Modernism: Expanding Markets, Publishers' Series and the Avant-Garde is the first study of European uniform reprint series that widened the market for modernist texts (or rather, texts that literary scholars now see as 'modernist'). We often think of *Mrs Dalloway* or *A Portrait of the Artist as a Young Man* as difficult books, originally published in small print runs for a handful of readers. But from the mid-1920s, these texts and others were available in a cheap format across Europe. Series of reprints such as the Travellers' Library, the Phoenix Library, Tauchnitz and Albatross sold modernism to a wide audience – thus transforming a little-read 'highbrow' movement into a mainstream phenomenon. By 'wide audience', I mean thousands of readers – much less than a mass-market readership, but much more than the small coteries that had read texts by Virginia Woolf, James Joyce and others in their original context of publication. Readers also encountered 'modernist' works alongside 'popular' literature, including detective fiction. The expansion of the readership for modernism was not only vertical (from 'high' to 'low') but also spatial – since publishers' series were distributed within and outside metropolitan centres in Britain, continental Europe and elsewhere. Many non-English native speakers discovered modernist texts in the original language – a fact that has been mentioned rarely in histories of modernism.

In a recent review essay, Ann Ardis notes that the field of modernist studies has been deeply transformed by the study of 'modernist print culture'. She gives the example of Peter Brooker and Andrew Thacker's three-volume

Oxford Critical and Cultural History of Modernist Magazines. For Ardis, this ambitious project is 'like the tip of an iceberg':

> the visible top mass of an even more massive body of related scholarship that is changing the way we think about the history of literary modernism's first emergence in a publishing ecosystem that was far richer, and far more complexly diversified, than the first several generations of bibliographic scholarship on modernism recognized, given the latter's exclusive focus on noncommercial little magazines, assumptions about the culture industry, and hagiographic stance toward 'the men of 1914'.[1]

It is certainly true that the rise of periodical studies has led to fascinating studies of little magazines – including influential digital projects such as the Modernist Journals Project.

Nearly two decades after Lawrence Rainey's *Institutions of Modernism*, the definition of 'institution' has also widened to include not only small presses and non-commercial magazines but also large-scale enterprises, such as mass-market magazines. At the 2015 Modernist Studies Association conference, for instance, a panel on the interwar fashion press featured papers on the British *Vogue*, *Harper's Bazaar* and *Eve: The Lady's Pictorial*.[2] Surveying the field of modern periodical studies, Patrick Collier notes 'the impressive range of periodicals':

> While a substantial number of the periodicals that appear as main foci of essays [published in the *Journal of Modern Periodical Studies*] could be aptly described as modernist or avant-garde, the list also includes newspapers such as the *Illustrated London News*, and mass-market magazines such as the *New Yorker*, *Esquire*, and *Scribners*, as well as the respectable political weekly *The Nation and Athenaeum*, and the aforementioned *PMLA* and *Mother Earth*.[3]

Collier points out that 'literary modernism, and particularly the values of avant-garde aesthetics and political radicalism congenial to the "New Modernisms", remain the leading conceptual frameworks through which periodicals of the early twentieth century are viewed'.[4] Even when scholars focus on apparently non-modernist artefacts, they continue to refer to modernism as an overall framework. For Collier, 'there is a more urgent need for mapping the much larger, nonmodernist locales of the vast landscape of early twentieth-century print culture than for filling in the blank spots on the already well-sketched map of modernism'.[5]

I find it problematic that 'print culture' often refers exclusively to periodicals, while other printed forms are neglected. Many scholars continue to focus on modernism's *first* emergence, and on periodicals rather than book publishers. We know much more about the *Egoist* magazine, which serialised Wyndham Lewis's *Tarr* in 1916–17, than about the Phoenix Library, which issued a cheap edition of the novel in 1928. And yet, Lewis entirely rewrote the novel especially for this edition, with the hope of appealing to a larger readership. In *Re-Covering Modernism* (2009), David Earle pointed out the lack of scholarship on 'reprint magazines and literary digests, reprint and circulating library hardback editions, pulp magazines, and paperbacks'.[6] For Earle, the 'academic prejudice of form' leads to an overemphasis on first editions and little magazines, and to the neglect of later, more popular forms of publication.[7] This has on impact on institutional archives, which have not traditionally collected printed materials that made 'modernism' available to the masses. As Earle puts it, there is a 'reciprocal relationship between the academy and the literary archives, that is, what is archived is that which is worth studying and what academia deems worth studying is that which is in the archives'.[8] While Earle's focus is mainly on mass-market magazines and post-Second World War paperbacks, the same observation is true for interwar series of reprints. With the exception of the British Library which holds the Tauchnitz collection, complete runs of reprint series are rare. I often relied on collectors and websites such as AbeBooks to get copies of dust jackets, which can seldom be found in university archives and libraries. I also started my own collections – thus imitating periodical scholars who have had to grapple with similar problems.[9]

Why should we pay attention to cheap reprint series? Why should university archives spend some of their limited resources collecting and cataloguing these series? And why should scholars spend time studying the Travellers' Library, the Phoenix Library and other similar publishing enterprises? One way to answer these questions is to look at authors. As the chapters in this book show, writers frequently contributed to the reprinting process. They often approached publishers directly, chose the physical format of their books and even revised their texts to target the mainstream audience reached by these cheap series. Moreover, reprint series shaped the reading experience of vast audiences in Europe and the rest of the world. These collections expanded the cultural horizon of readers who might have heard of Joyce and Lewis, but could not put their hands on the original editions (either because first editions were too expensive or were out of print). Since cheap series published difficult modernist works alongside all kinds of other texts, even readers who had never heard of the new literature could encounter books by Woolf, Joyce and others on display shelves in bookstores. These series had an important impact on the diffusion of a major literary movement, which has often been associated exclusively with small presses and little magazines.

The focus on original publication and first editions is deeply engrained not only in modernist studies, but also in bibliography and book history.[10] In a chapter of *The Cambridge Companion to the History of the Book*, Michael F. Suarez explains that degressive bibliographies are organised according to a numbering system that allows readers to trace the publication history of a text. In the original edition of Kirkpatrick's bibliography of Virginia Woolf, for example, 'A' represents the general category 'books and pamphlets'. A9 is the heading for *Mrs Dalloway*, so A9a is the first edition published by the Hogarth Press in 1925; A9b the first American edition (Harcourt Brace, 1925); A9c the re-impression issued by the Modern Library (1928); A9d the photo-offset reprint part of the Hogarth Press Uniform Edition (1929), and so on. Suarez points out that:

> degression typically (but not inevitably) means that, although the bibliographical details provided for the early printings of a work are as complete as possible, less bibliographical information is included for subsequent printings. The result, whether intended or not, is that later iterations of a work seem to be less important.[11]

As in the case of archives, what is in bibliographies is that which is worth studying and what academia deems worth studying is that which is in bibliographies. As Suarez notes, *Raymond Chandler: A Descriptive Bibliography* (1979) by Matthew Bruccoli has triggered a wave of new studies on this popular writer. The relationship goes both ways. In other words, 'Bruccoli's bibliography both reflected and contributed to an important book-historical phenomenon: the growing marketplace in the late 1960s and 1970s for collecting popular American literature and culture.'[12] There are few bibliographies of entire publishers' series, which partly explains the traditional lack of studies on these series.[13] For the Travellers' Library, New Adelphi Library, Phoenix Library and Albatross Modern Continental Library, I created bibliographical spreadsheets based on information in various catalogues and on the copies I examined in archives, libraries and my own collection. In her monograph on the New Canadian Library, Janet Friskney included an appendix with the list of titles published in this series. I have chosen not to do that here for practical reasons: my focus is on multiple series, and complete lists of titles would take up too much space. However, the rise of 'modernist print culture' as a research field highlights the need for a renewal of bibliographical tools. Too often, we have to rely on bibliographies that first appeared in print several decades ago. We need new bibliographical studies easily accessible on digital platforms, which would provide details on various publication venues – including mass-market magazines, hardback reprint series and paperbacks.

Not all older bibliographies privilege first editions. When Kirkpatrick's book was first published in 1957, the *Times Literary Supplement* reviewer claimed that it contained too much detail about later editions of Woolf's works:

Some bibliographically unimportant uniform and cheap editions receive what may seem undue prominence: for example, the value of a full collation of an American issue of *To the Lighthouse*, as published (with unchanged text) in a popular series twenty-two years after it first appeared, is perhaps doubtful.[14]

The fact that Kirkpatrick treated later editions seriously has been very useful for my own scholarship. For instance, she obtained the sales figures of the Modern Library editions of *Mrs Dalloway* and *To the Lighthouse*, probably from Random House.[15]

The Modern Library, a cheap series created in New York in 1917, was the focus of my first book, *Modernism, Middlebrow and the Literary Canon*. Bennett Cerf and Donald Klopfer, who bought the series from Horace Liveright in 1925, had international ambitions. However, copyright laws made it difficult for them to sell the Modern Library in Britain and their various attempts to find distributors came to nothing. In 1926, when the Modern Library issued James Joyce's *Dubliners*, it did not compete directly with the Travellers' Library edition published that same year in the United Kingdom. What is striking is that commercial publishers all over the world became interested in literary modernism at around the same time, in the mid- to late 1920s. A literary movement that had been confined to confidential venues was now available in cheap form and became a global commercial hit. The Modern Library was sold in the United States and Canada but also in South America, continental Europe and the Far East. British publishers distributed their series in the whole Empire and dominions. Resistance to the domination of the German publisher Tauchnitz on the Continent shows that international trade competition was often fierce.

The expansion of modernist studies has emphasised the sheer range of texts that falls within the category 'modernism' to the point of testing that category's limits. In my previous monograph, I argued that in the interwar period, the Modern Library blurred the boundary between 'modernism' and 'popular' literature. All the books had the same physical format, were advertised in the same periodicals, and reviewed at the same time. After the Second World War, with the rise of a new generation of American critics determined to separate 'highbrow' literature and mass culture, the Modern Library was increasingly seen as a debased commercial enterprise. By 'modernism,' then, I mean the literature of the early twentieth century, which addressed the social, economic and technological changes of that time. Although I focus mainly on Anglophone moderns, texts in translation were also included in publishers' series – thus contributing to their impact outside their countries of origins. For example, the Phoenix Library reprinted Marcel Proust's multi-volume *In Search of Lost Time*, creating interesting parallels with other titles in the series.

A reader in 1929 could go to a bookshop and find the two volumes of *Swann's Way* (#32 and 33), Clive Bell's *Since Cézanne* (#41) as well as Lewis's *Tarr* (#27). These titles offered insight on the modern movement in France, and its influence on Anglophone artists.

With the expansion of the canon to include a wide range of writers who responded to the condition of modernity, the distinction between 'modernism' and 'avant-garde' has disintegrated to the point where the two words are often taken to be quasi-synonyms. In this book, I reserve the term 'avant-garde' to the more radical forms of modernism. While the first version of *Tarr*, with its experimental style and controversial topic, belonged to the avant-garde, the version revised for the Phoenix Library had lost its most original stylistic aspects. In the 1920s, commercial publishers realised that texts initially perceived as radical could be sold to mainstream readers in cheap series.

THE RISE OF CHEAP REPRINT SERIES

In a 1946 article on the World's Classics series, Edmund Blunden gave a short summary of the rise of cheap reprint series in the nineteenth century. 'We must leave the full history of the subject to the industrious bibliographer', he added.[16] Such a history has never been written, in part because of the huge number of series issued during the second part of the century. But Victorianists such as Richard Altick and, more recently, Leslie Howsam, Jonathan Rose and Mary Hammond, have offered invaluable insight on 'sustained literary ventures' as the *Publishers' Circular* called them. For Howsam, 'a series may be defined as a named, sometimes numbered, group of books with a common theme, usually with uniform binding, and often uniformly priced, appearing under a general title'.[17] I would add that this 'common theme' is a marketing category constructed by the publisher. For instance, many series emphasised the notion of travel, which could be interpreted broadly as physical travel or travels of the mind. The coherence of a series was created by a uniform physical format and common marketing strategy, rather than by its list of titles.

The popularity of cheap series can be traced to an important change in copyright law at the end of the eighteenth century. As Altick points out, 'the momentous decision in *Donaldson v. Becket* (1774) ... killed the legal fiction of perpetual copyright'.[18] The case opposed Alexander Donaldson, a Scottish bookseller who sold cheap reprints, to a group of London booksellers and printers who accused him of having pirated their intellectual property. Donaldson claimed that under the Statute of Anne (1710), a work was freely available once the term of the copyright had expired. But for his opponents, it was a common-law right, therefore perpetual. Donaldson's victory led to a sharp increase in the number of reprints, beginning with John Bell's series 'Poets of Great Britain'.

Cheap prices were made possible by access to non-copyrighted texts but also by technological changes that deeply affected the publishing industry in the nineteenth century. Altick cites 'the use of steam-driven presses', 'the introduction of paper-making machines', which decreased the price of paper, 'the substitution of esparto and chemical woodpulp for expensive rags', and 'the invention of machine-made casings to replace hand-sewed bindings'.[19] These inventions made the production of books easier, faster and cheaper. Campaigners also insisted that education should not be the preserve of an elite, leading to the creation of mechanics' institutes and free libraries and to the 1855 repeal of the paper tax. Publishers marketed their books to aspirational readers, eager to self-educate and build their own libraries.

Not all publishers' series pretended to educate readers. Some, like Routledge's Railway Library, sold books with lurid covers to attract customers with the promise of mildly titillating entertainment. As Hammond notes, 'their brightly-coloured pocket-sized reprints, jammed with small print and adverts and sporting a dramatic illustration on the front cover, for decades enlivened the bookstalls and labelled them as cheap and cheerful, if . . . slightly shady'.[20] Born in 1849, the Railway Library was a long-lasting success: when it came to an end in 1898, it numbered nearly 1,300 volumes.

By the 1880s and 1890s, cheap series had become particularly significant and visible. Hammond argues that these *fin-de-siècle* series were rather different from their mid-century predecessors: 'the lurid sensationalism and cheapness of the railway reprint of a particular novel had become, in the hands of the right publisher, a sober, edifying and plain little book with a quite different emphasis'.[21] Soberly packaged series of classics were nothing new, but their renewed popularity is partly due to changing legislation on education. In 1880, school attendance became compulsory for all children until the age of ten, opening up new markets. Prices decreased sharply with the launch of W. T. Stead's Penny Poets and Penny Popular Novels in 1895–6. As Jonathan Rose notes, 'Stead proved that the demand for cheap classic reprints was enormous: by October 1897 there were sixty volumes of Penny Poets with 5,276,000 copies in print, and about 9 million copies of ninety Penny Novels.'[22]

The diversity of publishers' series meant that all kinds of books were presented as 'classics'. In order to establish a list of series, Altick excluded those that consisted mainly of contemporary texts, since only the passage of time could determine if a book was a classic or not. This is of course problematic, as Altick himself recognised: 'Obviously some books become established classics even within the lifetime of their authors, as did the novels of Scott and Dickens and the poetry of Byron and Tennyson, so that the demarcation between classics and recent books of evidently lasting popularity is vague indeed.'[23] Writing half a century later, Hammond gave a much broader definition: 'a book is a "classic" almost wholly because a particular publisher says it is'.[24] In other words, 'classic' is a marketing category used to target readers who value advice on what to read.

The explosion of cheap series was not limited to Britain. In *L'invention de la collection* (1999), Isabelle Olivero shed light on the popularity of inexpensive, small-format series in nineteenth-century France. She gave the example of the Bibliothèque Charpentier, created in 1838, which experimented with new practices including percentage royalties for authors. While the series had initially focused on contemporary texts by romantic writers, reprints dominated its list from the mid-1840s. The Bibliothèque nationale had a less elitist image. Made by and for working-class people, it contributed to the change in reading habits, including the transition from renting to buying books. French publishers also followed their foreign competitors closely. For instance, Louis Hachette imitated W. H. Smith by selling reprint series in his railway station vending kiosks.[25]

In Germany, Leipzig publishing houses such as Reclam and Tauchnitz launched cheap paperbound series in the mid-nineteenth-century. Created in 1867, Reclam's Universal-Bibliothek published thousands of titles – a wide scope which later inspired the British publisher J. M. Dent for his Everyman's Library. The firm of Christian Bernhard Tauchnitz started publishing books in 1837 and issued its first English edition in 1841. Only thirty-two volumes appeared during the following year, notes William Todd, 'but that number was to grow enormously until his firm could declare, in 1937, a total output of 5,290 volumes of English and American authors, or, on the average, about one every week over the preceding century'.[26] Tauchnitz launched its Collection of British and American Authors just before the establishment of an international copyright system. As Simon Nowell-Smith points out, 'under the act of 1844 Britain signed conventions with several German states in the forties, and under the act of 1852 with France, Belgium, Spain and other German states in the fifties, and with the States of Sardinia in 1861'.[27] From the start, Tauchnitz paid a lump sum to authors for the permission to reprint their texts on the Continent. This enabled the firm to establish good relationships with prominent writers, whose work was frequently pirated. For example, Dickens trusted Tauchnitz enough to send him his son Charley for a few months to learn German.

Education was at the core of the Tauchnitz brand, a brand that can be seen as 'middlebrow'. In 1886, the firm launched the Students' Tauchnitz Editions, which included texts in English, explanatory notes and a vocabulary list. In the late 1920s, this series published modern fiction by John Galsworthy, H. G. Wells, Arnold Bennett and Oscar Wilde, as well as G. K. Chesterton's collection of detective stories *The Innocence of Father Brown*. For students and other Tauchnitz readers, the series offered an opportunity to combine pleasure with education, to improve their language skills while reading exciting texts. Following Janice Radway, Joan Shelley Rubin and others, Faye Hammill and Michelle Smith have shown that 'self-improvement is the central ideal of middlebrow culture'.[28] Yet, the term 'middlebrow' is often used in a derogatory way, to designate a person or a thing that tries and fails to achieve high cultural standards. On 23 December 1925, the magazine *Punch* declared: 'The B.B.C. claim to have discovered a new type, the "middlebrow". It consists of people who are hoping that some day they will get used to the stuff they ought to like.'[29] With the rise of 'middlebrow' studies, scholars have used the term to designate the formal characteristics of texts with popular appeal and intellectual pretensions.[30] Others think it refers more clearly to a position in the literary field between 'high' and 'low' culture.[31] Tauchnitz, like many publishers' series, can be seen as a 'middlebrow' institution that mediated between various cultural levels. It included a wide range of texts, without making distinctions between titles on its list. In 1939, for example, Woolf's *Mrs Dalloway* and *Orlando* appeared among its '500 Best Titles' alongside *The Squeaker*, a mass-market crime novel by Edgar Wallace. Readers were encouraged to read as many Tauchnitz titles as possible, from high modernism to popular fiction.

The paperback format of Tauchnitz books made them easy to carry, thus reinforcing associations with travel and cosmopolitanism. Geographical mobility was linked to upward mobility. When George Eliot refused to allow her novel *Felix Holt* to be reprinted in Leipzig, she found in 'society' in Paris a 'deep regret' that the book was not in the Tauchnitz collection, 'the only medium by which the English text of English novels can get known on the continent'.[32] Tauchnitz books were read by the elite, and by large audiences who aspired to emulate the sophisticated lifestyle of those who frequently travelled and spoke several languages. With the development of modern transportation systems and the decrease in travel costs, tourism became a widespread middle-class activity. As Hammill and Smith have noted in their study of Canadian magazines, 'travel, in the earlier twentieth century, was a symbol of achievement, cultural literacy, *savoir faire*, and personal means'. This highlights the 'close connections between travel and the aspirational culture of the middle-brow'.[33] Other publishers' series made this association explicit in their title (the Travellers' Library) or advertisements.

CHEAP BOOKS AFTER THE NET BOOK AGREEMENT

Tauchnitz books appealed particularly to British tourists, who found it difficult to buy cheap, contemporary texts at home. The Net Book Agreement (1900) was designed to avoid price wars, as publishers and booksellers agreed on a fixed price at which books were to be sold to the public. The first challenge to this system came from *The Times*. In the early years of the twentieth century, the newspaper was in serious financial difficulties and a new manager, Charles

Frederic Moberley Bell, was appointed to revive its fortunes. As John Feather points out, Bell's plans 'included the *Times Literary Supplement*, one of his abiding successes, and The Times Book Club, which almost brought total disaster'.[34] Launched in 1905 for all subscribers, the Club was both a circulating library and a postal bookseller. Members could borrow books but also buy, at a discounted price, books that had previously been used as lending copies. 'In practice virtually new books were thus made available for public sale at huge discounts on their net prices', notes Feather.[35] This infuriated the trade and from October 1906, publishers refused to supply books to *The Times*.

The newspaper responded with a campaign to denounce the high price of books, appealing to its readers to send their own opinions. 'The fight of The Times Book Club is a fight for cheap literature', declared one letter signed 'A FREE TRADER'. 'I venture to predict that you will win, and the effect of your action in resisting this outrageous attempt to keep up the price of books will probably extend far beyond what is foreseen.'[36] One author encouraged British publishers to adopt the continental model of binding books in paper as a way to decrease prices:

> The French publishers are able to supply the public with good literary works at the price of 3f. 50c. per volume, often with maps – a price which presumably pays both themselves and the author. Cannot this be done in England? If the cloth binding is an obstacle, let it go; if our readers like our books, they will get them bound themselves; covers like those of the Tauchnitz volumes are good enough.[37]

This letter exemplifies readers' awareness of the continental book trade. Compared to France or Germany, Britain seemed to lag behind with its hardcover books sold for a fixed price. Another letter signed 'GLUE-BRUSH' shows the viewpoint of a worker in the book industry:

> I am merely a journeyman bookbinder, but I think I am as well qualified to express an opinion anent the above as certain journalists who will dogmatize with assurance, if not with knowledge, upon any subject under the sun. I am 31 years of age, and as far back as I can remember you could get a 6s. novel for 4s. 6d. To-day the price remains the same.

He went on to explain that technological changes had made the production of books much cheaper:

> Up till six or seven years ago we were able to get a fair living, but suddenly a large number of labour-saving machines appeared. To mention a few, we have the rounder and backer, the case-making machine, and lately the pasting-down machine. The rate of book producing is now enormously increased at greatly reduced cost.

If the number of books sold remained the same, many workers were no longer needed and struggled to find work:

> Therefore to keep us in work it is vitally necessary that more – much more – books be sold. But, owing to the policy of the publishers in keeping up the prices, no larger editions of new books are sold than when there was three times as much work in a book. I speak feelingly, as I have been out of work seven months this year and am still out. I sincerely hope, therefore, that *The Times* will succeed in their fight for cheap books, as this is the only thing that will help my trade.[38]

At around the same time, *The Times* started an association with the World's Classics, a cheap series that the Oxford University Press had acquired in 1905. 'Order your newsagent to deliver one volume of THE WORLD'S CLASSICS every week with your newspapers', declared one advertisement. 'You will enrich your Library with the wisest choice of standard books, charmingly bound, and the cost will hardly be perceptible.'[39] Here, *The Times* and Oxford University Press targeted readers who had not yet acquired the habit of going to bookstores to buy books. Direct selling by mail had developed in the United States, a country with vast distances between cities and too few bookstores (at least outside the East Coast). As Feather points out, *The Times* manager had met two American booksellers, Horace Hooper and W. M. Jackson, who introduced him to advertising techniques used to support mail-order operations.[40] The collaboration with the World's Classics exemplifies this attempt to create new markets by teaching customers habits such as book buying and collecting. Since the series was available in several bindings from one to four shillings, even the least well-off could afford to start a collection. The same advertisement explicitly addressed readers who lacked wealth and education: 'Where economy is a consideration the 1s. Binding, which is strong and comely, will spare the purse without offending the eye. This cheap form has been prepared specially for the benefit of poor students and for working men.' These customers were encouraged to display their taste and aspired social status by building their own library, one book at a time.

Paradoxically, this elite lifestyle could be achieved through an inexpensive series marketed to a large audience. 'A MILLION AND A HALF volumes of THE WORLD'S CLASSICS have been sold and the series is world-famous', declared another advertisement, before listing the reasons for this success:

> First, the books are really classics in the best sense – such as every one ought to have in his or her library; secondly, they are printed so carefully that they appeal to the scholar and the literary worker as much as to the general reader; thirdly, while the books cost little to buy, no trouble or

expense has been spared to present in worthy form 'the best thoughts of the best minds'.[41]

This echoes Matthew Arnold's famous definition of culture as 'the best which has been thought and said in the world'.[42] At the time when all kinds of books were included in publishers' series, the Oxford University Press reassured readers that a rigorous selection had weeded out undeserving classics. As an old and venerable academic press, Oxford University Press also used its scholarly aura to promise textual accuracy, and thus to widen its potential audience (from working men to scholars). These quality texts were packaged in a distinguished physical format, in contrast to more ephemeral series.

With their emphasis on education and social aspiration, The Times Book Club and the World's Classics shared the same 'middlebrow' positioning. In July 1906, one advertisement invited Book Club subscribers (as well as other *Times* readers) to order the 'entire series of 73 volumes'. The World's Classics was described as 'the cheapest, prettiest, and handiest form in which you can obtain the great classics of literature'.[43] There was a sense that culture took the form of a finite list, that it was sufficient to acquire these books to *appear* educated. As Janice Radway notes, American customers bought book sets 'not simply because they wanted to read them but also because they wished to display them as prized possessions'. The collection of uniform books 'would signify to visitors that this family placed a high premium on education, tradition, beauty, and taste'.[44] *Times* readers could of course buy individual volumes of the World's Classics, but they were encouraged to see the series as a coherent whole designed to be displayed on the shelf as a sign of taste and social respectability.

The Times eventually lost its campaign for cheap books as publishers united to defend the Net Book Agreement. In Autumn 1907, John Murray refused to supply the Book Club with *The Letters of Queen Victoria*. *The Times* vigorously attacked him, and Murray successfully sued for libel. The newspaper had to pay £7,500 in damages, a serious blow that added to its existing financial problems. Shortly after, the new owner, Lord Northcliffe, decided that a conflict with publishers would distract him from his main task of making the newspaper profitable again. *The Times* signed the Net Book Agreement in October 1908, thus ending its fight for cheap books.

What were the consequences of the generalisation of 'net books'? Unlike the United States, Britain largely remained a country of book borrowers until the 1930s. The high price of first editions also opened up markets for cheap reprints. For example, readers could buy non-copyrighted books in Nelson's Sixpenny Classics series, launched in 1903. By 1909, there were more than 100 cheap reprint series available.[45] In this competitive market, the series that proved the most enduring were not the cheapest, but those with the widest scope and the most distinguished physical format.

EVERYMAN'S LIBRARY: SETTING THE STANDARD

Joseph Malaby Dent (1849–1926) is best remembered today for Everyman's Library, the series of out-of-copyright reprints he launched in 1906 for one shilling – the same price as the World's Classics.[46] As Jonathan Rose puts it, Everyman's Library 'was not the first attempt at a cheap uniform edition of the "great books", but no similar series except Penguin Books has ever exceeded it in scope, and none without exception has ever matched the high production standards of the early Everyman volumes'.[47] Dent was the tenth child of a Darlington house painter. He left school at the age of thirteen and acquired his love of literature largely through self-education. After briefly working as a printer's apprentice, he then switched to bookbinding. In 1867, at the age of eighteen, he moved to London, where he opened his own bookbinding shop. Dent's admiration for fine craftsmanship would later influence his decision to market inexpensive books in a distinguished format.

In 1888, he founded a publishing firm, J. M. Dent and Company, at 69 Great Eastern Street. Dent's experience of autodidact culture made him aware of the demand for reliable texts in cheap editions. In 1894, he launched the successful Temple Shakespeare series priced at only one shilling a volume. Encouraged by this success, Dent went on to launch other series – including the Temple Dramatists and the Temple Classics in 1896 and the Mediaeval Towns Series in 1898. He also worked with contemporary writers (including Maurice Hewlett and H. G. Wells) and artists: *The Birth Life and Acts of King Arthur*, illustrated by the little-known Aubrey Beardsley, appeared in 1893–4.

In 1904, Dent started planning a new series of cheap books. As he later explained, his models were 'the French "Bibliothèque Nationale", or the great "Reclam" collection produced in Leipzig, of which you could buy a volume for a few pence'.[48] In Britain, cheap series of reprints were rarely well produced (with the exception of the World's Classics). Dent, who had been influenced by the Arts and Crafts movement, wanted his books to look good on the shelf. As Jay Satterfield puts it,

> each Everyman's Library title page was an act of typographical homage to the design principles of William Morris. Printed on quality paper (a blend of rag and wood pulp) with clearly set type, each literary category represented in the series sported flexible cloth covers in its own distinct color.[49]

For example, fiction appeared in red, poetry and drama in green and biography in lavender. This meant, of course, that Everyman's Library was not a perfectly uniform series. Its colour system enabled readers to arrange their books by genre, thus creating a classified home library.

The scope of Everyman's Library was another major difference with its competitors: a total of 152 titles appeared in 1906, under the editorship of Ernest Rhys. The success of the series depended on the availability of non-copyrighted books, and the Copyright Act of 1911 (which extended protection to fifty years after the author's death) was a serious, but non-fatal, blow. Everyman's Library also survived the difficult conditions of the First World War, including shortage of staff and paper.

Everyman's Library was sold in Britain, but also in the United States. In 1928, twenty-two years after the launch of the series, an advertisement in the *Saturday Review of Literature* gave 'six reasons for its indispensability to readers': (1) its scope (812 volumes, and 23,000,000 copies sold); (2) careful editing and introductions by well-known authors (3); a wide range of texts, with thirteen classified departments (including fiction, the largest department with 250 volumes); (4) value for money (many volumes had more than 400 pages); (5) handsome physical format with quality paper, binding and type; and (6) availability to a wide range of readers ('here are books that fit the Hand, the Mind, the Mood and the Purse of EVERYMAN').[50] Like the World's Classics, Everyman's Library targeted the widest possible audience, from working men to scholars.

Unlike the three-and-six-penny libraries launched in the mid-1920s, Everyman's Library shied away from controversial books. As Rose argues, 'Dent was a puritan who personally vetoed the inclusion of Smollett and *Moll Flanders*. "There is no reason why we should try to perpetuate the uncleanness of a very unpleasant age."'[51] After Dent's death in 1926, control of the firm passed to his sons and Everyman's Library finally published *Madame Bovary*, *The Decameron* and other daring classics. But modernist texts did not join the series until the 1930s: Virginia Woolf's *To the Lighthouse* appeared in 1938, for example.

THE WAYFARERS' LIBRARY: PUBLISHING 'CLEAN' MODERN LITERATURE

In early 1914, J. M. Dent launched another series of reprints, the Wayfarers' Library, sold for the same price as Everyman's Library. But unlike its predecessor, the new series focused on modern literature, excluding controversial or pessimistic texts. The first twelve titles were divided in several categories, with a different colour of binding for each section: General Fiction, Historical Fiction, Humour and Essays. 'The Wayfarers' Library embraces all that is healthy, clean and good in the lighter field of modern literature, ranging from works of pure romance to the best collective essays of the day', declared the text on the dust jacket. Newspapers relayed the announcement for the new series, often commenting on the exclusion of daring texts. 'On no account', wrote the *Times*

Literary Supplement, 'will "the iconoclastic problem novel" be allowed to insinuate itself into the Wayfarers' Library, the sole appeal of which is to those who prefer their books to be above suspicion'.[52] In other words, any middle-class household could display these books without anxiety: there was nothing too risqué to shock the vicar. In Canada and the British Empire, many newspapers welcomed the creation of a series of clean modern literature. 'Above all it is satisfying to note that there is a complete absence of the "problem novel," a species of production of which there has been a great deal too much', declared the Toronto *Globe*.[53] *The Times of India* shared this distaste for unhealthy modern fiction: 'The odious element which has crept into a large proportion of modern novels will not insinuate itself into the Wayfarers' Library.'[54] The *Manchester Guardian* was perhaps the only newspaper to express misgivings over Dent's policy. 'One fears that the "odious element that has crept into a large proportion of modern novels" is to be interpreted in such a way as will eliminate works representing one of the most characteristic developments of our time.'[55] However unpleasant, modern fiction was anchored in the present moment, and therefore presented an interest for readers.

The positioning of the Wayfarers' Library shows the widespread suspicion of modern literature in the early years of the twentieth century. Far from concerning only a handful of puritans, the audience for 'clean' literature was large enough to sustain a publishing enterprise that lasted sixteen years, until 1930. But what did Dent really mean by the 'odious element' in modern fiction? A good example is *Ann Veronica*, a 1909 novel by H. G. Wells (who, ironically, was one of the authors published in the Wayfarers' Library). The plot centres on Ann Veronica's revolt against her father, her participation in the suffragette movement, and eventually, her elopement with a married professor. A typical 'problem novel', *Ann Veronica* deals with themes such as female sexual desire, which seemed unpleasant to many readers. As Rachel Potter notes, 'Wells also broached the issue of literary censorship in the book.'[56] The view of the young woman's father, Mr Stanley, on censorship is ridiculed: he 'was inclined to think the censorship should be extended [from the British stage] to the supply of what he styled latter-day fiction; good wholesome stories were being ousted, he said, by "vicious, corrupting stuff" that "left a bad taste in the mouth"'.[57] Here, Wells seemed to anticipate problems with censorship: Macmillan refused to publish *Ann Veronica* (which appeared under the Unwin imprint), the editor of the *Spectator*, John St Loe Strachey, vigorously attacked the novel, and many libraries banned it from their shelves.[58] When the Modern Library was created in 1917, *Ann Veronica* was one of the first titles on its list. In contrast, Dent's series defined itself against a modern movement that dealt too frankly with social and political changes.

There was another aspect of modern literature that deeply bothered Dent and the imagined readers of the Wayfarers' Library: its pessimism, sometimes bordering on nihilism. Take Wells's *Tono-Bungay*, a 'condition of England' novel that the *English Review* had started serialising in December 1908. The plot follows George Ponderevo's rise to riches, as he helps his uncle build a business empire selling quack medicine. But George becomes increasingly disenchanted, and even contemplates suicide. The story he tells is one of decay and futility, at the personal level but also at the broader social level: 'I have called it *Tono-Bungay*, but I had better have called it *Waste*.'[59] Such fiction had no place on Dent's list. As the *Manchester Courier* declared:

> Mr Dent's aim all through his publishing career has been on the optimistic side. 'We don't want austerity,' he once remarked in explaining the ideals which guided him in making a book outwardly a sort of *con amore* possession; and in the same way, in explaining the principles which have guided the choice of the contents of his new library, he says in effect. 'We don't want the pessimist.'[60]

Many newspapers quoted the publisher's announcement: 'the trend of the Wayfarers' Library is optimistic and its sole object is to provide enjoyment for all who love a good wholesome book, whether on a journey or in the warm seclusion of the chimney corner'.[61] The reference to travel echoes the title of the series, which suggests a nomadic lifestyle. But the Wayfarers' Library also took the notion of travel metaphorically, promising escape and entertainment thanks to its selection 'in the lighter field of modern literature'.

The Wayfarers' Library was launched just a few months before the start of the First World War and included titles that presented the conflict as a heroic adventure. In 1916, for example, the Library reprinted John Alexander Steuart's *Cupid, V. C.*, about a female doctor who joins the Royal Army Medical Corps disguised as man. Advertised as 'a moving story of adventure in the great war', the novel seemed to subvert traditional gender roles, while in fact upholding readers' expectations. Indeed, the young doctor wants 'to take her share in the great task of healing and helping and works out her own romance by the way'.[62] This focus on nurture and love fitted well with social expectations for women.

The American magazine *Living Age* praised another war book published in the Wayfarers' Library, *Pebbles on the Shore* by 'Alpha of the Plough' (Alfred George Gardiner):

> The essays are charming, touched with the pathos and tragedy of the great war, yet not directly related to it. As the Preface suggests, they are 'pebbles gathered on the shore of a wild sea' but, although written in a stormy time, they show an understanding of Nature and of human nature which would make them pleasant reading at any time. They are varied in theme and sunny in spirit.[63]

'Sunny' books on the war were far from unusual. For example, the British writer 'Sapper' drew on his wartime experience to write realistic yet amusing short stories.[64] Unlike traditional series of classics, the Wayfarers' Library addressed contemporary issues. But it actively rejected the modernist project, particularly its most controversial and pessimistic aspects.

EXPANDING THE BOOK-BUYING PUBLIC

Despite the availability of cheap reprint series (including series of recent, copyrighted texts), the vast majority of British readers preferred to borrow rather than buy books. This trend dated back to the Victorian period, when for-profit circulating libraries such as Mudie's had an enormous impact on the book trade, influencing the price and format of new books. Scholars have often stressed the decline of these libraries after the end of the three-decker novel in the 1890s.[65] But 'even with their power diminished', notes Elizabeth Dickens, 'the circulating libraries of the early twentieth century, combined with the increasingly successful rate-supported public libraries, continued to exert influence over the economics of the book trade and the habits of readers'.[66] As new competitors such as Boots Book-lovers' Library (created in 1899) became widely popular, the older ones 'increased correspondingly in the struggle to maintain supremacy'.[67]

These for-profit libraries targeted middle-class customers, who were reluctant to rub shoulders with working-class patrons of free libraries. Boots Boot-Lovers' Library, for example, 'prided itself on the attractiveness and "hygiene" of its books and the ambience of its branches'.[68] Another major selling point was the offer of new and recent fiction (difficult to obtain in free libraries, which mostly stocked educational books). Circulating libraries were determined to exclude immoral books to avoid shocking their subscribers. In late 1909, in the wake of the *Ann Veronica* scandal, the managers of the big circulating London libraries (including Boots, W. H. Smith, The Times Book Club and Mudie's) issued a 'cry against "wicked" books, problem novels, and other "spicy" reading'.[69] They asked publishers to send books at least one week before the publication date, so that libraries could decide whether or not to offer them to their subscribers. Other forms of censorship included stocking controversial books but not displaying them on open shelves, as Nicola Wilson has shown.[70]

It was not until the 1930s and the rise of the twopenny libraries that working-class readers could borrow new books for a cheap subscription rate.[71] In his influential study of the book trade, Frank Mumby used the vocabulary of class to dismiss these cheaper libraries: 'compelled to adapt their policy to the demands of readers who, for the most part, were more familiar with cheap periodicals and novelettes, they could do little to raise the standard of literary taste'.[72] The wide geographical coverage of twopenny libraries also contributed to their success, as Harold Raymond of Chatto & Windus noted:

A few years ago circulating libraries were in the main confined to towns and were situated in the centre of those towns. Subscribers were limited to those who could afford to make frequent visits to the libraries or else pay substantial sums in postage. Nowadays branches of Twopenny Libraries are to be found in villages and in suburbs. As a result they can claim to have added appreciably to the book-reading public.[73]

These new readers seldom turned into book buyers (at least until the launch of the paperbacks). In 1929, one bookseller wrote an article criticising the trade's publicity campaign to encourage book buying: 'They [publishers], and the book trade in general, have got to tackle the admittedly difficult problem of dealing with the people who have not as yet been persuaded ever to buy books, let alone "Buy more books".'[74]

In order to steer people away from circulating libraries, publishers offered new products such as the 3s. 6d. series. The Travellers' Library, New Adelphi Library and Phoenix Library featured copyrighted texts (including controversial modern literature) in contrast to the market leader Everyman's Library, the Wayfarers' Library and other traditional series. The new series targeted an audience of middle-class readers familiar with Boots Book-lovers' Library, rather than the working classes who patronised free and twopenny libraries. At 3s. 6d., a Travellers' Library book was cheap compared to a first edition (generally sold for 7s. 6d.) – but it was not cheap for a manual worker or a shop assistant. A commodity priced at 3s. 6d. in 1930 would cost around £29 (labour value) or £52 (income value) in 2015.[75] Again, these series did not reach the mass market, but they were relatively affordable for middle-class customers.

Cheap Modernism is divided into five chapters, each focusing on a cheap reprint series that included modernist texts or authors. Chapter 1 looks at the introductions that T. S. Eliot and Virginia Woolf wrote for the Oxford World's Classics editions of Wilkie Collins's *The Moonstone* and Laurence Sterne's *Sentimental Journey* (both published in 1928). Oxford University Press generally shied away from literary experimentation. Nevertheless, by the late 1920s, Woolf and Eliot had become sufficiently well-known to attract readers of the World's Classics. They lent their reputation to boost sales of reprints and, in turn, they benefited from their association with a commercial publishing house with access to the American market. The World's Classics contributed to transforming the image of these modernist writers from obscure avant-gardists to members of the artistic establishment.

Chapter 2 starts in early 1926, with the debate between the home secretary William Joynson-Hicks and the MP Joseph Kenworthy over indecent books and plays. The *Bookseller*, the main magazine of the book trade, suggested putting 'sex novels' out of the view of women and young readers. It is in this context that two publishers launched new series of copyrighted texts, including titles by controversial authors. James Joyce's *Dubliners* and D. H. Lawrence's *Twilight in Italy* appeared in the Travellers' Library published by Jonathan Cape. Martin Secker's New Adelphi Library also included many titles by Lawrence. The success of these series proved that there was an untapped market for texts by the most subversive modern writers.

Chapter 3 focuses on the Phoenix Library, which published Wyndham Lewis's *Tarr* in 1928. Chatto & Windus's series not only made available modernism to a much larger audience, but also transformed the modernist text itself since Lewis extensively revised his novel for this edition. *Tarr* was published alongside a wide range of texts – including a cookery book, art books by Clive Bell and Roger Fry, and novels by Arnold Bennett.

Chapter 4 takes the examples of Tauchnitz and Albatross Modern Continental Library to study the continental diffusion of Anglophone modernism. The international nature of Tauchnitz particularly appealed to expatriate modernist writers such as Joyce. While Tauchnitz was initially reluctant to publish modernism, this changed under the leadership of Max Christian Wegner in the late 1920s. Wegner went on to co-found Albatross, a firm that not only popularised modernist texts, but was also shaped by modernism through its stylish covers and proclaimed cosmopolitanism.

Chapter 5 turns to the Hogarth Press Uniform Edition of Virginia Woolf's work. Despite her mistrust of the 'middlebrow' sphere, Woolf was fully aware that cheap reprints could help her reach common readers. In 1928, she collaborated with the Oxford World's Classics and the Modern Library. And in 1929, the Hogarth Press started publishing a collected edition of her work. This chapter, based on research in the Hogarth Press archive, shows that the Uniform Edition reached a wide readership in Britain and encouraged Woolf's American publisher, Harcourt Brace, to issue a similar edition. The Uniform Edition also sent a strong signal that Woolf was now a canonical writer whose work deserved to be 'collected'.

Many of the three-and-six-penny libraries and quality series were discontinued during the Second World War, at a time when paper rationing and distribution problems affected all publishers. An attempt to revive them after the war did not succeed. The conclusion addresses the following questions: why did European series associated with modernism fail to find a public in the years that followed the war? In what format did readers encounter modernist texts, at a time when modernism was institutionalised in the university system?

Notes

1. Ardis, 'Modernist Print Culture', p. 814.
2. 'Mediating Modernism and Modernity in the Interwar Fashion Press' (speakers: Vike Martina Plock, Alice Wood, Ilya Parkins), MSA conference, Boston,

20 November 2015. See also Hammill and Leick, 'Modernism and the Quality Magazines' and Leick, 'Popular Modernism'.

3. Collier, 'What is Modern Periodical Studies?', pp. 97–8.
4. Collier, 'What is Modern Periodical Studies?', p. 94.
5. Collier, 'What is Modern Periodical Studies?', p. 99. See also Collier, *Modern Print Artifacts: Textual Materiality and Literary Value in British Print Culture, 1890–1930s* (Edinburgh University Press, 2016).
6. Earle, *Re-Covering Modernism*, p. 3.
7. Earle, *Re-Covering Modernism*, p. 202. See also Earle, 'Pulp Magazines and the Popular Press'.
8. Earle, *Re-Covering Modernism*, p. 12.
9. 'Will Straw, Andrea Hasenbank, and Kirsten MacLeod are collectors and curators of their own objects of study, gathering materials that institutions have not traditionally thought worthy of archiving.' Hammill, Hjartarson and McGregor, 'Introducing Magazines', p. 8.
10. For examples of work across the fields of modernism and book history, see McGann, *Black Riders* and *The Textual Condition*; Bornstein, *Material Modernism*.
11. Suarez, 'Book History from Descriptive Bibliographies', pp. 211–12.
12. Suarez, 'Book History from Descriptive Bibliographies', p. 209. See also Bonn, 'American Mass-Market Paperbacks'.
13. See Andes, *A Descriptive Bibliography of the Modern Library*; Todd and Bowden, *Tauchnitz International Editions in English*. The two-volume *The Culture of the Publisher's Series*, edited by John Spiers, highlights a recent rise of interest in these series.
14. Rota, 'Mrs Woolf's Writings'.
15. This information is not in the archive deposited at Columbia University.
16. Blunden, 'World's Classics'.
17. Howsam, 'Sustained Literary Ventures', p. 5.
18. Altick, 'From Aldine to Everyman', p. 6.
19. Altick, 'From Aldine to Everyman', p. 8.
20. Hammond, *Reading*, p. 86.
21. Hammond, *Reading*, p. 86.
22. Rose, *Intellectual Life*, p. 131.
23. Altick, 'From Aldine to Everyman', p. 7.
24. Hammond, *Reading*, p. 94.
25. Finkelstein and McCleery, *An Introduction to Book History*, p. 90.
26. Todd, 'Firma Tauchnitz', p. 8.
27. Nowell-Smith, *International Copyright Law*, p. 41.
28. Hammill and Smith, *Magazines, Travel, and Middlebrow Culture*, p. 12.
29. Quoted in 'Middlebrow, n. and adj.,' *OED Online*, Oxford University Press, December 2015, accessed 29 February 2016.
30. See Humble, *The Feminine Middlebrow Novel* and Brown, *Comedy and the Feminine Middlebrow Novel*.
31. See Hammill and Smith's definition: 'What we find much more useful is to consider the middlebrow as a mode of circulation, reception, and consumption of cultural products, and also as a space where high and popular culture meet, and where art encounters consumerism.' *Magazines, Travel, and Middlebrow Culture*, p. 10.
32. Quoted in Nowell-Smith, *International Copyright Law*, p. 59.
33. Hammill and Smith, *Magazines, Travel, and Middlebrow Culture*, p. 14.
34. Feather, *A History of British Publishing*, p. 184.
35. Feather, *A History of British Publishing*, p. 184.
36. 'Publishers and the Public', *The Times*, 10 October 1906, p. 5.

37. 'To the Editors of *The Times*', *The Times*, 28 February 1907, p. 11.
38. 'Publishers and the Public', *The Times*, 18 October 1906, p. 8.
39. Advertisement for the World's Classics, *The Times*, 2 July 1906, p. 4.
40. Feather, *A History of British Publishing*, p. 184.
41. Advertisement for the World's Classics, *The Times*, 12 June 1906, p. 12.
42. Arnold, *Culture and Anarchy*, p. viii.
43. Advertisement for the World's Classics, *The Times*, 11 July 1906, p. 1.
44. Radway, *A Feeling for Books*, p. 159.
45. Keating, *The Haunted Study*, p. 434.
46. These two series sold for double the price of Nelson's Sixpenny Classics, which shows that many customers were ready to pay more for well-produced books.
47. Rose, 'J. M. Dent and Sons'.
48. Dent, *The House of Dent*, p. 123.
49. Satterfield, *The World's Best Books*, p. 26.
50. Advertisement for Everyman's Library, *Saturday Review of Literature*, 21 April 1928, p. 799.
51. Rose, *Intellectual Life*, p. 134.
52. 'Everyman's New Venture', *Times Literary Supplement*, 15 January 1914, p. 26.
53. 'Books of the Day', *Globe* [Toronto], 12 May 1914, p. 6.
54. 'A New Library', *The Times of India*, 8 July 1914, p. 9.
55. 'Books and Bookmen', *Manchester Guardian*, 26 February 1914, p. 6.
56. Potter, *Obscene Modernism*, p. 26.
57. Wells, *Ann Veronica*, pp. 370–1.
58. See Jaillant, *Modernism*, p. 26.
59. Wells, *Tono-Bungay*, p. 482.
60. Mumby, 'Books that Count'.
61. 'Books of the Day', *Globe* [Toronto], 12 May 1914, p. 6.
62. Advertisement for the Wayfarers' Library, *Manchester Guardian*, 11 May 1916, p. 3.
63. 'Books and Authors', *Living Age*, 8 December 1917, p. 637.
64. See Jaillant, 'Sapper'.
65. Griest, *Mudie's Circulating Library*, pp. 213–24; Feltes, *Modes*, p. 77; Keating, *The Haunted Study*, pp. 279–80.
66. Dickens, 'Permanent Books', p. 170. John Passmore Edwards and other philanthropists also funded libraries. See Morris, 'Edwards, John Passmore (1823–1911)', *Oxford Dictionary of National Biography*.
67. Winterton, 'Circulating Libraries', p. 62.
68. Wilson, 'Boots Book-Lovers' Library', p. 429.
69. 'Improper Books: Great Libraries Take Action', *Evening Post* [Wellington, New Zealand], 13 January 1910, p. 8.
70. Wilson, 'Boots Book-Lovers' Library', p. 438.
71. See Hilliard, 'The Twopenny Library'.
72. Mumby, *Publishing and Bookselling*, pp. 320–1.
73. Raymond, *Publishing and Bookselling*, p. 20.
74. Kay, 'On the Selling of Books'.
75. 'Labour value is measured using the relative wage a worker would use to buy the commodity. This measure uses the earning index. Income value is measured using the relative average income that would be used to buy a commodity. This measure uses the GDP per capita.' Officer and Williamson, 'Five Ways to Compute the Relative Value of a UK Pound Amount, 1270 to Present'.

I

'INTRODUCTIONS BY EMINENT WRITERS': T. S. ELIOT AND VIRGINIA WOOLF IN THE OXFORD WORLD'S CLASSICS SERIES

'For over 100 years Oxford World's Classics have brought readers closer to the world's great literature', declares a statement at the beginning of recent books in the series. 'The pocket-sized hardbacks of the early years contained introductions by Virginia Woolf, T. S. Eliot, Graham Greene, and other literary figures which enriched the experience of reading.' Indeed, in 1928, Woolf and Eliot wrote prefaces to Laurence Sterne's *Sentimental Journey* and Wilkie Collins's *The Moonstone* respectively. Two decades later, Greene contributed a foreword to the Oxford World's Classics edition of Henry James's *The Portrait of a Lady*. These introductions increased the appeal of older works, and continue to serve the reputation of the World's Classics as a major cultural enterprise.

This chapter focuses particularly on the late 1920s, at the time when Humphrey Milford (manager of the London branch of Oxford University Press) commissioned introductions by Woolf and Eliot. 1928 was a turning point in the history of modernism – the moment when commercial publishers published modernist writings that had previously been confined to little magazines and small presses.[1] This was the year when the Modern Library reprinted Joyce's *A Portrait of the Artist as a Young Man* and Woolf's *Mrs Dalloway* in the United States. However, the Modern Library was very different from traditional series of classics such as Everyman's Library and the World's Classics. It was sold as a daring series of 'complete and unabridged' texts for readers who wanted to keep abreast of modern literature. The fact that *Portrait of the Artist* was reviewed as 'slightly pornographic' was unproblematic for the Modern Library, since Joyce's subversive reputation contributed to the commercial appeal of the series.[2]

In contrast, the World's Classics published mostly out-of-copyright works and shied away from controversy. Oxford University Press, whose London branch bought the World's Classics from Grant Richards in 1905, was known for its Bibles, scholarly works and anthologies, not for literary experimentation.[3] The group of Delegates who ran the press from Oxford were extremely reluctant to include contemporary fiction on the Oxford University Press list. Although the London office had a large autonomy, its successive managers preferred to avoid any conflict with Oxford. 'If I once begun to publish novels', wrote Milford to the novelist Constance Holme, 'well, I don't know what would happen. (The Delegates would probably discharge me, to begin with).'[4] In practice, Oxford World's Classics included a few contemporary novels, but none of them could be described as experimental or daring. In Mary Hammond's words, 'the books had to be inoffensive to the lower- and middle-class family reader'.[5] The World's Classics editors refused to reprint certain books (Zola and Maupassant did not appear on the list until 1933, with the publication of *French Short Stories*). They also expurgated some texts, including the *Twenty-Four Tales of Tolstoy* translated by Louise and Aylmer Maude – which became *Twenty-Three Tales* when the story 'Françoise' was dropped.[6] This kind of censorship aimed at protecting 'innocent' readers of the World's Classics – namely young people, women, and the lower classes. 'Well into the twentieth century a double standard prevailed', Peter Sutcliffe notes. 'Expensive complete texts could be made available for the élite, for "ripe scholars": for the masses expurgated editions would be required reading for many years to come.'[7]

So why would such a staid series include an introduction by T. S. Eliot, a writer with 'a sustained interest in rotting orifices'?[8] Why would a series associated with an old English university value the opinion of Woolf, who repeatedly criticised the patriarchal structure of the academic system? My central argument is that, by the late 1920s, Woolf and Eliot had become well-known names recognisable by the lower middle class, the self-educated and other readers of the World's Classics. In Pierre Bourdieu's terminology, Woolf and Eliot now had the 'power to consecrate' old books, moving them to the centre of literary discussion and increasing their sales.[9] The Oxford World's Classics not only commissioned new introductions to Eliot and Woolf, but also reprinted some of their other works in the early 1930s. The second series of *Selected Modern English Essays* (1932), edited by Milford, contained Woolf's 'The Patron and the Crocus' (as well as an essay on T. S. Eliot, by C. Williams). *English Critical Essays, Twentieth Century* (1933, edited by Phyllis Jones) included Woolf's 'Modern Fiction' and Eliot's essay on Samuel Johnson's poems *London* and *The Vanity of Human Wishes*. Poems by Eliot also appeared in *A Book of American Verse*, edited by A. C. Ward (1935).

Considering the cultural importance and longevity of the World's Classics, it is surprising that the series has attracted so little scholarly interest. Even the three-volume *History of Oxford University Press* does not feature any chapter on the World's Classics (although there are related essays on educational and classical books, and on the origins of the London branch of the press).[10] The few sources of information on the series include a succinct account in Sutcliffe's 1978 book and a more detailed analysis in Hammond's chapter, '"People Read So Much Now and Reflect So Little": Oxford University Press and the Classics Series' in her *Reading, Publishing and the Formation of Literary Taste in England, 1880–1914* (2006). Since Hammond focuses on Henry Frowde (the manager of Oxford University Press's London business) and his role in the early development of the World's Classics, she has little to say on the original creator Grant Richards, or on Frowde's successor Humphrey Milford. This chapter aims to put the introductions by modernist writers in the broader context of the history of the World's Classics, a series sold to a wide audience. It thus contributes to scholarship on the relationship between high modernism and the marketplace, and on Eliot's and Woolf's non-fiction writings.[11]

GRANT RICHARDS, HENRY FROWDE AND THE WORLD'S CLASSICS

Drawing on N. N. Feltes's work, Mary Hammond describes Grant Richards, who created the World's Classics in 1901, as an 'enterprising' publisher – as opposed to the 'list' publisher Oxford University Press.[12] Richards (1872–1948) was only twenty-four years old when he created his own firm with the help of his family – including his uncle, the writer Grant Allen.[13] As a young publisher with a name to make, Richards could not set his sights on well-known authors, but he showed an aptitude to attract promising writers at the beginning of their careers. He thus published Laurence Housman's *Spikenard* (1898), G. K. Chesterton's first book *The Wild Knight and Other Poems* (1900) and Arnold Bennett's *Fame and Fiction* (1901). Like John Lane and other enterprising small presses, Richards did not shy away from controversial literature. He offered to take on James Joyce's *Dubliners* in 1906, but backed out when the printer objected to certain passages. As Robert Scholes notes, 'much of his caution in dealing with *Dubliners*, as a matter of fact, stemmed from his precarious financial situation at the time'.[14] These financial difficulties had partly originated in the launch of the World's Classics five years earlier. As a small, undercapitalised publisher, Richards was ill-equipped to respond to the enormous and unexpected demand for his inexpensive reprints. 'When I started the series', Richards later said, 'the trade generally prophesied failure for it. Success, however, was immediate, increasing and continued, and the series might almost be said to be running its rivals off the field.'[15]

How can we account for this success, at a time of heightened competition from other cheap series? Since Richards mainly selected popular non-copyrighted books, he could not count on the uniqueness of his list: *Jane Eyre*, the first book included in the World's Classics, had also appeared in Walter Scott's Camelot series in 1889 and in Bliss, Sands & Co.'s Burleigh Library in 1896. However, as Richard Altick has shown, many Victorian cheap series were poorly produced: 'Strenuously small (and often badly worn) type; thin margins, sometimes crowded with legends advertising tea, baking powder, or patent medicines; poor paper; paper wrappers; flimsy sewing – these were too often the result of the pressure to cut prices.'[16] To distinguish the World's Classics from its competitors, Richards paid particular attention to the material aspect of the books while keeping prices low: 'Size five x three-and-a-half inches, their standard bulk one-and-a-half inches, stamped with a gilt spine decoration by Laurence Housman, they sold at no more than 1s. cloth and 2s. skiver leather.'[17]

In an effort to carve a unique niche for the World's Classics, Richards thought of including works by living authors – as long as they agreed on a reduced royalty rate compatible with the small profit margins of the series. Following Grant Allen's advice, he contacted the philosopher Herbert Spencer, who replied that the offer was too low to be considered.[18] Richards had better luck with Theodore Watts-Dunton, whose 1898 bestseller *Aylwin* joined the World's Classics in 1904. As the leading critic of poetry for the *Examiner* and, from 1876, the *Athenaeum*, Watts-Dunton was a well-connected and respected literary man. Richards suggested that he write an introduction to his book: 'This would be of considerable interest to the wide public your book will reach in the World's Classics, and would also draw fresh journalistic notice to the edition.'[19] As Hammond points out, introductions were already a well-established feature of classics series, appearing in Cassell's National Library, Routledge's World and Railway Libraries, Chandos Classics, the Minerva Library of Famous Books and the Temple Classics.[20] But writers generally introduced older classics, not recent bestsellers such as *Aylwin*.

By the time of Richards's bankruptcy in 1905, the World's Classics included sixty-five titles. To sustain the rapid expansion of the series, Richards went heavily into debt. According to *Publishers' Circular*, 'he had to borrow £8,000 off creditors on charges covering the series of books entitled "The World's Classics," the leases of 2 Park Crescent, and 48 Leicester Square, and other property'.[21] The main part of the Richards estate was acquired by Alexander Moring, who then negotiated with Henry Frowde of Oxford University Press for the sale of the World's Classics.[22]

After October 1905, the image of the series underwent a major shift. No longer owned by an entrepreneurial publisher with a taste for subversive texts, the World's Classics was now associated with a prestigious university press. However, Frowde's name appeared on the imprint, 'to distinguish these sorts of books, and perhaps to distance them, from those published by the Clarendon Press' in Oxford.[23] The positioning of the series was therefore ambiguous, reflecting both an ambition to advertise links with Oxford while avoiding any embarrassment to the Board of Delegates.

Shortly after purchasing the series, Frowde asked Watts-Dunton to publicise his strategy for the new Oxford World's Classics in the *Athenaeum*. The announcement should articulate a three-point plan: 'that new vigour would now be infused into the series, that important additions are to be made, that as in other series printed at the Oxford University Press writers can rely on the accuracy of the text'.[24] First, in his effort to regenerate the series, Frowde commissioned introductions that would 'lift some of the new volumes a little above the bare reprint style'.[25] As Frowde explained, these introductions were written by 'eminent writers'.[26] Frowde thus contacted Edmund Gosse, asking him to suggest one or two new books he would like to introduce (Gosse eventually wrote the foreword to Thackeray's *Pendennis*, published in 1907).[27] The same kind of request appears repeatedly in Frowde's correspondence. He was happy to leave a great deal of freedom to the potential contributor, as long as the texts selected were in the public domain and 'popular in character, for the first cost of production is not turned until from 10,000 to 15,000 have been sold'.[28] The *name* of the writer who penned the preface was, to a certain extent, more important than the texts themselves. As Bourdieu argued, 'the consecrated writer is the one who has the power to consecrate and to win assent when he or she consecrates an author or a work – with a preface, a favourable review, a prize, etc.'[29] The 'consecration' process worked in two ways: writers of introductions brought new prestige to old books (and to the World's Classics series), and in turn, these classics increased the cultural aura of already-distinguished authors.

In addition to renowned writers, Frowde also asked distinguished scholars to contribute introductions. Although he insisted that the World's Classics imprint was for 'popular books' not schoolbooks or educational works (as published by the Clarendon Press),[30] Frowde seemed nevertheless eager to appeal to the school market and to self-educated readers. Introductions by well-known academics would not only boost the prestige of the series, but also increase sales. 'We shall be much gratified to see your name associated with the series, and an introduction from your pen will materially help the sale of the book', wrote Frowde to the Master of University College Oxford.[31]

Introductions by famous names, as well as new additions, allowed the World's Classics to compete with Everyman's Library, created by J. M. Dent in 1906. In a letter to Watts-Dunton, Frowde wrote: 'Dent is making a great splash with his series, and the specimens which I have seen are certainly deserving of success.' Since Dent planned to eventually include a staggering 1,000 volumes in Everyman's Library, Frowde was determined to considerably increase the World's Classics list. He asked Watts-Dunton 'for a list of any works which occur to you which ought to be included, and the best name in each case for an introduction'.[32] In a report to the Delegates written two years after the purchase of the series, Frowde noted that sixty-one new titles had been added to the initial list of sixty-five World's Classics books. In total, 250,000 volumes were sold each year, including one-third in leather. 'The success of the venture has, no doubt, been to some extent affected by the gigantic proportions of Everyman's Library which Mr Dent has since issued', wrote Frowde, 'but notwithstanding this our sales are being fairly well maintained'.[33]

The third point of Frowde's strategy to develop the World's Classics relied on the accuracy of texts. One of the first things Frowde did after acquiring the series from Grant Richards was to have the volumes 'very carefully read' to correct misprints.[34] Frowde used the distinguished scholarly reputation of Oxford to differentiate the World's Classics from other cheap series. More than twenty years later, his successor, Humphrey Milford could present the World's Classics editions of Tolstoy as 'reliable translations' in a market saturated with cheap editions 'so unreliable that they ought not to be encouraged'.[35]

Frowde followed Grant Richards's practice to issue the World's Classics in various formats sold at different prices. In spring 1906, he launched the first pocket editions, printed on thin paper for holiday, travel and outdoor use. This was probably a way to side-step competition from Everyman's Library, whose books had a larger size.[36] World's Classics were also available in thick paper, for a more durable presence in a personal library. Copies in either thickness were sold in cloth and leather bindings. The 1907 catalogue gives an indication of this diversity in paper, binding and price.[37] The thick-paper edition was bound up in ten different styles, as Table 1.1 shows.

Table 1.1: Bindings and prices (in shillings and pence) for each edition of the World's Classics, 1907.

Thick-paper edition	Pocket edition
Cloth (1/-)	Art cloth (1/-)
Sultan red leather (1/6)	Sultan red leather (1/6)
Buckram (paper label) (1/6)	¼ Vellum (4/-)
¼ Parchment (1/8)	
Lambskin (2/-)	
Parchment (2/6)	
¼ Vellum (4/-)	
½ Calf (4/-)	
Whole calf (5/6)	
Three calf (5/6)	

This broad choice of physical formats sat rather uncomfortably with the proclaimed uniformity of the World's Classics. As Frowde told the Delegates, 'a popular series issued under a general title ought to consist of volumes uniform in size, binding, and <u>price</u>'.[38] Frowde gave the examples of the Rulers of India Series and the Fireside Dickens Series, whose variations in prices had been 'detrimental' to the success of the former and 'unfortunate' for the latter. Frowde and Milford (who took over in 1913) probably used the various physical formats of the World's Classics to target different niches of readers. For example, thick-paper editions bound in calf leather were well suited for those who wanted to build their own libraries, but not for travellers and low-income readers. The thick-paper edition was dropped in 1917 and by 1928 the World's Classics series was issued only in the pocket edition, in two bindings priced at 2s. for cloth and 3s. 6d. for sultan red leather.

HUMPHREY MILFORD AND T. S. ELIOT'S INTRODUCTION TO THE MOONSTONE

The turn towards more physical uniformity was accompanied by a relative modernisation of the list. Under Richards's and Frowde's leadership, the World's Classics had included works and introductions by writers associated with the Victorian era. Watts-Dunton's death in 1914 nearly coincided with the arrival of Humphrey Milford at the head of the London branch. While Richards and Frowde had started working in their adolescence, Milford went to the University of Oxford to study classics. Unlike the first two, he was an Oxford insider, selected by Charles Cannan, then secretary to the Delegates of the Oxford University Press.[39] Amy Flanders suggests that 'while Frowde's trade experience and entrepreneurship had served the London business well, Cannan perhaps felt that Milford's academic credentials would better suit the ever-growing list of literary and educational titles'.[40] Indeed, Milford kept a lifelong interest in literature and followed contemporary developments by reading the *Times Literary Supplement*, the *London Mercury* and the *Criterion* (founded by T. S. Eliot in 1922).[41] Like Eliot, Milford also enjoyed various forms of popular culture. An avid reader of detective and mystery stories, he once told the politician Godfrey Collins: 'I began *The Footsteps that Stopped* – what an excellent title – late one evening, and found myself at past midnight at the most exciting part, when a belated (and of course "wrong-number") telephone-bell rang and terrified me out of wits!'[42]

In 1924, Milford added an anthology of 'uncanny tales', *Ghosts and Marvels*, in the World's Classics. M. R. [Montague Rhodes] James, a noted medievalist and author of antiquarian ghost stories, prefaced the book. The editor of the anthology, V. H. Collins, selected one of James's stories ('Casting the Runes'), as well as tales by Daniel Defoe, Walter Scott, George Eliot, H. G. Wells, Algernon Blackwood, Barry Pain and others. Like other World's Classics, *Ghosts and Marvels* was sold in Britain, the United States and throughout the British Empire. An advertisement from the Indian branch of the Oxford University Press declared that this 'book of many thrills . . . will please the lovers of the *Supernatural*'.[43] *The Times of India* also described it as 'a fine parcel of creepy stories'.[44] In 1927, the first printing of 10,000 copies had sold out, and two additional printings of 5,000 and 10,000 copies were ordered.[45]

The success of *Ghosts and Marvels* encouraged Milford to add more popular short stories to the World's Classics. *Crime and Detection*, published in 1926, included stories by Edgar Allan Poe, Arthur Conan Doyle, Arthur Morrison, Richard Austin Freeman, Ernest Bramah, G. K. Chesterton, H. C. Bailey, E. W. Hornung and Barry Pain. According to one advertisement, *Crime and Detection* contained 'a delightful introduction (which will conquer the prejudices of the firmest disliker of introductions)'.[46] In this clearly written preface, the Magdalen historian E. M. [Edward Murray] Wrong argued that the detective story could be traced back to the Bible: in the Apocrypha, for example, 'Daniel's cross-examination saves Susanna from the false witness of lecherous elders.'[47] Having placed detective fiction in the long history of Western literature, Wrong then went on to praise the Victorian writers who had reinvented the genre: Wilkie Collins's *The Woman in White* (reprinted in the World's Classics in 1921) 'made a happy connexion between villainy and detection' and *The Moonstone* was 'more orthodox because more of a pure puzzle'.[48] Wrong's foreword was so influential that fifteen years later, the American publisher and mystery scholar Howard Haycraft could describe it as a 'memorable introduction' that 'remains the most succinct of all statements of detective story principles'.[49] Haycraft also anthologised the preface in his collection of critical essays, *The Art of the Mystery Story* (1946).

It was highly uncommon for cheap series of classics to include detective fiction (*Fourteen Great Detective Stories*, largely inspired by *Crime and Detection*, was published in the Modern Library in 1928 and *Tales of Detection*, edited by Dorothy Sayers, appeared in Everyman's Library only in 1936). As Haycraft put it, *Crime and Detection* was not only the first anthology on the subject 'to be compiled in accordance with critical principles', it also had an introduction that 'marked the earliest attempt of a purposive historical and analytical survey and summation of the medium'.[50] *Crime and Detection* was thus a unique product that caught the attention of many reviewers. *Contemporary Review* declared that 'it was a good idea but a difficult task' to add detective stories to the World's Classics. The journalist commended the selection, but found Wrong's connection between the prophet Daniel and detective fiction rather 'far-fetched'.[51] The *Times Literary Supplement* devoted its leading article to a long discussion on detectives, which was then reproduced in the American magazine the *Living Age*. The *Times Literary Supplement* reviewer, Harry Pirie-Gordon (13th Laird of Buthlaw), praised

Oxford University Press 'for reissuing in cheap editions the finer achievements of the Old Masters of this form of craft'. According to him, *Crime and Detection* was interesting precisely because it contained many older texts written before the invention of modern technologies:

> In this way we can readily compare the technique of those who thrill us now with that of the men who kept our sires and grandsires awake till dawn with the prowess of heroes who landed each criminal fish in turn without the assistance of finger-prints or chemical reagents, telegraphic warnings over the official tape-machine to all police stations, wireless messages to shipmasters upon the high seas, photography, the telephone, or any means of locomotion more rapid than a hansom cab.[52]

This focus on tradition fitted well with the image of the World's Classics, and with Wrong's account of the long history of the detective genre.

Crime and Detection was presented as a collection of venerable classics written by 'Old Masters', but also as an anthology of thrilling tales grounded in modernity. The dust jacket thus showed a drawing of an executioner, in a purified composition of angular shapes and black lines (Figure 1.1).[53] A similar style was used in a poster that grouped together *Ghosts and Marvels* and *Crime and Detection*, marketed as 'short stories for the holidays' (Figure 1.2). These striking modern illustrations highlight an evolution in the positioning of the World's Classics. Milford trod a fine line between tradition and modernity. On the one hand, he was heavily invested in preserving the image of the World's Classics as a respectable, conservative series but, on the other, he was aware of the intensely competitive nature of the reprint market. In 1926, the year *Crime and Detection* was published, Jonathan Cape launched the Travellers' Library, which offered recent texts for a modest price. Milford chose to position the World's Classics somewhere between Everyman's Library and the Travellers' Library, by incorporating aspects of the new art and new literature without losing sight of the World's Classics core mission of providing family-friendly books to a large audience of middle-to-lower-class readers.

Crime and Detection was an immediate bestseller: nine months after its release, nearly 10,000 copies had already been sold.[54] A comparison with *Ghosts and Marvels* shows that both books eventually reached a total sale of around 25,000 copies each. In 1927, Milford published a second selection of tales, *More Ghosts and Marvels*, with a first printing of 10,000.[55] He then issued the second series of *Crime and Detection*. With these books, Milford had proved that detective fiction and ghost stories could be marketed as 'world's classics' without endangering the credibility of the series.

It is in this context that Milford decided to add Wilkie Collins's *The Moonstone* to the World's Classics. In December 1926, Harold Raymond of Chatto & Windus confirmed that Collins's preface to the second edition was

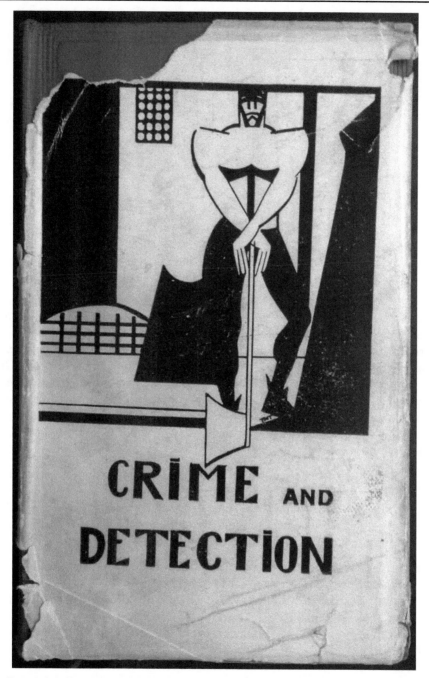

Figure 1.1 Dust jacket, *Crime and Detection*, Oxford World's Classics (c. 1926) (unknown illustrator). By permission of Oxford University Press.

Figure 1.2 Poster, *Ghosts and Marvels* and *Crime and Detection*, reproduced in the *Bookseller*, August 1926, p. 32.

free to be used.[56] The novel itself had been out-of-copyright since 1910, and was already available in several publishers' series (including Nelson's Classics and Harrap's Standard Fiction Library). However, Milford was confident that a preface by a well-chosen writer could create interest in the book. In January 1927, Milford read T. S. Eliot's praise of *The Moonstone* in the *New Criterion* ('The great book which contains the whole of English detective fiction in embryo . . .; every detective story, so far as it is a good detective story, observes the detective laws to be drawn from this book').[57] Milford wrote to the author:

> I am about to add it to the World's Classics series, and it would give me great pleasure if you would write an introduction – pleasure both in being associated with your name, and in having the *Moonstone* properly discussed. It remains so much the greatest of detective novels that someone ought to do it justice among the populace.[58]

Here we see a reference to the name of the consecrated writer, and to his power to re-evaluate a work that has so far been neglected.

Eliot was delighted by Milford's letter, which came with a gift of the World's Classics books (including *The Woman in White*). He replied on the same day to accept the offer, pending the authorisation of Faber, who had an option on all his non-periodical work. Eliot also mentioned that he was working on a long article on Collins for *The Times*, and suggested that *Armadale* should be added to the World's Classics.[59] In mid-April, Milford, desiring to publish the book as soon as possible, asked Eliot to submit his preface within three to four weeks.[60] Eliot took less than that, and sent his preface on 1 May 1927 along with a cover letter:

> I am afraid that you may find it rather short for your purpose. But I found that if said more in a general way, about Collins or about this form of fiction, it seemed to cease to be an Introduction to this book; and if I said more particularly about this book I was telling the new reader more than he wanted to know in advance. It is difficult to write a long introduction to a single novel, and I doubt whether many readers want it.[61]

For Eliot (and for Woolf), an introduction was at best an invitation to read the book and, at worst, a pedantic discourse that would create a boundary between readers and the novel.

Eliot was well aware of the role of scholars in the Oxford World's Classics series. One of the volumes sent by Milford, William Congreve's *Comedies*, was edited and introduced by Bonamy Dobrée, a professor of English at the Egyptian University in Cairo. Eliot's distrust of academia probably explains his reluctance to write a long introduction, which risked turning the reader away from the novel. His own experience of academic life, including graduate work at Oxford, had been far from happy. He once wrote to his friend Conrad Aiken: 'I hate university towns and university people, who are the same everywhere, with pregnant wives, sprawling children, many books and hideous pictures on the walls . . . Oxford is very pretty, but I don't like to be dead.'[62] As Gail McDonald argues, Eliot was convinced that erudition was not enough to explain a work of art: the creation of poetry and criticism could bring insights not available through traditional academic disciplines.[63]

As we have seen, the Oxford World's Classics had a rather ambiguous positioning. Although it was published by a university press and included many academic contributors, it was sold to a large audience of non-specialist readers (the 'populace' mentioned by Milford in his first letter to Eliot). The opportunity to reach a wide readership certainly appealed to Eliot. While he has often been presented as an elitist writer who wrote difficult poems for a small coterie of readers, Eliot, in fact, deplored the divide between high and low culture. The importance of addressing a broad audience is a central theme in 'Wilkie Collins and Dickens', published on the front page of the *Times Literary Supplement* in August 1927. 'Those who have lived before such terms as "high-brow fiction," "thrillers" and "detective fiction" were invented', wrote Eliot, 'realize that melodrama is perennial and that the craving for it is perennial and must be satisfied.'[64] As David Chinitz puts it, 'Eliot describes the disjunction between the "high" and the "popular" as a sort of iron curtain that has only recently descended across the arts.'[65] For Eliot, Collins's melodramatic plots appealed to all kinds of readers and ensured his literary legacy. Even long after his death, *The Woman in White* – 'the greatest of Collins's novels' – continues to be a novel that 'every one knows'.[66] Eliot also praised *The Moonstone* as 'the first and greatest of English detective novels',[67] which became 'the first, the longest, and the best of modern English detective novels' in the introduction to the World's Classics edition.[68] The editor of the *Times Literary Supplement*, who published Eliot's article in August for 'holiday reading',[69] must have been delighted by the light and enthusiastic tone of the piece. 'Best' and 'greatest' are recurring words. Eliot does not directly criticise contemporary writers for being too obscure or 'highbrow', but reminds them that 'the first – and not one of the least difficult – requirements of either prose or verse is that it should be interesting'.[70]

Although Milford had planned to publish *The Moonstone* shortly after receiving Eliot's introduction, the book did not appear until March 1928.[71] The 2,500-word introduction is a more focused version of the 3,500-word article. In particular, Eliot made cuts to the discussion on the divide between high and low culture. He also expanded his comparison between *The Moonstone* and contemporary detective novels: 'Modern detective writers have added the use of fingerprints and such other trifles, but they have not materially improved upon either the personality or the methods of Sergeant Cuff.'[72] This observation resembled Harry Pirie-Gordon's review of *Crime and Detection* in the *Times Literary Supplement*. For both Eliot and Pirie-Gordon, the detective's use of new technologies did not necessarily make the novel more interesting. 'Sergeant Cuff is the perfect detective', wrote Eliot, 'Our modern detectives are most often either efficient but featureless machines, forgotten the moment we lay the book down, or else they have too many features, like Sherlock Holmes.'[73] Eliot's analogy between human beings and machines is reminiscent of the typist in *The Waste Land* who 'smooths her hair with automatic hand, / And puts a record on the gramophone'.[74] As Tim Armstrong argued, the 'mechanized body or the body attached to a machine' is a central theme of modernism.[75] Far from celebrating this penetration of the body by emerging technologies, Eliot bemoans the lost era of the fallible detective who solved crimes unaided by modern means.

In his review of *The Moonstone* in the American magazine the *Dial*, Gilbert Seldes agreed with Eliot that contemporary detectives lacked the personality of a Sergeant Cuff.[76] Seldes had known Eliot for a long time (they first met at Harvard in 1912) and as the managing editor of the *Dial* between 1921 and 1924, Seldes oversaw the publication of *The Waste Land* in the magazine.[77] An early admirer of Eliot's and Joyce's work, he nevertheless enjoyed popular culture. A few months before reviewing *The Moonstone*, Seldes had written on *Fourteen Great Detective Stories*, an anthology published in the Modern Library series.[78] He even wrote his own detective stories, which Eliot asked him to send over for possible publication by Faber in Britain.[79] As Michael Kammen puts it, Seldes 'never ceased to believe that high culture and popular culture could beneficially converge'.[80]

Drawing on Eliot's introduction, Seldes deplored that writers like S. S. Van Dine considered a murder as essential to the detective novel: 'In *The Moonstone* the diamond itself is made interesting by the prologue giving its bloody history and giving, as Mr Eliot says, the sense of fatality for the whole book.'[81] In an endnote, Seldes explained that he had already publicly disagreed with Van Dine on this issue.[82] Eliot's foreword thus allowed him to bring new arguments to this ongoing discussion. In short, Milford's plan to have *The Moonstone* 'properly discussed' had been entirely fulfilled: thanks to its preface, the book re-emerged, both in Britain and in the United States, as central to the canon of detective fiction.

The title of the review, 'Mr Eliot's Favourite', highlights the aura of the writer, whose name was enough to attract the attention of readers. Like Hollywood stars advertising their favourite soap, Eliot's recommendation of a particular book was a guarantee of increased sales. This explains why his introduction was mentioned on many, if not all advertisements for the World's Classics.[83] Although *The Moonstone* was not a quick success like *Ghosts and Marvels* and *Crime and Detection*, it sold steadily over a long period of time (see the Appendix to this chapter). The book was still available in the series in the mid-1960s, with a dust jacket that referred to the introduction by T. S. Eliot (Figure 1.3). Overall, Milford made an excellent bargain by paying fifteen guineas for a preface that continued to boost the sales and cultural prestige of the series for several decades.[84]

Eliot's introduction has been so enduring in part because of its striking statements that can be turned into blurbs. An editor himself, Eliot often wrote blurbs for Faber & Faber book-jackets.[85] He was certainly aware that a phrase such as 'the first, the longest, and the best of modern English detective novels' (repeated twice in the introduction) could boost the sales of *The Moonstone*. However, Eliot probably felt that such enthusiastic declarations had to be used cautiously. Too many introductions, with too many 'best' and 'greatest', would have a decreasing effect on readers, and could even endanger his position as a consecrated writer. In the preface to Djuna Barnes's *Nightwood* (1936), Eliot declared:

> When the question is raised, of writing an introduction to a book of a creative order, I always feel that the few books worth introducing are exactly those which it is an impertinence to introduce. I have already committed two such impertinences; this is the third, and if it is not the last no one will be more surprised than myself.[86]

Here, Eliot gave the image of a modest writer, who had no authority to judge literary masterpieces. The purpose of the introduction, Eliot said, was simply to encourage the reader to read the book. In other words, a good preface was nothing more than an expanded blurb. 'In describing *Nightwood* for the

Figure 1.3 Dust jacket, *The Moonstone*, Oxford World's Classics (c. 1966). By permission of Oxford University Press.

purpose of attracting readers to the English edition', Eliot explained, 'I said that it would "appeal primarily to readers of poetry". This is well enough for the brevity of advertisement, but I am glad to take this opportunity to amplify it a little.'[87] Eliot's introductions can therefore be seen as advertising materials that would circulate his name and help increase the sales of the books.

VIRGINIA WOOLF'S INTRODUCTION TO SENTIMENTAL JOURNEY

One year after approaching Eliot, Humphrey Milford wrote to Virginia Woolf about the proposed World's Classics edition of Laurence Sterne's *Sentimental Journey*.[88] 'I should be delighted if you would consent to write a recommendatory introduction for the "common reader"', declared Milford.[89] Ironically, this ordinary reader could be reached through a series published by Oxford University Press and edited by an Oxford-educated man. It seems surprising that Woolf, who deeply resented the authority of university men, would have contributed to a series so much associated with an elitist academic system.[90] For Woolf, the 'common reader' differed 'from the critic and the scholar': 'He reads for his own pleasure rather than to impart knowledge or correct the opinions of others.'[91] Woolf thought that readers should make their own decisions on the value of a text, without any guidance from so-called 'experts'. So why did she agree to write not one but two introductions to cheap editions published by Oxford World's Classics and the Modern Library in 1928? In my monograph on the Modern Library, I argue that Woolf wanted to widen her audience in the United States.[92] This chapter develops my argument by looking at the Oxford World's Classics, a series well distributed in the United States.

Woolf, who had started reviewing books for the *Times Literary Supplement* in her early twenties, was already familiar with the World's Classics series. In 1917, she praised the series' publication of Tolstoy's *The Cossacks and Other Tales of the Caucasus*. She agreed with the translators, Louise and Aylmer Maude, that Tolstoy was 'the greatest of Russia's writers'.[93] Woolf's attraction to Russian literature would lead her to take language lessons, and even contribute to translations of books published by the Hogarth Press.[94] Woolf did not only review World's Classics books, she also owned many titles in this series (including Tolstoy's *Plays* and *What then Must we Do?*).[95] Her essay 'Modern Fiction' – reprinted in the World's Classics in 1933 – also celebrated the influence of Russian writers on Anglophone literary modernism.

In addition to Russian literature, Woolf often wrote about her interest in Sterne's work. As early as 1905 she described *Sentimental Journey* as a pioneering book, well suited for contemporary readers: 'Sterne, when he invented the title of *Sentimental Journey*, not only christened but called into existence a class of book which seems to grow more popular the more we travel and the more sentimental we become.'[96] Four years later, Woolf wrote a long review of Sterne's biography which was published on the front page of the *Times Literary Supplement*.[97] In Woolf's critical writings, Sterne appears as one of the first truly modern English writers. In 1919, she wrote: 'English fiction from Sterne to Meredith bears witness to our natural delight in humour and comedy, in the beauty of earth, in the activities of the intellect, and in the splendour of the body.'[98] Considering Woolf's well-documented admiration for Sterne, it is not surprising that E. M. Forster suggested, in his *Aspects of the Novel* (1927), that there was a strong affinity between the two writers.[99]

Milford, who had included Forster's essay 'Philo's Little Trip' in his *Selected Modern English Essays* (1925), probably got the idea to contact Woolf after reading *Aspects of the Novel*. In Milford's correspondence and in the World's Classics catalogue, Forster and Woolf are often linked together. In 1929, Milford asked Forster to write the introduction to Jane Austen's *Persuasion* in the World's Classics, and sent him 'a copy of one of the latest volumes, the *Sentimental Journey* with Virginia Woolf's introduction'.[100] Forster declined, but his work later appeared alongside Woolf's in *Selected Modern English Essays, Second Series* (1932) and in *English Critical Essays, Twentieth Century* (1933). In bringing the names of Forster, Woolf and Eliot to his catalogue, Milford therefore updated the image of the World's Classics, from a traditional series of classics to a modernist institution of a sort.

The presence of Woolf also signalled a timid turn towards more women in the series. Although the early World's Classics had included the works of Charlotte Brontë, George Eliot, Jane Austen and Elizabeth Gaskell, those who wrote introductions were, with very few exceptions, men. For instance, Theodore Watts-Dunton wrote the preface to Brontë's *The Professor* and to Eliot's *Works III* (both published in 1906, shortly after Henry Frowde took over the series). However, Frowde was not hostile to having women write prefaces. When he was planning to add Washington Irving's *A Chronicle of the Conquest of Granada*, he contacted Gertrude Atherton, a prolific American writer. As Frowde explained, the World's Classics books 'have a very large circulation and many distinguished authors are consequently willing to contribute introductions although the fee I am able to offer is so small'.[101] Atherton seemed unimpressed, and never contributed to the series. The gender imbalance of the World's Classics list did not change much in the following years. Milford thus refused to publish Mary Wollstonecraft's *A Vindication of the Rights of Woman*, with an introduction by George Catlin (Vera Brittain's husband). 'In England, at least', Milford told Catlin, 'women have secured political equality, and I believe very few of us can no longer feel any strong interest in the subject.'[102] Despite this lack of interest in the suffrage movement, Milford slightly increased the representation of women in the World's Classics. Indeed, his collaboration with Woolf in 1928 was followed by multiple attempts to add introductions by Rebecca West and Edith Sitwell.[103] From 1931, Milford also reprinted several novels by Constance Holme, the first living female author to join the series. In addition, Phyllis Jones edited *English Critical Essays, Twentieth Century* (1933), which included essays by Woolf and Eliot. Although the World's Classics remained a male-dominated series, it was no longer closed to contemporary female authors and contributors.

After receiving Milford's letter in January 1928, Woolf asked him to confirm that she would be able to publish a version of the introduction in America before it came out in book form.[104] The year before, Irita Van Doren had invited Woolf to write a series of reviews for the October 1927 issues of the *New York Herald Tribune* Sunday *Books* supplement. The newspaper, which Joan Shelley Rubin has described as 'middlebrow', reached a circulation of 289,000 in 1928.[105] This was a unique opportunity for Woolf to increase her 'visibility in the US', as Beth Daugherty puts it.[106] Another advantage was that American editors paid more money than their British counterparts.[107] Woolf was thus eager to repeat this experience and publish another article in a mass-market newspaper read in America and elsewhere.

Milford replied that since the World's Classics edition would also be sold in the United States, he would prefer it if the article did not appear 'long in advance of the book'.[108] He was perhaps thinking of Eliot's *Times Literary Supplement* article on Wilkie Collins and Dickens, published so long before the publication of *The Moonstone* that it could not be used to advertise the book. When it became clear that Woolf's essay would appear in September in the *New York Herald Tribune*, Milford asked that the editors mentioned that it was a reprint of the introduction to *Sentimental Journey*.[109] 'Whether they do so or not you will no doubt be able to make use of the article to boost our edition', wrote Milford to the American branch of Oxford University Press.[110] In short, the publication of the introduction in America was beneficial to Woolf (who was eager to increase her audience there) but also to the World's Classics, a series with global ambitions.

In October 1928, three weeks after the release of the *New York Herald Tribune* article, the publisher Harcourt, Brace brought out the first American edition of *Orlando* with a first printing of 6,350 copies.[111] The book soon became a bestseller and contributed to Woolf's growing celebrity in America.[112] That same month, Woolf delivered two lectures on Women and Fiction at the University of Cambridge (later revised and published as *A Room of One's Own*). In November and December, *Sentimental Journey* and *Mrs Dalloway* were published in the World's Classics and the Modern Library series, and sold to a wide audience of common readers. Fellow modernist writers also expressed an interest – for example, Wyndham Lewis owned a copy of *Sentimental Journey*.[113] The British side of Oxford University Press issued the book with a first printing of 5,000 copies.[114] Since the World's Classics did not have to pay royalties on the text itself, the edition of *Sentimental Journey* could be sold for only 80 cents in the United States.[115] That was even cheaper than the 95-cent Modern Library edition, which reprinted Woolf's copyrighted novel. The dust jackets of both the World's Classics and Modern Library editions mentioned the introduction by Woolf to increase the appeal of the volumes.[116]

The two prefaces present striking similarities. In both cases, Woolf places the reader at the centre of her analysis. In the foreword to *Sentimental Journey*, she writes: 'the writer is always haunted by the belief that somehow it must be possible to brush aside the ceremonies and conventions of writing and to speak to the reader as directly as by word of mouth'.[117] She argues that Sterne was able to create a conversation with readers, instead of treating them as passive listeners. In the introduction to *Mrs Dalloway*, Woolf gives fragments of interpretation on the text but she frames her discussion in reference to readers: 'even so when everything had been brought to the surface, it would still be for the reader to decide what was relevant and what not'.[118] Woolf was well aware that a wide public would read these introductions, and she eagerly sought to engage with her new readers.

In January 1929, the *Times Literary Supplement* published a long article on the World's Classics edition of *Sentimental Journey*. 'As a pocket volume in "The World's Classics", to which it has been added by Mr Humphrey Milford with a generous type and margins', declared the reviewer (Arthur Sydney McDowall), 'the little novel may seem to glide by us in a flash'. The review, entitled 'Mrs Woolf and Sterne', focused mainly on the relationship between the two writers. In particular, it explored the modernity of Sterne's work: 'Certainly he might recognize something of himself in the varied sensibility, the personal expressiveness, the audacities of modern fiction.' While Sterne appeared as an ancestor to modern literature, Woolf was placed in the long canon of English literature: 'Is there no analogy to Sterne in the undertones of *To the Lighthouse* or the elastic brilliance of *Orlando*?'[119] The World's Classics series therefore contributed to Woolf's reputation as a major writer, comparable to Sterne.

Woolf's collaboration with the World's Classics was also noticed in the United States. In an article entitled 'We Love the Modernists', the *Christian Science Monitor* stated that the New York office of Oxford University Press had sent them several books, including Sterne's work. This package came in response to an earlier article on series of classics that had failed to acknowledge the World's Classics, which 'are authoritatively edited, well printed, neatly bound and cost only 80 cents'. The journalist replied that they had no objection to mentioning the World's Classics in the newspaper. 'Nor had we waited until now to read Virginia Woolf's introduction to the *Sentimental Journey* in this edition.'[120] The tone suggests that no educated American reader could have missed such an important book. Moreover, the *Washington Post* reviewed *English Critical Essays, Twentieth Century* (1933), which included Woolf's 'Modern Fiction'. 'There is nothing stuffy' about the book, stated the reviewer, before referring to the essays as 'all very good reading on a quiet night'.[121] *English Critical Essays* was also listed among recently added titles in a *New York Times* advertisement, which showed passengers on a

Figure 1.4 Advertisement for the World's Classics, *New York Times Book Review*, 3 June 1934, p. 19. By permission of Oxford University Press.

steamship reading the World's Classics books (Figure 1.4). Here, the cheap series was associated with leisure, luxury and taste – but also with portability ('a PERFECT POCKET FORMAT').

Having established her name in the American market, Woolf refused to write another introduction for the World's Classics and other publishers' series. In 1930, E. M. Forster declined to introduce Jane Austen's *Persuasion* (as he told Milford, the more he thought about the book, the more he hated it).[122] Milford then turned to Woolf, who also rejected the offer.[123] Shortly after, Woolf refused to write a preface to Anne Thackeray Ritchie's novels in the Travellers' Library. 'I find these short introductions very difficult to do, and unsatisfactory from the writer's point of view', she told Jonathan Cape.[124] As Hammond notes in her chapter on the World's Classics, 'attempts were made – and refusals received – from the 1930s to at least the 1950s'.[125] In 1950, Milford's successor, Geoffrey Cumberlege, asked for permission to put a selection from Virginia Woolf's essays in a single volume of the World's Classics. 'I think it would be good if some of her representative essays could be made available to a wider public than they may so far have reached', he told Harold Raymond, who now represented the Hogarth Press as an associate company of Chatto & Windus.[126] But Leonard Woolf firmly rejected the proposal.[127] It seems that for Virginia and her husband, cheap reprint series could bring little to an already-established writer. When Woolf was trying to increase her stature in America, classics series offered her access to a wide market of common readers. But once she had obtained the recognition she was looking for, these series no longer served her purpose and risked competing with the inexpensive editions published by the Hogarth Press.

Although Woolf and Eliot wrote only one preface for the Oxford World's Classics, the books they introduced remained in the series for decades and sold to thousands of readers. Figures are available for the UK market, and show that *Sentimental Journey* and *The Moonstone* sold more than 17,000 and 23,000 copies respectively in the thirty years between 1928 and 1957. It is impossible to give a precise account of the increased sales generated by the modernist writers' introductions, but we do know that during this period *The Moonstone* sold around 10,000 more copies than *The Woman in White* (which did not feature a new introduction). *Selected Modern English Essays, Second Series* and *English Critical Essays, Twentieth Century* did even better, with nearly 26,000 copies sold between 1932 and 1957 for the former, and 31,000 copies between 1933 and 1957 for the latter (see Appendix, Figure 1.5).[128] These sales figures were comparable to those of the most successful titles in the series.[129]

The collaboration between modernist writers and the World's Classics had an important cultural impact, not only in Britain but also in the United States. Eliot's introduction to *The Moonstone* seemed such an effective selling point that it was soon imitated. In 1937, the Modern Library launched its own edition of *The Moonstone* and *The Woman in White* in a single 'Giant' volume, with an introduction by Alexander Woollcott. '*The Moonstone* was the first full-length detective novel. It is still the best', declared a blurb by Woollcott printed on the dust jacket. This was, of course, reminiscent of Eliot's 'the first, the longest, and the best of modern English detective novels'. This phrase and its variant 'the first and greatest of English detective novels' have continued to be used in the marketing of *The Moonstone*. The latest edition in the Oxford World's Classics includes it as a blurb on the back cover. In the introduction, John Sutherland also comments on his illustrious predecessor. 'Literary pontiff that he was, Eliot was less than well equipped to pronounce on the excellences of pulp fiction', writes Sutherland before arguing that *The Moonstone* is neither the first nor the best detective novel.[130] Eliot's superlatives have nevertheless become intrinsic to *The Moonstone* (even competitors to the World's Classics quote them on marketing materials). Eliot's praise for *Armadale*, which initially appeared in the introduction to *The Moonstone*, is also used for the Penguin edition of the novel. Eliot's introduction to the World's Classics edition has helped to sell cheap books for more than eighty years.

APPENDIX

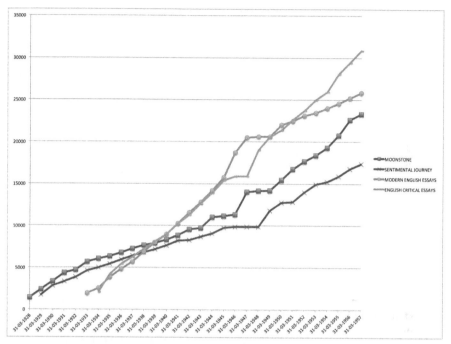

Figure 1.5: Cumulated sales figures, UK: Oxford World's Classics editions of *The Moonstone* (1928), *Sentimental Journey* (1928), *Selected Modern English Essays, Second Series* (1932), *English Critical Essays, Twentieth Century* (1933).

NOTES

1. Jaillant, *Modernism*, pp. 63–4, 85.
2. Pinto, 'We Have Been Reading Lately'.
3. In particular, the press published the influential *Oxford Book of English Verse*, edited by A. T. Quiller-Couch (Virginia Woolf had a copy of the 1900 edition in her library). King and Miletic-Vejzovic, eds, 'The Library of Leonard and Virginia Woolf'.
4. Milford to Holme, 21 December 1931, Letter books of Humphrey Milford, OUP.
5. Hammond, *Reading*, p. 103.
6. Hammond, *Reading*, pp. 104–5.
7. Sutcliffe, *The Oxford University Press*, p. 143; Hammond, *Reading*, p. 104.
8. Potter, *Obscene Modernism*, p. 103.
9. Bourdieu, *The Field of Cultural Production*, p. 42; Hammond, *Reading*, p. 113.
10. Gadd, Eliot and Louis, eds, *The History of Oxford University Press*.
11. For more on the 'vertical expansion' of modernist studies towards popular culture, see Mao and Walkowitz, 'The New Modernist Studies,' p. 744. For more

on Eliot's and Woolf's non-fiction, see Kaufmann, 'A Modernism of One's Own: Virginia Woolf's *TLS* Reviews and Eliotic Modernism'.

12. Hammond, *Reading*, p. 95.
13. Sims, 'Grant Richards: Publisher', p. 16.
14. Scholes, 'Grant Richards to James Joyce', p. 140.
15. Richards to Herbert B. Turner & Co, 2 January 1904, Letter book Vol. 4, GR.
16. Altick, 'From Aldine to Everyman', p. 15.
17. Horder, 'Grant Richards', p. 42. On the material form of the series, see also Birchall, 'The World's Classics'.
18. Richards to Charles Holme, 17 December 1903, Letter book Vol. 4, GR.
19. Richards to Watts-Dunton, 18 November 1903, Letter book Vol. 4, GR.
20. Hammond, *Reading*, p. 111.
21. 'Mr Grant Richards's Affairs', *Publishers' Circular*, 22 April 1905, p. 434.
22. Frowde bought the copyright, but also the stock and plates of the World's Classics. Contract between Moring and Frowde, October 1905, Letter books of Henry Frowde, OUP.
23. Flanders, 'The Press in London', p. 140.
24. Frowde to Watts-Dunton, 18 December 1905, Letter books of Henry Frowde, OUP.
25. Frowde to Watts-Dunton, 18 December 1905, Letter books of Henry Frowde, OUP.
26. Frowde to Watts-Dunton, 19 April 1906 and 18 December 1905, Letter books of Henry Frowde, OUP.
27. Frowde to Gosse, 7 May 1906, Letter books of Henry Frowde, OUP.
28. Frowde to George Wyndham, 6 November 1906, Letter books of Henry Frowde, OUP.
29. Bourdieu, *The Field of Cultural Production*, p. 42.
30. Frowde to Watts-Dunton, 12 January 1906, Letter books of Henry Frowde, OUP.
31. Frowde to the Master of University College Oxford, 23 September 1909, Letter books of Henry Frowde, OUP.
32. Frowde to Watts-Dunton, 30 January 1906, Letter books of Henry Frowde, OUP.
33. Frowde to Charles Cannan, 27 November 1907, Letter books of Henry Frowde, OUP.
34. Frowde to Watts-Dunton, 12 January 1906, Letter books of Henry Frowde, OUP.
35. Milford to George Stephen, 22 June 1928, Letter books of Humphrey Milford, OUP.
36. Milford to H. Z. Walck, 14 August 1943, WC Misc. (to June 1962), Ref. LOGE 000260 Box LG34, OUP.
37. Quoted in 'The World's Classics', 12 August 1943, WC Misc. (to June 1962), Ref. LOGE 000260 Box LG34, OUP.
38. Frowde to the Delegates, 22 November 1905, Letter books of Henry Frowde, OUP.
39. Maw, 'Milford, Sir Humphrey Sumner (1877–1952)', *Oxford Dictionary of National Biography*.
40. Flanders, 'The Press in London', p. 144.
41. Milford to F. V. Morley, 10 May 1928; Milford to Abel Chevalley, 5 January 1927, Letter books of Humphrey Milford, OUP.
42. Milford to Collins, 2 October 1926, Letter books of Humphrey Milford, OUP.
43. Advertisement for the Oxford University Press, *The Times of India*, 11 March 1927, p. 15.
44. 'Current Topics', *The Times of India*, 15 January 1925, p. 8.
45. Production and sales figures, *Ghosts and Marvels*, OUP.

46. Advertisement for the Oxford World's Classics, *Spectator* 137 (1926), 400.
47. Wrong, 'Introduction' to *Crime and Detection*, p. ix.
48. Wrong, 'Introduction' to *Crime and Detection*, p. xii.
49. Haycraft, *Murder for Pleasure*, p. 273.
50. Haycraft, ed., *The Art of the Mystery Story*, p. 18.
51. Unindexed back matter, *Contemporary Review*, 1 July 1926, p. 811.
52. Pirie-Gordon, 'Detectives', *Times Literary Supplement*, p. 529.
53. I am grateful to Roxann Bilger for sending me a copy of the dust jacket.
54. Production and sales figures, *Crime and Detection*, OUP.
55. Production and sales figures, *More Ghosts and Marvels*, OUP.
56. Raymond to Gerard Hopkins, 3 December 1926, File *The Moonstone*, Ref. 010117 Box OP1365, OUP.
57. *New Criterion*, January 1927, p. 140. Quoted in *Letters of T. S. Eliot*, vol. 3, p. 395, n. 3.
58. Milford to Eliot, 31 January 1927, File *The Moonstone*, Ref. 010117 Box OP1365, OUP.
59. Eliot to Milford, 31 January 1927, File *The Moonstone*, Ref. 010117 Box OP1365, OUP. Quoted in *Letters of T. S. Eliot*, vol. 3, pp. 395–6.
60. Milford to Eliot, 12 April 1927, Letter books of Humphrey Milford, OUP.
61. Eliot to Milford, 1 May 1927, File *The Moonstone*, Ref. 010117 Box OP1365, OUP. Quoted in *Letters of T. S. Eliot*, vol. 3, p. 493.
62. Eliot to Aiken, 31 December 1914. Quoted in *Letters of T. S. Eliot*, vol. 1, p. 74.
63. McDonald, *Learning to Be Modern*, p. 44.
64. Eliot, 'Wilkie Collins and Dickens', p. 525.
65. Chinitz, *T. S. Eliot and the Cultural Divide*, p. 55.
66. Eliot, 'Wilkie Collins and Dickens', p. 525.
67. Eliot, 'Wilkie Collins and Dickens', p. 525.
68. Eliot, 'Introduction', *The Moonstone*, p. v.
69. Eliot to Milford, 1 May 1927, File *The Moonstone*, Ref. 010117 Box OP1365, OUP. Quoted in *Letters of T. S. Eliot*, vol. 3, p. 493.
70. Eliot, 'Wilkie Collins and Dickens', p. 526.
71. It is probable that Bruce L. Richmond, editor of the *TLS*, asked for this delay, so that Eliot's article would be seen as original and exclusive rather than an advertisement for the forthcoming World's Classics edition. Milford mentions his negotiation with Richmond in his letter to Eliot, 3 May 1927, File *The Moonstone*, Ref. 010117 Box OP1365, OUP.
72. Eliot, 'Introduction', *The Moonstone*, p. xii.
73. Eliot, 'Introduction', *The Moonstone*, p. xii.
74. Eliot, *The Waste Land*, p. 32.
75. Armstrong, *Modernism, Technology, and the Body*, p. 86.
76. Seldes, 'Mr Eliot's Favourite', p. 437.
77. Chinitz, *T. S. Eliot and the Cultural Divide*, p. 60.
78. Seldes, 'Extra Good Ones'. See also Jaillant, *Modernism*, p. 75.
79. Eliot to Seldes, 12 April 1927, Box 5, T. S. Eliot collection, HRC.
80. Kammen, *The Lively Arts*, p. 10.
81. Seldes, 'Mr Eliot's Favourite', p. 439.
82. Seldes, 'Mr Eliot's Favourite', p. 440.
83. See for example, *Times Literary Supplement*, 8 March 1928, p. 161; 22 March 1928, p. 199; and 22 November 1928, p. 871.
84. Milford to Eliot, 31 January 1927, File *The Moonstone*, Ref. 010117 Box OP1365, OUP.
85. Evans, 'Guru-in-Chief'.

86. Eliot, 'Introduction', *Nightwood*, p. 1.
87. Eliot, 'Introduction', *Nightwood*, pp. 1–2.
88. The Scholartis Press published a fine edition of *Sentimental Journey* with an introduction by Herbert Read shortly after the Oxford World's Classics edition.
89. Milford to Woolf, 6 January 1928, File *Sentimental Journey*, Ref. 010120 Box OP1365, OUP.
90. It should be noted that Woolf had many friends among 'university men', including Dadie Rylands, G. Lowes Dickinson and Bertrand Russell.
91. Woolf, *The Common Reader*, p. 11.
92. Jaillant, *Modernism*, pp. 83–4.
93. Woolf, 'Tolstoy's *The Cossacks*'.
94. See Beasley, 'On Not Knowing Russian'.
95. King and Miletic-Vejzovic, eds, 'The Library of Leonard and Virginia Woolf'.
96. Woolf, 'Journeys in Spain'.
97. Woolf, 'Sterne'.
98. Woolf, 'Modern Novels'. This article was later reprinted under the title 'Modern Fiction'.
99. Forster, *Aspects of the Novel*, pp. 30–3.
100. Milford to Forster, 11 October 1929, Letter books of Humphrey Milford, OUP.
101. Frowde to Atherton, 15 April 1907, Letter books of Henry Frowde, OUP.
102. Milford to Catlin, 12 June 1928, Letter books of Humphrey Milford, OUP.
103. Milford to Secretary Clarendon Press, 15 October 1930, Letter books of Humphrey Milford, OUP; 'ACW' to H. Z. Walck, 6 December 1945, File Henry James: *The Portrait of a Lady*, Ref. 010149 Box OP 1367, OUP.
104. Woolf to Milford, 11 January 1928, File *Sentimental Journey*, Ref. 010120 Box OP1365, OUP.
105. Rubin, *The Making of Middlebrow Culture*, p. xvi. Kluger and Kluger, *The Paper*, p. 232. Quoted in Tyler, 'Cultural Conversations', p. 46.
106. Daugherty, 'The Transatlantic Virginia Woolf', p. 9.
107. Tyler, 'Cultural Conversations', p. 45.
108. Milford to Woolf, 12 January 1928, Letter books of Humphrey Milford, OUP.
109. Milford to Woolf, 16 August 1928, File *Sentimental Journey*, Ref. 010120 Box OP1365, OUP.
110. Milford to Oxford University Press American Branch, 16 August 1928, File *Sentimental Journey*, Ref. 010120 Box OP1365, OUP.
111. Kirkpatrick and Clarke, *A Bibliography of Virginia Woolf*, p. 63. Woolf's article was published on 23 September, *Orlando* on 18 October 1928.
112. 'There were five re-impressions totalling 14,950 copies between November 1928 and February 1933.' Kirkpatrick and Clarke, *A Bibliography of Virginia Woolf*, p. 63.
113. This copy is now held at the Harry Ransom Center, University of Texas at Austin.
114. Production and sales figures, *Sentimental Journey*, OUP.
115. However, the press paid fifteen guineas to Woolf for the introduction to the World's Classics edition. Milford to Woolf, 6 January 1928, File *Sentimental Journey*, Ref. 010120 Box OP1365, OUP.
116. Jaillant, *Modernism*, pp. 87, 91.
117. Woolf, 'Introduction', *Sentimental Journey*, p. vii.
118. *The Essays of Virginia Woolf*, vol. 4, p. 549.
119. McDowall, 'Mrs Woolf and Sterne'.
120. Sloper, 'Bookman's Holiday'.
121. Hall, 'No End of Books'.
122. Milford to Forster, 14 March 1930, Letter books of Humphrey Milford, OUP.

123. Milford to Secretary Clarendon Press, 21 March 1930, Letter books of Humphrey Milford, OUP.
124. Woolf to Cape, 1 May 1931, JC.
125. Hammond, *Reading*, p. 111, n. 77.
126. Cumberlege to Raymond, 3 July 1950, Folder World Classic Suggestions, Ref. LOGE 000267 Box LG35, OUP.
127. Raymond to Cumberlege, 18 July 1950, Folder World Classic Suggestions, Ref. LOGE 000267 Box LG35, OUP.
128. Production and sales figures, OUP.
129. For example, Henry Fielding's *The Adventures of Joseph Andrews*, with an introduction by L. Rice-Oxley, sold nearly 27,000 copies from 1929 to 1957. Production and sales figures, OUP.
130. Sutherland, 'Introduction', p. vii.

2

POCKETABLE PROVOCATEURS: JAMES JOYCE AND D. H. LAWRENCE IN THE TRAVELLERS' LIBRARY AND THE NEW ADELPHI LIBRARY

In February 1926, a long essay on 'The Poisoning of Youth' appeared in the *English Review*. John Rudd, a librarian at a boy's school, simply refused to provide the books that the students asked for, books by 'the most advertised moderns' – including H. G. Wells, Arnold Bennett, Rose Macaulay, John Galsworthy and Warwick Deeping.[1] For Rudd, the treatment of love and sex in modern fiction made it unsuitable for teenage boys. The imagery of food and health runs throughout the essay: boys have been 'brought up on the healthy diet of Kipling, Marryat, Ian Hay, Wells (early period)' and they 'want diet more suitable to their years'.[2] But the lack of morality in modern books risked poisoning the 'bright and clever and healthy lad'.[3] Rudd gives the example of Deeping's 1925 bestseller *Sorrell & Son*, a novel with 'immoral' and 'rebellious' female characters.[4] Reading this kind of fiction could give the boys the impression that emancipated women have sexual desires and want to 'have a good time'.[5] To prevent corrupting young readers, Rudd asked novelists to write cleaner books and publishers to fulfil their educational mission. His essay shows that issues of obscenity and censorship applied to all kinds of texts, including texts that we now see as 'middlebrow'. If Rudd could present Deeping as a problematic writer, it is not difficult to imagine what he would have thought of James Joyce or D. H. Lawrence.

Of course, Rudd was not the first one to denounce the poisonous effect of modern fiction. Rachel Potter notes that 'prussic acid, strychnine, and arsenic; leprosy, excrement, and open sewers' were 'some of the more colourful images conjured up by nineteenth- and twentieth-century commentators to capture the noxious effects of obscene literature'.[6] The Obscene Publications Act of 1857, and the subsequent 'Hicklin ruling' that defined obscenity as the tendency 'to deprave and corrupt those whose minds are open to such immoral influences', were used to censor a wide range of books.[7] This official censorship was complemented by actions from members of the book trade (printers, publishers, booksellers, librarians) to prevent the diffusion of questionable books. Despite these strict controls, concerns over obscenity did not disappear. In early 1926, the debate between the home secretary William Joynson-Hicks and the MP Joseph Kenworthy led to a series of articles on indecent books and plays. The *Bookseller*, the main magazine of the book trade, explored several solutions to the problem of 'sex novels', including putting these books out of the view of young and female readers. It is in this context that two publishers launched new series of modern, copyrighted texts, including titles by controversial authors. James Joyce's *Dubliners* and D. H. Lawrence's *Twilight in Italy* were among the first books that Jonathan Cape selected for his Travellers' Library. Martin Secker also reprinted many titles by Lawrence in his New Adelphi Library – starting with *The Captain's Doll* in 1926.

This chapter argues that the success of Cape's and Secker's series proved that there was a large market for the most contentious modern writers – Joyce and Lawrence. It is important to remember that when Lawrence appeared in the Travellers' Library and the New Adelphi Library, his name was intertwined with obscenity (his novel *The Rainbow* was seized by police in 1915, which led to a debate in the House of Commons). When *Dubliners* and *A Portrait of the Artist as a Young Man* were reprinted in the Travellers' Library (in 1926 and 1930 respectively), *Ulysses* was still banned in Britain and in other Anglophone countries. Despite the ban, Eleni Loukopoulou notes that 'during the 1920s, Joyce's work continued to circulate and be read (within both avant-garde circles and the literary establishment)'.[8] My chapter shows that far from being restricted to an elite readership, *Dubliners* and later *Portrait of the Artist* were read by a large audience in the Travellers' Library. The three-and-six-penny libraries used the modernists' subversive reputation as a selling point to market Joyce and Lawrence to a wide public. The first section of this chapter examines the 'Indecent Books' debate in early 1926, at the time when the Travellers' Library and the New Adelphi Library were launched. I then focus on the inclusion of Joyce's *Dubliners* and *Portrait of the Artist* in Jonathan Cape's series and of Lawrence's work in Martin Secker's series. Finally, I turn to the paperbacks, which contributed to the decline of the three-and-six-penny libraries in the 1930s.

THE 'INDECENT BOOKS' DEBATE (1926)

The home secretary from 1924 to 1929, William Joynson-Hicks (nicknamed 'Jix'), has been remembered as a hardliner who pushed for more censorship. 'He was the most prudish, puritanical, and protestant home secretary of the twentieth century', writes F. M. L. Thompson,

> He led the campaign to suppress the hedonistic permissiveness of metropolitan life in the 1920s, attempting to stem 'the flood of filth coming across the Channel' by rooting out the pornography of *The Well of Loneliness*, D. H. Lawrence's books and pictures, works on birth control, the translation of the *Decameron*, sundry publications condemned as 'pseudo-sociological', and the like, the policy being defended in his 1929 pamphlet *Do We Need a Censor?*

For Thompson, Joynson-Hicks was associated with 'extreme puritanism and illiberalism'.[9] In fact, far from being extreme, the home secretary's concerns over obscenity were shared by many – at least in 1926.[10]

In February of that year, the Lieutenant-Commander Kenworthy, a Liberal MP, raised a series of questions about morality and public order in the House of Commons. 'Better regulation and supervision' were needed in London parks open after dark, Kenworthy said.[11] Joynson-Hicks recognised that there had been 'one or two unfortunate incidents': the month before, Sir Basil Thomson – the former Director of Intelligence at the Home Office – had been arrested for misbehaving himself with a young woman (perhaps a prostitute) in Hyde Park.[12] But Joynson-Hicks refused to take measures, such as closing the parks earlier, which would penalise the entire community. One week later, Kenworthy asked the home secretary to explain what his department was doing to prevent the publication and sales of obscene books. Joynson-Hicks replied:

> The Home Office in this matter keeps in close touch with the Director of Public Prosecutions and the police authorities, and effective action is being taken wherever possible. I am advised that, speaking generally, the law is reasonably adequate, and the difficulties which arise in enforcing it are due not so much to any defect in the law itself, as to differences of opinion in the minds of magistrates as to what in any particular case constitutes punishable indecency within the law.[13]

Indeed, the legal definition of obscenity was so vague that magistrates did not necessarily agree on what books should be banned. This was not a new problem. 'For some years after the Hicklin test [1868]', Katherine Mullin points out, '"obscenity" remained an unstable term, often invoked, frequently blurring into "indecency," but nonetheless resisting clear legal definition'.[14]

Joynson-Hicks had little interest in changing a law that left a large autonomy to authorities to suppress questionable books.

Pressed by Kenworthy and by the London Public Morality Council to take action against dirty books and plays, Joynson-Hicks gave a restrained response in two letters published in *The Times*.[15] He recommended educating the public to 'raise the standard of taste and judgement'. This would eliminate the market for 'border-line cases', i.e. controversial books that could not be described as 'really pornographic'. However, he refused to ask publishers to set up a censorship committee that would examine all books before publication. As Lisa Sigel notes, members of the Home Office were often less conservative than the London Public Morality Council, a private organisation 'willing to take matters of morality to the lunatic fringe'.[16] The Bishop of London, speaking for the Council, then suggested that Joynson-Hicks call 'a conference of reputable publishers with a view to the establishment of a standard or informal censorship, as was done in the case of films in 1917'.[17]

The book trade quickly reacted to these suggestions, which targeted mainstream publishers rather than the underground producers of pornography. One commentator wrote in the *Bookseller* that 'such [a] censorship committee' would be impossible to set up:

> I have yet to meet a publisher who would welcome an arrangement that at any moment might impose on him the invidious job of vetoing, or helping to veto, a book which some brother-publisher had approved and accepted, and was ready and anxious to put on his list.[18]

Forcing publishers to censor each other was presented as a bad solution to a real problem. Indeed, many booksellers remained uneasy with a perceived flow of problematic books. Some of them decided to 'put in the background all suggestive novels and only sell them when specially asked for by adults'.[19] Others went even further and refused to sell daring books, even to adults, a solution that was not without risks. As one article puts it, 'it is a pity that when the multiple firms refuse facilities for the sale of these books, the business falls into the hands of the competing booksellers who have no such qualms'.[20] Since publishers could not be expected to censor each other, and booksellers could do little to prevent the sale of daring books, Joynson-Hicks's appeal to raise the level of public education and taste seemed to many the best solution.[21]

The 'Indecent Books' debate of 1926 highlights a mainstream concern over obscenity. A major trade magazine such as the *Bookseller* did not include a single article defending freedom of expression. Among members of the book trade, the dominant view seemed to have been that public authorities should exercise control over the diffusion of suggestive books. If that control failed, booksellers were perfectly entitled to put these books under their counter, and to sell them only on request (if at all). In the long run, readers had to be educated to improve the general standard of taste, but until then, censorship was necessary. In this context, 'Jix' was not seen as an extreme puritan. Writing in 1933 – after the ban on Radcliffe Hall's *The Well of Loneliness* and the confiscation of a manuscript of poems by Lawrence[22] – Joynson-Hicks's biographer wrote that he 'pursued a middle course, failing to satisfy the reformers [such as the London Public Morality Council], and angering those who, in the name of art, demanded freedom'.[23] Most publishers were careful not to stray too far from this middle course, and risk being tainted by allegations of obscenity.

JAMES JOYCE IN THE TRAVELLERS' LIBRARY

So why did Jonathan Cape decide to include works by provocateurs such as James Joyce in his Travellers' Library? In this section, I show that Cape was prepared to take calculated risks to create interest in his new series. Never an anti-censorship crusader, he selected relatively uncontroversial titles by controversial authors. He also moved at a slow pace, waiting four years after the publication of *Dubliners* to add *A Portrait of the Artist as a Young Man* to the series.

Jonathan Cape shared many similarities with Grant Richards and other 'enterprising' publishers (see Chapter 1). Like Richards, Cape started working when he was a teenager and had little formal education. And like Richards, Cape was interested in James Joyce's work – although he found *Ulysses* a 'penance' and rejected, perhaps against his will, *A Portrait of the Artist as a Young Man* when he was working for the publisher Duckworth & Co.[24] The son of a builder, Cape's rise in the publishing industry was long and torturous, and he was forty years old when he created his own firm in 1919. Shortly after that, he secured the reprint rights for the 'spicy novels of Elinor Glyn', which he produced 'in huge quantities as shilling paperbacks'.[25] Like Richards, Cape did not shy away from daring texts – as long as the risk of censorship seemed remote.

In 1924, Harriet Shaw Weaver sold the Egoist Press, and Cape bought the rights to Joyce's *A Portrait of the Artist as a Young Man*, *Chamber Music* and *Exiles*. The first printing of *Portrait of the Artist* in the 7s. 6d. edition was only 1,250 copies. Although Cape did not initially anticipate a large market, the book sold well, and there were five printings between 1924 and 1926.[26] Unlike the Egoist Press, Cape spent large sums on advertising. In a letter to Sylvia Beach, he offered a royalty rate of 15 per cent to Joyce: 'This is a lower percentage than what you and Miss Weaver have been paying him but my different methods of publication have to be taken into account – the expenses of travelling and advertising are very high. I hope that Mr Joyce will agree to this.'[27] Cape could not offer the high royalty rate paid by the Egoist Press and Shakespeare & Company, but he did advertise the book in large-circulation newspapers. One advertisement in *The Times* featured a blurb by H. G. Wells:

'A book to buy and read and lock up, but not a book to miss. A most memorable novel.'[28]

In 1926, Cape decided to launch his own series of classics, the Travellers' Library, sold for three shillings and six pence (approximately half the price of an original edition). In the mid-1920s, as noted earlier, buying recent books was still not a common practice. As Nicola Wilson points out, 'the circulating libraries were the main way in which the majority of readers got hold of newly published fiction for most of the first half of the twentieth century'.[29] Libraries such as W. H. Smith, Boots Book-lovers' Library, Mudie's Select Circulating Library, The Times Book Club, and Harrods offered a good choice of books in a comfortable environment designed to appeal to the middle classes. In a paper presented before the Society of Bookmen in 1926, E. Winterton described the libraries as 'a modern development, compared with other branches of book distribution'.[30] For Winterton, the libraries 'greatly increas[ed] the number of readers, and have made what at one time was considered a luxury to become one of the everyday necessities of the educated public'.[31] The enduring success of the circulating libraries was a source of concern for many publishers and booksellers. In an article entitled 'Why People Do Not Buy More Books', the *Bookseller* magazine explained that 'middle-class folks get their books from libraries instead of buying them because they cannot afford what they think to be high prices, and as the flats of to-day are so small there is no room for a presentable book-case'.[32] With the launch of the 3s. 6d. series, the middle classes who patronised the circulating libraries could now buy recent books with small sizes well suited to small flats. This contributed to a larger trend towards an expanding book-buying public. 'One seems to notice more people reading books in trains, tubes, and so forth nowadays than one noticed a few years ago', declared the *Bookseller*.[33]

Cape understood the need to *educate* ordinary people to buy books. One advertisement for the Travellers' Library featured a dialogue between two men:

> 'You really must read it, it's wonderfully good.'
> 'Yes, I've heard about it. Will you lend it to me?'
> 'I haven't got a copy now. I had one, but some one borrowed it, and so far it hasn't come back.'
> 'I'd buy a copy, only I'm awfully hard up these days and books are so expensive.'
> 'You can get it for three and six pence. It's in The Travellers' Library.'
> 'Oh! is it. I'll get it then. I like that series so much. I've bought a lot of them for presents and for myself.'[34]

Here, the first impulse to borrow a book is replaced with the decision to buy it in a cheap form. This kind of narrative to produce a new habit is a strategy that is still used in today's business world: Twitter and Square co-founder Jack Dorsey has talked about 'user narratives', whose plot, place and action can be translated into triggers to buy products.

While cheap books had long been available in well-produced series such as Everyman's Library and the Oxford World's Classics, the Travellers' Library distinguished itself from its competitors by including many copyrighted texts. It was a good way for Cape to use his backlist, and to give a second life to novels that had first been published years ago. But launching a new series in a crowded market was not an easy decision to make for an undercapitalised publisher. 'In the course of his work a publisher takes risks which would make the men in most businesses shudder', stated Cape's magazine *Now & Then*, 'and one of the greatest risks a publisher can take is in the issue of a series of this kind'.[35] While the World's Classics series had contributed to Grant Richards's bankruptcy, the success of the Travellers' Library helped Cape consolidate his position in the book trade.

Cape and his colleagues paid particular attention to the uniform physical format of the series. As they put it,

> the appearance, shape, and durability of the volumes in a series of this kind is clearly of the greatest importance, the more particularly as errors of judgment or taste cannot be remedied after any volumes are published or uniformity would not be maintained.[36]

All Travellers' Library books had a blue cloth binding, with the title and author's name stamped in gold on the spine. The yellow dust jacket was designed to catch the eye of prospective customers in bookshops (Plate 1).[37] 'The wrapper itself', declared the *Bookseller*, 'has a "quality" touch about it that is at the same time inviting, and embodies the now established "Cape" idea of printing the price on the perforated corner of the wrapper – a little piece of thoughtfulness that makes a Cape book particularly suitable as a gift book.'[38] The colophon of the series, which appeared on dust jackets, title pages, bindings and on advertisements also served to improve brand recognition (Figure 2.1). Designed by Percy Smith, this logo represented 'a faun as the traveller, carrying a modification of the Jonathan Cape vase of fruits'.[39] In the Antiquity, fauns were described as guiding humans in need – as in Aesop's fable *The Satyr and the Traveller*. This classical reference seems surprising for a series of modern texts. But it also allowed Cape to position the Travellers' Library as a series of *classics*, rather than mere reprints of recent texts.

The name of the series highlights a central element of its brand story – the association with travel and discovery. As Faye Hammill and Michelle Smith put it, 'travel is a part of the middlebrow, aspirant psyche – a symbol of achievement, cultural literacy, *savoir-faire*, and personal means'.[40] The Travellers' Library was presented as an ideal companion for the refined English

Figure 2.1 Travellers' Library Colophon (spine, binding of *Twilight in Italy* [1926]). By permission of Penguin Random House UK.

venturing outside the country's borders. '*The Travellers' Library*', declared the writer Laurence Housman,

> will be a selection of books very urbane, very civilized in character – or at any rate very English, so as to provide antidotes to all the ills which a crossing of the Channel, or still more of the Atlantic, is sure to bring in its train.[41]

Not only did the small format of Travellers' Library books (7 x 4¾ inches) make them easy to pack in a suitcase, they also provided the comfort of civilisation to those travelling to foreign countries. Cape's series was sold in Britain, in India, in Australia and even in South Africa. 'Have you a friend who travels?' asked one advertisement with a blurb from the *Natal Advertiser*, a South African newspaper.[42] Here, the cosmopolitanism and sophistication of the traveller was paralleled with the global diffusion of the Traveller's Library.

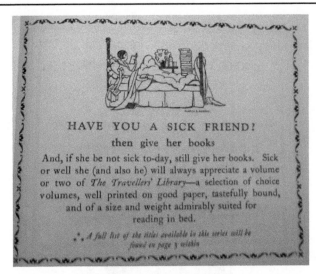

HAVE YOU A SICK FRIEND?

then give her books

And, if she be not sick to-day, still give her books. Sick or well she (and also he) will always appreciate a volume or two of *The Travellers' Library*—a selection of choice volumes, well printed on good paper, tastefully bound, and of a size and weight admirably suited for reading in bed.

⁂ *A full list of the titles available in this series will be found on page 3 within*

Figure 2.2 Advertisement for the Travellers' Library, *Now & Then*, 22 (1926), 37. By permission of Penguin Random House UK.

The series was associated with physical travel and globalisation, but also, as the *Observer* put it, 'with voyages of the spirit, exploration of the imagination in the darkness that surrounds us'.[43] One advertisement recommended giving these books to a sick friend: 'Sick or well she (or he) will always appreciate a volume or two of *The Travellers' Library* – a selection of choice volumes, well printed on good paper, tastefully bound, and of a size and weight admirably suited for reading in bed' (Figure 2.2). The accompanying illustration showed an elegant female reader in her bed, which reinforced the traditional association between women and the domestic sphere. In short, Cape targeted not only actual travellers but also all those interested in the travels of the mind.

This broad definition of 'travel' allowed Cape to select a wide range of books. A typical description of the Travellers' Library stated: 'It is famed for its clever combination of literary quality with catholicity. Its scope allows, without discomfort, the juxtaposition of high-spirited books of pure adventure and works of mature scholarship.'[44] Joyce's and Lawrence's texts were not isolated in a 'highbrow' ghetto: they were read alongside a wide range of texts. Among the titles published in 1926 were W. H. Davies's *The Autobiography of a Super-Tramp* (#3 in the series), Sinclair Lewis's *Babbitt* (#4), Joyce's *Dubliners* (#14), Ernest Bramah's *The Wallet of Kai-Lung* (#18), Lawrence's *Twilight in Italy* (#19) and H. G. Wells's *The Dream* (#20).

When *Dubliners* joined the series in late 1926, Joyce was already a well-known name in Britain. In February, a young publisher, Geoffrey Bles, had issued *James Joyce, his First Forty Years* by Herbert S. Gorman. As one advertisement put it, 'this is the first book to appear on the author of *Ulysses* – a work which, very properly prohibited, is very widely read'.[45] This statement ridiculing censorship laws should be read in the context of the 'Indecent Books' debate. Despite calls for cleaner books, *Ulysses* was described as 'a work which is recognised as a masterpiece by some of the greatest living writers'.[46] Gorman's book was widely reviewed, in literary periodicals and in mainstream newspapers across the country. The *Times Literary Supplement* deplored the contrast between Gorman's 'unreadable' writing and Joyce's meticulous attention to style.[47] The *Yorkshire Evening Post* was more enthusiastic, describing Gorman's book as 'a very useful aid to the comprehension' of *Ulysses* – a book that 'has had more influence upon modern letters, and has been more widely discussed, than any other literary production of the age'.[48] The *Aberdeen Press and Journal* also insisted on the centrality of Joyce in modern literature. *Ulysses* was presented as 'the subject of discussion and curiosity on the part of those who have never been able to secure a copy and who are intrigued by the whispered comments of the initiates'.[49] This tension between widespread curiosity and difficulty of access to Joyce's work opened up new opportunities for Cape: although *Ulysses* could not be sold in Britain, its reputation could be used to promote *Dubliners* and *A Portrait of the Artist as a Young Man* to intrigued readers.

Cape and his colleagues selected titles by well-known modern writers that would create interest in the Travellers' Library, without attracting the attention of censors. The *Observer* thus declared:

> A new name in the series is that of Mr D. H. Lawrence, whose *Twilight in Italy* presents him in his least controversial aspect. During the coming week, another provocative figure, Mr James Joyce, will be added to the list with his *Dubliners*.[50]

Here, the subversive image of the modernist writers is contrasted with the uncontroversial nature of the Travellers' Library titles. The travel book *Twilight in Italy* had not the same shock value as *The Rainbow*. 'This volume of travel vignettes in North Italy was first published in 1916', stated the dust jacket. 'Since then Mr Lawrence has increased the number of his admirers year by year. In *Twilight in Italy* they will find all the freshness and vigour of outlook which they have come to expect from its author.'[51] Cape avoided any reference to Lawrence's polarising reputation, including the fact that the travel book had initially been published in the wake of the *Rainbow* scandal. Likewise, British readers were encouraged to view *Dubliners* as an uncontroversial work. A catalogue bound at the end of Travellers' Library books described Joyce's work as 'a collection of fifteen short stories by the author of *Ulysses*. They are all of them brave, relentless and sympathetic pictures of Dublin life; realistic, perhaps, but not crude; analytical, but not repugnant.'[52]

This description both emphasises the reputation of Joyce, the author of the still-banned *Ulysses*, and tames the complicated history of *Dubliners* (a book that remained unpublished for ten years after Grant Richards declined it). In short, Cape was capitalising on the aura of the modernist celebrity, while downplaying the association with obscenity.

It is interesting to compare Cape's strategy with that of the Modern Library, which published a cheap edition of *Dubliners* in 1926 for the American market. Like the Travellers' Library, the Modern Library presented Joyce as the famous author of *Ulysses* ('the greatest product of the realistic movement in literature').[53] But the Modern Library went further than Cape in describing *Dubliners* as a daring modern book. The dust jacket of the Modern Library edition thus stated:

> DUBLINERS was written in 1905, and the author spent the next seven years trying to make his publisher live up to a contract to bring out the book. For the reader who has never sampled Joyce, DUBLINERS is an ideal introduction.

Many reviewers repeated the publisher's claim that *Dubliners* was the first step to discovering Joyce's work. 'With the publication of *Dubliners* in the low-priced Modern Library series, it becomes an easy matter for the average reader, who has heard much of *Ulysses* but has never seen a copy, to learn what manner of writing man James Joyce may be', stated the *St Louis Post Dispatch*.[54] Another reviewer described the book as 'short stories for any one whom you wish to lead by easy steps – sort of Gradus ad Parnassum – to *Ulysses*'.[55] This was a surprising claim, considering the fact that *Ulysses* was still banned. But the reviewer was simply making explicit what was implicit in the Modern Library's marketing strategy. From 'ideal introduction' to Joyce's work, *Dubliners* became seen as a prerequisite to reading *Ulysses*, a book that was not legally available. This association between the two texts was coherent with the daring image and anti-censorship positioning of the Modern Library.[56] In contrast, Jonathan Cape strived to keep the Travellers' Library free from any taint of obscenity. Readers who might fear that Joyce's work was too 'crude' and 'repugnant' were reassured that there was nothing scandalous about *Dubliners*.

When Cape published Radcliffe Hall's novel about lesbianism, *The Well of Loneliness* (1928), he again used the same kind of cautious strategy designed to keep the censor at bay. One advertisement in the *Spectator* described *The Well of Loneliness* as 'a new long novel by the author of *Adam's Breed* which was awarded both the *Femina Vie Heureuse Prize* and the *James Tait Black Memorial Prize*'. A quotation by Havelock Ellis, a famous sexologist, also emphasised the 'high level of distinction' of the book.[57] Hall was therefore presented as the consecrated, prize-winning author of a serious and tasteful novel.

An advertisement for the Travellers' Library appeared just below, thus creating a visual association between Hall's novel and the series. However, Cape carefully marketed *The Well of Loneliness* as a novel for a small audience. The first printing consisted of only 1,500 copies, sold for fifteen shillings each (more than four times the price of a Travellers' Library book).[58] According to Jonathan Rose, 'review copies were sent only to magazines and newspapers that were likely to give it a fair reading'. But in August 1928, James Douglas, the editor of the *Sunday Express*, condemned the book as obscene and demanded its suppression. Cape reacted by sending the novel to the home secretary with some favourable reviews, offering to stop the publication if Joynson-Hicks deemed it obscene. This reaction shows Cape's lack of experience: having so far avoided entanglements with the censors, he naively believed that 'Jix' might defend the book. When the contrary happened, Cape hastily announced that he would cease publication, in an effort to avoid prosecution and distance the firm from any association with obscenity.[59] 'The stigma of being responsible for the publication of an "obscene" book is best answered by our record', declared the magazine *Now & Then*. The firm was not ready to challenge the decision of the Home Office, which 'would have been costly, both in time and money'.[60]

However, Cape also subleased the rights of the novel to the Pegasus Press in Paris, which printed the book from the same plates and sent copies to England. When the *Daily Express* denounced this, a Cape representative replied that the firm 'was not connected in any way with the Paris publication'.[61] This cat-and-mouse game ended badly for Cape, with a trial that the firm lost – resulting in the lengthy ban of Hall's novel. The *Well of Loneliness* episode shows that Cape was certainly not an anti-censorship warrior: he tried to maximise profit while avoiding controversy. In other words, he lacked the mix of ideological conviction and love of publicity that prompted American publishers such as Horace Liveright and Bennett Cerf to fight for the right to publish subversive books.

There is evidence to show that James Joyce found Cape's prudent strategy frustrating. In a 1929 letter to T. S. Eliot, Joyce reported that Cape had initially expressed interest in publishing Stuart Gilbert's study on *Ulysses*, before arguing that the English public was not interested in Joyce's magnum opus. Joyce told Eliot that 'possibly such an interest can be created'.[62] By the end of 1929, Cape had already printed 10,000 copies of *Dubliners* in the Travellers' Library (the total printing figure reached 16,000 copies in 1941).[63] This was an impressive success for a book whose first edition had sold only a few hundred copies.[64] Although Cape was not ready to create interest in *Ulysses* (especially not after the *Well of Loneliness* fiasco), he eventually decided to add another Joyce title to the Travellers' Library.

Why did Cape wait four years after the publication of *Dubliners* to include

A Portrait of the Artist as a Young Man in the series? In October 1930, Cape justified his decision in a letter to Sylvia Beach that I discovered at the University at Buffalo:

> You have on more than one occasion suggested that A PORTRAIT OF THE ARTIST AS A YOUNG MAN should be published in the TRAVELLERS' LIBRARY. I have held back from doing this because we had a fair stock of the 7/6d edition and further I was a little afraid that after the effect of the cheap edition had worn off we would be selling not many more copies at 3/6d than we would sell if the book remained at 7/6d. However I think that the time has now come to put the book into the TRAVELLERS' LIBRARY and this we have now done.[65]

Interestingly, it was Beach who encouraged Cape to issue a cheap edition of *Portrait of the Artist*. She later persuaded Albatross Library to issue an inexpensive edition of *Ulysses*.[66] Ironically, Beach, who had published *Ulysses* in a limited edition in Paris, did not see Joyce as a coterie writer. In *Institutions of Modernism*, Lawrence Rainey takes the example of the 1922 Shakespeare & Company edition of *Ulysses* to argue that 'literary modernism constitutes a strange and perhaps unprecedented withdrawal from the public sphere of cultural production and debate, a retreat into a divided world of patronage, investment and collecting'.[67] This might have been the case in the early 1920s, but by the end of the decade even Beach recognised that Joyce could reach a wide market.

In 1930, Cape finally agreed with Beach that it was time to release a Travellers' Library edition of *Portrait of the Artist*. Earlier that year, Faber & Faber had issued Stuart Gilbert's study of *Ulysses*, and *Anna Livia Plurabelle* (an extract from *Work in Progress*). Another extract, *Haveth Childers Everywhere*, was published by Henry Babou and Jack Kahane in Paris and circulated in Britain. The flow of largely appreciative reviews and articles on Joyce[68] may have contributed to the exasperation of one professor of history, who resigned from the Newcastle Literary and Philosophical Society 'because the society has arranged lectures dealing with certain modern authors whose works, he says, may not unjustifiably be called "indecent"'. In addition to Joyce, the professor criticised D. H. Lawrence 'whose works are hopelessly oversexed' and Aldous Huxley, 'a writer of dirty-minded matter'. His 'fight for decency and purity' met with indifference.[69] 'Professor's Protest Ignored', declared the *Manchester Guardian* – two weeks after the publication of the Travellers' Library edition of *Portrait of the Artist*.[70] Between 1930 and 1939, Cape printed 12,000 copies of the novel in this cheap edition.[71] Although works by Joyce were not the most successful titles in the series (see Appendix), they sold in the thousands – as compared to the hundreds of copies of the first editions.

D. H. LAWRENCE IN THE NEW ADELPHI LIBRARY

While Cape has been presented as a 'pioneer' of the three-and-six-penny library,[72] this narrative obscures the role of Martin Secker, who launched the New Adelphi Library in late 1925 – a few months before the Travellers' Library. The name of the series was a reference to the street where Secker had established his business ('Number Five John Street Adelphi' was printed on his title pages). In early 1926, at the height of the 'Indecent Books' debate, Secker reissued Lawrence's *The Rainbow* – which had been banned eleven years earlier – and advertised the first volumes in his new cheap series including Norman Douglas's *Fountains in the Sand* (#1 in the series) and Lawrence's *The Captain's Doll* (#6). Such a list would have seemed unsuitable to many readers: Douglas was then living in Italy, having left Britain after being charged with sexually assaulting several boys, and Lawrence was often seen as a sexually-obsessed writer.

Secker became Lawrence's publisher in 1918, with the release of *New Poems*. After publishing *The Lost Girl* (1920), Secker undertook *Women in Love* (1921), a daring novel that had been rejected by several publishers, and *The Rainbow* in 1926. These novels were sold to a relatively small audience for the high price of nine shillings. Secker was initially reluctant to publish Lawrence's works in cheap editions. When Jonathan Cape approached him to reprint *Sea and Sardinia* in the Travellers' Library, Secker declined the offer and informed Lawrence that he would publish a 7s. 6d. edition instead. 'Why always so expensive?', wrote Lawrence to Curtis Brown. 'And never the slightest bit of push. Never half alive!'[73] At this point, Lawrence was growing increasingly impatient with his publisher. In November, he told his agent:

> What I feel about Secker is that he is so obscure, and his range is so definitely, and, I'm afraid, for ever limited and circumscribed. I like him personally. I don't want to leave him. But I feel that, even for *his* sake, if I am ever to get a wider public, some other publisher will have to help break down the fence.[74]

Lawrence's dissatisfaction (and his involvement with other publishers) should not obscure the fact that Secker was already trying to reach a wider readership.[75] On 8 May 1926, Secker wrote to Curtis Brown to suggest cheaper editions of the earlier work.[76] The 3s. 6d. pocket edition of Lawrence's novels was then launched in 1927. Short stories and non-fiction were included in the New Adelphi Library. By 1934, ten titles by Lawrence had appeared in the series: *The Captain's Doll* was followed by *Sea and Sardinia* (1927), *Fantasia of the Unconscious* (1930), *Mornings in Mexico* (1930), *David* (1930), *Psychoanalysis and the Unconscious* (1931), *Assorted Articles* (1932), *Studies in Classic American Literature* (1933), *Reflections on the Death of a*

Porcupine (1934) and *Twilight in Italy* (1934). To Lawrence's delight, this last had been a success in the Travellers' Library: 11,000 copies were printed from 1926 to 1933.[77]

Like the Travellers' Library, the New Adelphi Library featured a distinguished physical format. 'Slender books in an elegant green binding, that slip easily into the pocket', wrote the *Times Literary Supplement*.[78] The *Observer* also used the vocabulary of distinction and taste: 'very attractive they are, with the dignified uniformity of their page and their green covers'.[79] The *Daily Express* emphasised the excellent quality/price ratio of the series:

> for three-and-six pence Martin Secker has turned out a volume that is in its way a small édition de luxe – a book that is neatly bound and beautiful to look at, that is printed on thin paper and in choice type, that is small enough to put in the pocket and elegant enough to place on the library shelf, and that is in all ways a most desirable volume to possess.[80]

The reference to 'édition de luxe' is interesting, considering the fact that texts by Lawrence and others had first appeared in expensive and limited editions. The New Adelphi Library offered an opportunity for the ordinary reader to buy their own piece of luxury for only three shillings and six pence.

The logo of the series, a reference to the first name of the publisher, showed Saint Martin using his sword to cut his coat in two, to give to a beggar. In the 1930s, it started appearing not only on the bindings and advertisements but also on dust jackets, which had so far been plain and generic. As J. B. Krygier points out, the new jackets bore many similarities with the Modern Library typographical dust jackets (Figure 2.3).[81] It is probable that Secker knew about the Modern Library when he launched the New Adelphi Library, a series that also included copyrighted texts. In the 1920s, Secker was regularly in touch with Thomas Seltzer, Lawrence's American publisher. The Russian-born Seltzer was an uncle of Albert Boni – who created the Modern Library in 1917 with Horace Liveright. Lawrence's *Sons and Lovers* appeared in the Modern Library in 1923 and stayed for more than fifty years in the series. The publication of *The Rainbow* in 1927 (and of *Women in Love* ten years later) confirmed the Modern Library's anti-censorship positioning. 'Ironically enough, it was the vain effort of a self-appointed censor to supress *The Rainbow* that first called to the attention of the general public the enduring qualities of the book', declared a text printed on the front of the 1927 dust jacket. In addition to Lawrence, Norman Douglas appeared in both series. *South Wind* and *Old Calabria* were published in the Modern Library in 1925 and 1928, and in the New Adelphi Library in 1927 and 1930 – another sign that Secker partly modelled his series on his American competitor.

Unlike the Modern Library, the New Adelphi Library (and the Travellers' Library) avoided any direct condemnation of censorship. Indeed, Secker made

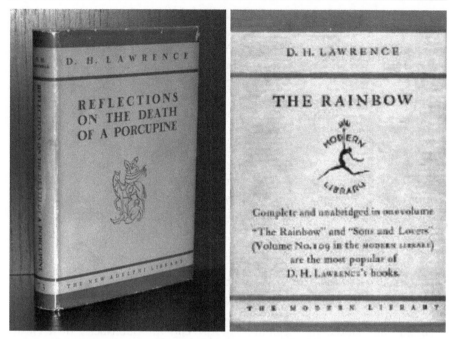

Figure 2.3 Dust Jackets, *Reflections on the Death of a Porcupine*, New Adelphi Library (1934); *The Rainbow*, Modern Library (c. 1929). By permission of Penguin Random House UK and Penguin Random House LLC.

a clear separation between Lawrence's daring novels published in the uniform edition at 3s. 6d. and his less controversial writings published for the same price in the New Adelphi Library. The publisher was presumably targeting different audiences with these two pocket editions: modern readers attracted to Lawrence's subversive reputation would turn to the uniform edition of his novels, while less adventurous readers would get an introduction to Lawrence in the New Adelphi Library. The series thus offered a roadmap to read Lawrence's work, starting with his less daring writings.

Unsurprisingly, it was not the New Adelphi Library but the Uniform Pocket Edition of Lawrence's novels that attracted the attention of the censor. Christopher Pollnitz's research in the Home Office files shows that in March 1930, the month when Lawrence died, a note asked if *The Rainbow* should be prosecuted a second time.[82] A reference to a 'Cutting from *Times Literary Supplement* 6/3/30' can also be found in the file. That day, the newspaper carried an advertisement for Lawrence's work, including *The Rainbow* and other novels in the 3s. 6d. uniform edition. Under the heading 'Essays & Travel', three New Adelphi Library titles (*Sea and Sardinia*, *Mornings in*

Mexico and *Fantasia of the Unconscious*) were listed as either available or in preparation. If the Home Office had decided to press charges against Secker for the publication of *The Rainbow*, the New Adelphi Library would have been isolated from the taint of obscenity. But no action was taken, and one month after Lawrence's death Secker published a 3s. 6d. edition of *Pansies* (the poems that had been seized in 1929) as part of the uniform edition of Lawrence's poetry.

The New Adelphi Library stayed in print for a decade, but never rivalled the scope of the Travellers' Library. By 1935, when Secker went bankrupt, the series included around eighty volumes (one of the last titles was Maurice Magnus's *Memoirs of the Foreign Legion*, with an introduction by Lawrence). In contrast, the Travellers' Library included more than 200 books by that time, a number that remained stable until the demise of the series during the Second World War.

From Hardback Series to Paperbacks

The two series suffered from the competition of paperbacks in the 1930s. Michael Howard notes that 'while paperbacks, being only reprints of long-established books, could not threaten the price structure of new publications, their advent marked the beginning of the end for publishers' own cheap editions'.[83] However, Penguin – the leader of the paperback revolution in Britain – did not reprint texts by Lawrence and Joyce until the mid-1940s. *Sea and Sardinia* was the first Lawrence title to be 'Penguinised' in 1944, followed by *The Prussian Officer* (1945), *Sons and Lovers* (1948), *The Rainbow* (1949) and ten other titles published in 1950 for the twentieth anniversary of Lawrence's death. Joyce appeared on the Penguin list in 1943 with *Modern Irish Short Stories*, but *Dubliners* was not included until 1956.[84]

Why did Allen Lane, who had published the first British edition of *Ulysses* in 1936, wait so long to add Joyce to the Penguin list? It is all the more surprising that out of the first Penguin titles published in 1935, several had originally been published by Cape. For example, Ernest Hemingway's *A Farewell to Arms* had been available in Cape's Florin Books series (sold for two shillings since 1932). Beverley Nichols's *Twenty-Five* and E. H. Young's *William* were available in the Travellers' Library. Cape later said that he thought that Penguin was doomed to fail, and he had better accept Lane's offer for the reprint rights before this impending bankruptcy.[85] It is likely that Lane did not ask to reprint *Dubliners* and *Portrait of the Artist* because he thought their audience was too limited. As Raymond MacKenzie notes, the variety of the Penguin list was 'calculated to appeal to the widest range of readers possible'. While Lane was prepared to publish *Ulysses* with a first printing of 1,000 copies,[86] he was perhaps not convinced that *Dubliners* and *Portrait of the Artist* could sell the 17,000 to 20,000 copies necessary for a Penguin title to break even. Moreover, the Penguin list 'was dominated by respectable but not intimidating authors and titles'.[87] Lane perhaps thought that Joyce was too intimidating, too associated with a 'highbrow' sphere, for the Penguin list.

Yet, by the mid-1930s, Jonathan Cape had demonstrated that Joyce's texts could be sold to a large audience of ordinary readers. The success of *Dubliners* and *Portrait of the Artist* in the Travellers' Library convinced Cape to publish these titles in even cheaper editions, well suited to the difficult economic context. In 1934, the two texts were included in the Flexibles series, using sheets from the Travellers' Library editions. Advertised as 'a new series with a washable, pliable binding', Flexibles books were sold for two shillings and six pence.[88] In 1936, Cape issued another edition of these two titles, this time in the Half Crown Fiction series. Cape was targeting various audiences with these multiple editions. Although a Flexibles or Half Crown Fiction book was five times more expensive than a Penguin paperback, it was still three times cheaper than a regular edition (often sold for seven shillings and six pence). In other words, Cape had made Joyce's texts widely available, without reaching the mass market targeted by Allen Lane.

There is yet another possible reason why Lane waited nearly a decade to publish Joyce (and Lawrence) under the Penguin imprint. Although Lane was not afraid of the censor (as the publication of *Ulysses* shows), he wanted to position Penguin as a respectable, middle-of-the-road imprint. As J. E. Morpurgo notes,

> Allen was ready and even eager to march Penguin to the frontiers of British taste but, properly sensitive for the reputation that the firm had established in its first decade, he would not move one step beyond that line until he was convinced that he could take at least a large minority of his readers with him.[89]

This led to a conflict with the American branch of Penguin, whose managers were pushing for more controversial books with sensational covers. When Victor Weybright, who was running the American house, suggested adding the salacious Southern writer Erskine Caldwell to the list, Lane responded that they should change the name of the imprint to Porno Books.[90] He objected to the content as well as to the covers of novels by Caldwell, James M. Cain, James T. Farrell and William Faulkner (*Sanctuary* had joined the American list in 1947). 'He was', Weybright later wrote, 'still far from being a convinced general publisher of serious modern literature that might offend the parsons and squeamish readers of the United Kingdom. As the years ran on he changed his mind, but too late to keep in step with us in New York.'[91] Although this accusation is largely unfair to Lane, it is certainly true that he was careful not to go too far and alienate Penguin readers with controversial texts.

Allen Lane's prudent attitude highlights the real achievements of Jonathan Cape and Martin Secker, who as early as the mid-1920s published titles by Joyce and Lawrence in cheap editions. Morpurgo argues that the three-and-six-penny series 'were unashamedly representative of high literature' and 'could not be classed as truly cheap editions'.[92] Although books in the Travellers' Library, the New Adelphi Library and other similar series were seven times more expensive than Penguin paperbacks, they were sufficiently cheap to reach a wide market of common readers eager to discover modern literature. Cape and Secker published modernist texts for a large audience at the time when the reputation of Joyce and Lawrence was intertwined with obscenity. In 1950, Cape relaunched the Travellers' Library with *A Portrait of the Artist as a Young Man* among the first titles (*Dubliners* was added later that year). Between the creation of the Travellers' Library in 1926 and its relaunch twenty-four years later, Joyce had made the transition from little-read provocateur to classic writer – a transition to which Cape greatly contributed. The year 1950 is also when Penguin published ten titles by Lawrence to commemorate the twentieth anniversary of his death. While Secker had popularised Lawrence's work in the 1920s and 1930s, Penguin was now making his work 'available to a post-war generation which does not know them' – as David Garnett noted in the *Observer*.[93] Ten years later, the publication and subsequent trial of *Lady Chatterley's Lover* shed light on Penguin's evolution towards a more daring positioning. At the trial, the prosecutor said to the jury: 'You may think it must tend to deprave the minds certainly of some, and maybe many, of the persons who are likely to buy it at the price of 3s. 6d. and who read it, with 200,000 copies already printed and ready for release', and he continued: 'Would you approve of your young sons and daughters – because girls can read as well as boys – reading this book?'[94] Once again, modern fiction was associated with the poisoning of youth – a danger made all the more serious by the diffusion of 'obscene' books in cheap form.

APPENDIX

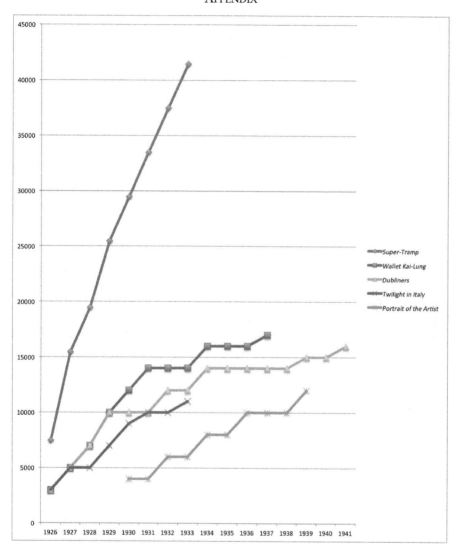

Figure 2.4 Cumulated printing figures: Travellers' Library editions of Davies's *The Autobiography of a Super-Tramp* (1926), Bramah's *The Wallet of Kai-Lung* (1926), Joyce's *Dubliners* (1926) and *A Portrait of the Artist as a Young Man* (1930) and Lawrence's *Twilight in Italy* (1926).

NOTES

1. Rudd, 'The Poisoning of Youth', p. 216.
2. Rudd, 'The Poisoning of Youth', p. 216.
3. Rudd, 'The Poisoning of Youth', p. 217.
4. Rudd, 'The Poisoning of Youth', p. 218.
5. Rudd, 'The Poisoning of Youth', p. 219.
6. Potter, 'Introduction', p. 1.
7. Ormerod, Smith and Hogan, *Smith and Hogan's Criminal Law*, p. 1058.
8. Loukopoulou, 'Joyce's Progress through London', p. 686.
9. Thompson, 'Hicks, William Joynson-', *Oxford Dictionary of National Biography*.
10. It was not until 1928 that a 'hardening of the government's censorship practices' led to increased mail surveillance and prosecution. See Colligan, *A Publisher's Paradise*, p. 49.
11. 'House of Commons', *The Times*, 12 February 1926, p. 7.
12. 'The Hyde Park Case', *The Times*, 5 January 1926, p. 7.
13. 'House of Commons', *The Times*, 19 February 1926, p. 9.
14. Mullin, 'Poison More Deadly than Prussic Acid', p. 25.
15. 'The Sale of Indecent Books', *The Times*, 4 March 1926, p. 11. 'Home Secretary and Clean Plays', *The Times*, 4 March 1926, p. 11.
16. Sigel, 'Censorship in Inter-War Britain', p. 66.
17. 'Undesirable Plays and Books', *The Times*, 13 March 1926, p. 14.
18. Omnium, 'Under Cover'.
19. Ramsden, 'Correspondence'.
20. 'A Bookseller's Censorship', *Bookseller*, March 1926, p. 104.
21. 'The real remedy is the slow and gradual improvement of public opinion on these matters, a result which we may safely think is being realised by degrees.' 'The Sale of Indecent Books', *Bookseller*, March 1926, p. 19.
22. Sagar and Boulton, eds, 'Introduction', pp. 5–6.
23. Taylor, *Jix, Viscount Brentford*, p. 248.
24. Howard, *Jonathan Cape*, p. 69; *Letters of James Joyce*, vol. 2, p. 371.
25. Rose, 'Jonathan Cape Limited'.
26. Production ledger, JC.
27. Cape to Beach, 14 April 1924, James Joyce collection, UB.
28. Advertisement for Jonathan Cape Ltd, *The Times*, 7 November 1924, p. 7.
29. Wilson, 'Circulating Morals', p. 53.
30. Winterton, 'Circulating Libraries', p. 61.
31. Winterton, 'Circulating Libraries', p. 62.
32. 'Why People Do Not Buy More Books', *Bookseller*, March 1926, p. 19.
33. *Bookseller*, May 1926, p. 28.
34. Advertisement for the Travellers' Library, *Manchester Guardian*, 22 March 1928, p. 7.
35. 'The Travellers' Library', *Now & Then*, 23 (1927), 31.
36. 'Notes on Book-Making', *Now & Then*, 21 (1926), 25.
37. 'The yellow flash of the Travellers' Library stretching along a shelf or two is by now a friendly and familiar feature in the bookseller's shop – their blue and gold no less so at home.' 'The Life and Letters Series', *Now & Then*, 37 (1930), 18.
38. 'Travellers' Library', *Bookseller*, May 1926, p. 56.
39. 'Notes on Book-Making', *Now & Then*, 21 (1926), 29.
40. Hammill and Smith, 'About the Project'.
41. Housman, 'What Books for Travellers?', p. 9.

42. Advertisement for the Travellers' Library, *Manchester Guardian*, 28 June 1928, p. 7.
43. Advertisement for the Travellers' Library, *Observer*, 23 May 1926, p. 6.
44. Dust jacket, Anderson, *Horses and Men*.
45. Advertisement for Geoffrey Bles, *The Times*, 5 February 1926, p. 8.
46. Advertisement for Geoffrey Bles, *Sunday Times*, 14 February 1926, p. 8.
47. Review of *James Joyce, His First Forty Years*, by Herbert S. Gorman, *Times Literary Supplement*, 18 March 1926, p. 219.
48. 'Our Books of the Week: James Joyce – A New Thriller', Review of *James Joyce, His First Forty Years*, by Herbert S. Gorman, and *The Crimson Feather*, by Maude Crossley and Charles King', *Yorkshire Evening Post*, 18 February 1926, p. 6.
49. 'James Joyce: The Mysterious Author of *Ulysses*', *Aberdeen Press and Journal*, 12 April 1926, p. 2.
50. Advertisement for the Travellers' Library, *Observer*, 31 October 1926, p. 7.
51. Dust jacket, Lawrence, *Twilight in Italy*.
52. Catalogue, Anderson, *Horses and Men*.
53. Dust jacket, Joyce, *Dubliners*.
54. 'By the Author of *Ulysses*', *St Louis Post-Dispatch*, 18 December 1926, n.p.
55. 'Better than Cards or Calendars', *Outlook*, 19 December 1928, n.p.
56. Jaillant, *Modernism*, pp. 22–3.
57. Advertisement for *The Well of Loneliness*, *Spectator*, 21 July 1928, p. 113.
58. Production ledger, JC.
59. Jonathan Cape, 'Letter', *The Times*, 23 August 1928, p. 13.
60. '*The Well of Loneliness*', *Now & Then*, 29 (1928), 23–4.
61. 'Banned Book Republished', *Daily Express*, 4 October 1928, p. 1.
62. Joyce to Eliot, 2 July 1929, *Letters of James Joyce*, vol. 3, p. 511. Quoted in Loukopoulou, 'Joyce's Progress through London', p. 686.
63. Production ledger, JC.
64. 'Financially [*Dubliners*] is, like my other books, a fiasco – 450 copies sold to date in the United Kingdom.' Joyce to John Quinn, 10 July 1917, *Letters of James Joyce*, vol. 1, p. 105. Approximately 746 copies had been bound in the edition published by Grant Richards in 1914. Slocum and Cahoon, *A Bibliography of James Joyce*, p. 12.
65. Cape to Beach, 15 October 1930, James Joyce collection, UB.
66. 'I think that your suggestion that *Ulysses* should be published in the ALBATROSS LIBRARY is excellent. I am quite sure that we should reach a very extensive public with our edition and a public that previous editions have never touched.' Max Christian Wegner to Beach, 6 September 1932, James Joyce collection, UB.
67. Rainey, *Institutions of Modernism*, p. 75.
68. See, for example, 'Mr Joyce's Experiments. Rev. of *Anna Livia Plurabelle and Haveth Childers Everywhere*, by James Joyce', *Times Literary Supplement*, 17 July 1930, p. 588, and 'A Guide to *Ulysses*. Rev. of *James Joyce's Ulysses: A Study*, by Stuart Gilbert', *Manchester Guardian*, 1 July 1930, p. 7.
69. 'Modern Authors: Professor Resigns in Protest', *Sunday Times*, 28 September 1930, p. 17.
70. 'Professor's Protest Ignored', *Manchester Guardian*, 3 October 1930, p. 9.
71. Production ledger, JC.
72. Nicolson, 'These Pocket Editions', p. 522.
73. Lawrence to Curtis Brown, 18 May 1926, *Letters of D. H. Lawrence*, vol. 5, p. 460.
74. Lawrence to Curtis Brown, 13 November 1926, *Letters of D. H. Lawrence*, vol. 5, p. 575.

75. Lawrence was involved with many publishers and other actors of the book trade, juggling possibilities in interesting ways (see, for example, the publishing history of *Lady Chatterley's Lover*).
76. *Letters of D. H. Lawrence*, vol. 5, p. 481, n. 2.
77. Production ledger, JC; Lawrence to Secker, 27 May 1927 and 3 February 1928, *Letters from D. H. Lawrence to Martin Secker*, pp. 88, 101.
78. 'New Editions', *Times Literary Supplement*, 26 November 1925, p. 799.
79. 'Next Week's Diary', *Observer*, 26 September 1926, p. 9.
80. Quoted in 'The Price of Books', *Sunday Times*, 12 December 1926, p. 9.
81. Krygier, 'Modern Library and Everyman's Library Simulacra?'.
82. Pollnitz, 'The Censorship and Transmission of D. H. Lawrence's "Pansies"', p. 62.
83. Howard, *Jonathan Cape*, p. 165.
84. *Portrait of the Artist* was published in America in 1948 under the Penguin Signet imprint.
85. Howard, *Jonathan Cape*, p. 164.
86. Slocum and Cahoon, *A Bibliography of James Joyce*, p. 34.
87. MacKenzie, 'Penguin Books'.
88. Advertisement for Jonathan Cape Ltd, *Times Literary Supplement*, 5 July 1934, p. 467.
89. Morpurgo, *Allen Lane*, p. 228.
90. Morpurgo, *Allen Lane*, p. 227.
91. Morpurgo, *Allen Lane*, p. 228.
92. Morpurgo, *Allen Lane*, p. 84.
93. Garnett, 'D. H. Lawrence'.
94. 'Sensuality Commended Almost As A Virtue – Prosecution', *The Times*, 21 October 1960, p. 4.

3

REWRITING *TARR* TEN YEARS LATER: WYNDHAM LEWIS, THE PHOENIX LIBRARY AND THE DOMESTICATION OF MODERNISM

Four years before his death, Wyndham Lewis wrote to the modernist scholar Hugh Kenner:

> In *Tarr* I had in view a publique d'élite who could be addressed in blank verse, and the style of the poème en prose might suddenly be used, or be employed for half a page. Down to Fielding or Thackeray in England, and in all the great Russian novelists it was an aristocratic audience which was being addressed.

Lewis added: 'In *Tarr* (1914–15), I was an extremist.'[1] This image of a difficult, uncompromising novel for an elite could well apply to the first version of *Tarr* – completed in 1915 and published by the Egoist Press in Britain and by Knopf in the United States in 1918. But in 1928, Lewis accepted an offer to reprint his novel in the newly created Phoenix Library, sold for only three shillings and six pence. Lewis was reluctant at first, complaining about the low compensation he would receive. But he then threw himself into the project and decided to rewrite the entire novel. At that time in his career, Lewis was eager to address not a 'publique d'élite' or an 'aristocratic audience', but a large audience who had never read *Tarr* before.

Scholars have often discussed the merit of the 1928 edition over the earlier versions. 'Just ask any one of the two dozen Lewis scholars in the world which of the versions of *Tarr* is the best or most complete text', wrote John Xiros Cooper. 'Be prepared for a lively response.'[2] While some might prefer the less polished Egoist or Knopf texts, it is likely that very few university teachers choose these versions for their courses. When Scott Klein edited a reprint edition of *Tarr* in the Oxford World's Classics series, he selected the 1928 text. As he put it, 'Lewis intended *Tarr* to be known solely in its revised version.'[3] Although the differences between the 1918 and 1928 texts have been extensively studied, the Phoenix Library is mentioned only in passing (if at all).[4] This gap in scholarship is all the more surprising given that Lewis self-consciously recorded his engagement with the publisher's series. 'This is the copy of the american edition of "Tarr" on which I made the corrections for the revised edition of "Tarr" published in Chatto & Windus' "Phoenix" library.' This inscription in Lewis's hand, dated April 1929, appears on the title page of the Knopf edition of Tarr held at the University at Buffalo.[5] While Lewis scholars have largely neglected the Phoenix Library, book historians have paid more attention to this series. Andrew Nash rightly notes that the republication of *Tarr* 'marks a moment of transferral of a text from a small, elite readership to a mainstream commercial market'.[6] But his discussion on *Tarr* is limited to one paragraph in a chapter that focuses on various aspects of interwar publishing in Britain. Nash also briefly mentions *Tarr* in an interesting essay on the Phoenix Library.[7]

In this chapter, I want to replace the Phoenix Library at the centre of the discussion on the 1928 *Tarr*. I propose to examine the revised version as a material artefact as well as a stylistic testimony on the 'taming' of modernism. Writing for the large audience that would read his novel in a cheap format, Lewis made his style much more accessible and less confusing for the common reader. *Tarr* is therefore a prime example of the late 1920s domestication of an earlier, utopian modernist form. Drawing on archival research in the Chatto & Windus records at the University of Reading, I take the example of *Tarr* to argue that the Phoenix Library not only made available modernism to a much wider audience, but also transformed the modernist text itself. The first section of this chapter briefly examines the genesis and publication of the ur-*Tarr*. The second part looks at the creation of the Phoenix Library and its role in the diffusion of modernism. The third section focuses more specifically on the inclusion of the revised *Tarr* in the series in 1928. The final part sheds light on the advertising, distribution and reception of this cheap edition, an edition that reached a much wider audience than the 1918 texts.

THE THREE 'FIRST' TARRS

In 1915, the thirty-three-year-old Wyndham Lewis finished *Tarr*, a satire of bohemian life in Paris. In his autobiography, *Blasting and Bombardiering*, Lewis presented the period 1914–1915 as a high point in his career as painter and writer. The first issue of the provocative little magazine *Blast*, published just before the declaration of war, had attracted a great deal of attention. As the leader of the Vorticist movement, Lewis was 'on constant exhibition': 'Everyone by way of being fashionably interested in art, and many who had never opened a book or brought so much as a sporting-print, much less "an oil", wanted to look at this new oddity, thrown up by that amusing spook, the Zeitgeist.'[8] Lewis probably exaggerated his popularity. In *Institutions of Modernism*, Lawrence Rainey argues that 'contemporary critics were neither angered nor provoked by *Blast*. They were simply bored, and not because *Blast* was an incomprehensible novelty, but because it was all too familiar.'[9] For Rainey, Vorticism was generally seen as a pale imitation of Futurism, led by the charismatic Filippo Marinetti. Even Lewis admitted that the invitations he received brought him little rewards, financial or otherwise: 'As a result of these sociable activities I did not sell a single picture.'[10]

Lewis also had trouble finding a publisher for *Tarr*, a novel that deals with casual sex, rape, murder and suicide. In late November 1915, John Lane, who had published *Blast*, rejected *Tarr*, as being 'too strong a book'.[11] The novel was then turned down by another publisher, Werner Laurie, before being accepted by Harriet Shaw Weaver, who serialised it in the little magazine *The Egoist* from April 1916 to November 1917. Lewis, who had joined the army, asked his friend Ezra Pound to prepare a publishable text of *Tarr* for the American edition. As Paul O'Keeffe notes, Pound's

> task was made difficult because parts of the original typescript, edited down for serialisation, had apparently gone astray at *The Egoist*'s print-ers in West Norwood. As a result he was forced to plug gaps with printed pages from the September 1916, February, April and June 1917 issues of *The Egoist*.[12]

The American edition was published by Alfred Knopf in June 1918, shortly before it appeared in England under the Egoist imprint. As John Xiros Cooper puts it, 'there were three "first" *Tarrs*, all of them different'.[13]

Even by the standards of small-scale institutions of modernism (little maga-zines and small presses), *Tarr* was not a commercial success. Harriet Shaw Weaver, who paid £50 for the serialisation rights, 'still had a £36 deficit in 1924'.[14] For the publication in book form (priced at six shillings), Weaver refused to pay any royalties until her costs had been covered. She sold 729 copies of the book out of a first printing of 1,000, and lost £22.[15] It is unlikely that the Knopf edition, priced at $1.75, sold much more than the Egoist edition, and no cheap reprint of *Tarr* appeared in the United States during Lewis's lifetime.[16] Although the first versions of *Tarr* reached a small number of readers, the critical reception was generally enthusiastic. *Tarr* was praised by young critics, including Ezra Pound, Rebecca West and T. S. Eliot. 'There can be no question of the importance of *Tarr*', wrote Eliot in *The Egoist*. 'In the work of Mr Lewis we recognize the thought of the modern and the energy of the cave-man.'[17] A press release issued by Harriet Shaw Weaver shows that positive reviews appeared not only in little magazines, but also in the mainstream press (including *The Times*, the *Morning Post*, the *Manchester Guardian* and the *Glasgow Herald*).[18] Many people had heard of *Tarr*, but had never read the book – which was only available in relatively expensive editions published by small presses.

In the 1920s, Lewis suffered setbacks that threatened his position in the artistic world. As Paul Edwards points out, 'his *Tyros and Portraits* exhibition made little impact, his money ran out, and he failed to complete the necessary complement of advanced experimental works needed for a projected show in Léonce Rosenberg's gallery L'Effort Moderne in Paris'.[19] Lewis deeply resented his growing dependence on the patronage of friends and art collectors. His career as a writer was also in decline. Having published no books between 1919 and 1926, he was being eclipsed by the other 'men of 1914', James Joyce and T. S. Eliot. It was not until the late 1920s that Lewis staged a comeback.[20] In 1926, his new publisher, Chatto & Windus, issued *The Art of Being Ruled*. This was the start of a long collaboration with Charles Prentice, the senior partner of the firm. Encouraged by Prentice, Lewis became increasingly productive. 'The year 1927 was Lewis' *annus mirabilis*', notes Jeffrey Meyers.

> He published *The Lion and the Fox*, his Machiavellian interpretation of Shakespeare's tragedies, in January; the first number of the *Enemy*, his third magazine, in February; *Time and Western Man*, his most important non-fictional work, in September; the second number of the *Enemy* in September; and *The Wild Body*, his thoroughly revised comic stories of Brittany, in November.[21]

It is in this context of renewed artistic activity that Prentice offered to reprint *Tarr* in the Phoenix Library.

THE PHOENIX LIBRARY AND THE DIFFUSION OF MODERNISM

Charles Prentice was then a young publisher who had worked at Chatto & Windus since the end of the war. When he was away fighting in France, his father – a well-known Scottish solicitor – had bought him a partnership at the firm. Prentice was in charge of book design until 1926, when he became senior partner. In their essay on the writer T. F. Powys and Chatto & Windus, Andrew Nash and James Knowlson describe Prentice as a 'remarkable publisher' who gave 'support and advice, inspiration and friendship' to many authors including Wyndham Lewis, Samuel Beckett, Norman Douglas, David Garnett, Richard Hughes, Sylvia Townsend Warner and Richard Aldington.[22] Prentice also frequently corresponded with Aldous Huxley, whose successful association with Chatto & Windus began in 1920.[23] By the end of the decade, the firm decided to publish its backlist of Huxley's books in a uniform, cheap series of reprints. 'We are launching [the Phoenix Library] at the end of January [1928]', Prentice wrote to Huxley. 'It is a sort of Pocket library at 3/6d., more or less the same kind of thing as Secker's Adelphi Library and Cape's Traveller's [sic] Library.'[24] Like these two inexpensive series, the Phoenix Library would include copyrighted texts published in a distinguished but small format.

The Phoenix Library departed from its competitors in at least two aspects. First, Chatto & Windus could rely on its prestigious backlist, which included books by Huxley but also Lytton Strachey, Arnold Bennett, C. E. Montague and others. Moreover, well-known writers would each be associated with a distinctive colour in binding. As the firm told the literary agent Eric Pinker, Huxley and Montague would 'retain an individuality of their own, but at the same time get the advantages which such a series gives to books within it'.[25] Books by Montague were thus bound in red cloth, Huxley in blue and Strachey in green. In short, the Phoenix Library combined two seemingly contradictory marketing strategies: an emphasis on the *distinctiveness* of selected authors but also an insistence on the *uniformity* of the series.

Apart from the colour of their binding, all Phoenix Library books looked the same and were sold for the same price (a more expensive leather edition was soon abandoned).[26] The illustrator Thomas Derrick (1885–1954) designed the uniform dust jacket. Educated at the Royal College of Art, where he exhibited his work and later became an instructor of decorative painting for five years, Derrick had a varied artistic production. His work included murals, stained glass, portraiture, posters for the London Underground and artwork in publications such as *Punch*.[27] The wrapper he designed for the Phoenix Library was bright red, a colour that, 'owing to a novel process', would 'not easily fade'.[28] As Chatto & Windus explained to the editor of the *Times Literary Supplement*, 'the publishers believe that, by the devise [sic] of using, as here, printers' ink instead of stationers' dye they have produced dustcovers that are more likely to wear well than any others of a similar series now on the market'.[29] In addition to differentiating the Phoenix Library from its competitors, the jacket served to unify the series. Once wrapped, each Phoenix Library book looked the same (in spite of their bindings in various colours). As Chatto & Windus explained to Pinker, 'a mass of uniform colour on a bookseller's shelf catches the eye, and thus attracts purchasers' (Figure 3.1).[30]

In addition to the dust cover, Derrick designed the emblem of the series, the Phoenix. In a discussion of the Modern Library's own emblem (a torchbearer figure), Jay Satterfield notes: 'the colophon's twentieth-century revitalization as a quality trademark was symptomatic of literature's commodification, although it drew on a tradition of fine printing consciously detached from commercial interests by its aesthete progenitors'.[31] Likewise, the Phoenix

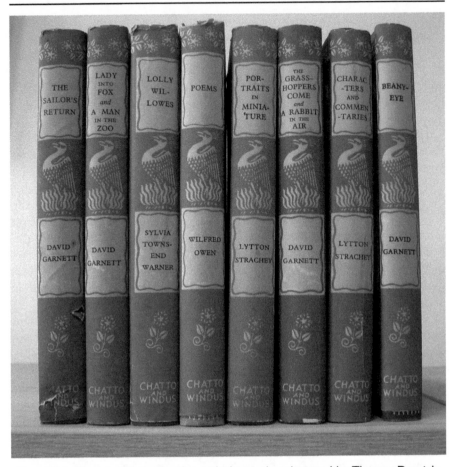

Figure 3.1 Phoenix Library books, with dust jacket designed by Thomas Derrick. By permission of Penguin Random House UK.

Library's colophon increased the cultural capital of the series while also serving as a distinctive trademark – appearing on dust jackets, covers, title pages and advertisements (Figure 3.2). Chatto & Windus explicitly described the Phoenix as 'the symbol of rebirth' – a fitting emblem for a series of modern literature.[32] As Andrew Nash puts it, 'the ornithological image anticipates the success of the Penguin paperbacks, which would hatch less than a decade later'.[33] Derrick also designed the gold decorations on the binding-cases. The Phoenix Library's high standard of production was coherent with Chatto & Windus's distinguished reputation for the quality of their book design.

Like other publishers' series, the Phoenix Library included a wide range of texts: bestselling novels by Lytton Strachey, Aldous Huxley, Richard

Figure 3.2 Advertisements for the Phoenix Library, *Times Literary Supplement* (a) 25 April 1929, p. 334 and (b) 21 February 1935, p. 100. By permission of Penguin Random House UK.

Aldington and David Garnett, plays by A. A. Milne and Richard Hughes, popular science (including several titles by Julian Huxley), political essays, and even a cookery book. As Prentice told the co-author of *The Gentle Art of Cookery*, a Phoenix Library edition of the book would 'have a good chance of capturing the cultivated and educated public to which it primarily appeals – whereas in a fat form at 3s. 6d. it would be jostled and jumbled between Mrs

Beeton, *Good Housekeeping*, The Olio Book etc. etc. etc.'[34] In other words, the Phoenix Library would raise *The Gentle Art of Cookery* above its competitors – as a well-written text for a sophisticated audience. 'You may wonder why on earth we are including a cookery book in such a literary assembly', wrote Harold Raymond (the firm's other senior partner) to one colleague. 'You will see that the book has a decided literary savour, and I do assure you that any number of the recipes have a savour that is more than literary.'[35] Here, the repetition of 'literary' highlights a key aspect of the marketing of the series – the fact that the Phoenix Library was sold as a distinguished series for all those who could not, or would not, pay more than three shillings and six pence for a book.

The Phoenix Library also included modernist titles that had so far been restricted to a small audience. As Chatto & Windus told Roger Fry, 'by an inclusion in the library *Vision and Design* stands a chance of reaching a wider public than that definitely concerned with the study of aesthetics'.[36] In 1928 and 1929, Clive Bell's *Art* and *Since Cézanne* as well as Fry's *Vision and Design* were reprinted in the series and sold to a large readership, thus raising awareness of recent developments in modern art. The firm printed 5,000 copies of *Since Cézanne* in June 1929; 8,000 copies of *Vision and Design* between February 1928 and September 1929; and 10,000 copies of *Art* between December 1927 and December 1930.[37] These figures show that books on modern art could sell as well as, or even better than, a cookery book such as *The Gentle Art of Cookery* (8,000 copies were printed in the first six years after publication).[38]

In addition to popularising modern art, the Phoenix Library opened up new markets for the new poetry. The first anthology of poems published in the series was *Twentieth-Century Poetry*, edited by the poet and bookseller Harold Monro, who was closely associated with the modernist movement. In his monthly *Poetry Review* (launched in 1912), Monro had published Ezra Pound's manifesto, 'Prolegomena' and F. S. Flint's study of recent French poetry, 'two contributions which gave rise to Pound's brief imagist movement'.[39] Monro was also friendly with Wyndham Lewis, whose Rebel Arts Centre was just round the corner from his Poetry Bookshop.[40] The bookshop was a well-known meeting place for poets in the 1910s and 1920s – including T. S. Eliot and his *Criterion* club. In his introduction to the Phoenix Library anthology, Monro predicted that Eliot would be a very influential figure 'up to 1940'.[41] Poets represented in the anthology included Eliot, Pound, H.D., W. B. Yeats as well as Siegfried Sassoon and Wilfred Owen.[42] In a letter to Monro, Pound noticed a 'good strong antimilitarist vein' in the anthology.[43]

Monro's anthology was widely reviewed – including in mass-market newspapers. 'Easily the best of the anthologies of modern verse is *Twentieth Century Poetry* ... chosen by Harold Monro, himself a poet of rare distinction', declared the *Morning Post*. 'It is not an anthology compiled from anthologies, but the product of a wide and diligent investigation of all the original sources.'[44] In a long review published in the *Evening Standard*, the influential critic Arnold Bennett wrote that although he could not understand the influence of T. S. Eliot on younger poets, he had been 'much impressed by *Twentieth Century Poetry*':

> I read it with increasing respect and pleasure . . . on the whole its contents are surprisingly beautiful. There are more good poets around than I had supposed. *Twentieth Century Poetry* is the best anthology of the moderns that I have seen. It ought to sell. If it sells it will be talked about. If it is talked about, the cause of poetry will be advanced.[45]

It is likely that this review (which was reproduced in other newspapers, including the *Liverpool Echo* and the *Manchester Evening News*) contributed to the commercial success of the book.[46] When Prentice contacted Monro about the anthology project, he warned him: 'there is not much money in the idea for either of us, unless the sales go beyond the 10,000 mark'.[47] *Twentieth-Century Poetry* sold much more than that. As the Chatto & Windus stock book shows, a total of 27,500 copies were printed in the three years following publication.[48] This edition 'was followed in 1933 by a new edition revised and enlarged by Alida Monro, of which there have again been four reprints, the final issue being in 1950'.[49]

Chatto & Windus was not the first commercial publisher to realise that modernism could be marketed to a wide audience. As a latecomer in the field of 3s. 6d. quality series, Chatto & Windus had to create a list significantly different from its competitors. One way of doing that was to include daring books that would be talked about. The Phoenix Book Company, which sold the Phoenix Library directly to customers,[50] used the vocabulary of class and taste to describe the series as an 'aristocrat among pocket libraries':

> Its very format exhales the spirit which animates its editors in their selective pursuit. Aldous Huxley, Lytton Strachey, J. B. S. Haldane, Roger Fry – the PHOENIX LIBRARY is noted for its lively presentation of the modern attitude to life. Many of its books have created (and still create) world-wide discussions and *acrid controversy*.[51]

To a large extent, the Phoenix Library can be seen as a British equivalent to the Modern Library – a series that had always specialised in controversial modern literature. This positioning was rather surprising, in view of Chatto & Windus's reputation as a respectable 'list' publisher.[52] As Nash and Knowlson point out, Charles Prentice 'was a kind, sensitive man who disliked any kind of controversy, let alone the deep hostilities involved in legal disputes'.[53] Yet, under Prentice's leadership, the Phoenix Library published modern books that were then considered daring and controversial, including Richard Aldington's *Death of a Hero* and Wyndham Lewis's *Tarr*.

TARR IN THE PHOENIX LIBRARY

It is possible that Prentice decided to reprint *Tarr* after reading a review by Arnold Bennett, which appeared in the *Evening Standard* in April 1927. '*Tarr* had good chapters – chapters that were worth writing', wrote Bennett. 'It was, however, in the somewhat Teutonic lump, doughy, and at last unreadable.'[54] In a long response to the editor of the *Evening Standard*, Lewis openly presented himself as Bennett's *enemy*.[55] This controversy in a mass-market newspaper was a great publicity coup for Lewis. Yet, those readers who wanted to check if *Tarr* was, indeed, 'unreadable' would have had great difficulties finding a copy of the book.

In spring 1928, when Prentice suggested including *Tarr* in the Phoenix Library, he probably thought that it would be a straightforward matter. Surely, the impoverished Lewis would be glad to receive a cheque – however small – for a novel that the Egoist Press had remaindered long ago. However, Prentice's offer of £150 for the outright sale of *Tarr* infuriated Lewis:

> This can only mean (1) that is an unsatisfactory offer or (2) that your firm is disappointed with its author: as I cannot entertain the first alternative I am compelled to believe the second and that I find very discouraging. As I am hard-up I must sell *Tarr* now and 300 pounds for an outright sale of that book is not, I feel, out of the way. 250 pounds is the lowest that [?] in the present circumstances I shall be able to accept for an outright sale. Considered as an advance on royalties I do not see . . . that for <u>Tarr</u> I could just now fix the figure lower than 200 pounds – for that could imply that I considered <u>Tarr</u> worth less today than a book of collected stories one year ago. I may add that were I not in need of money I wouldn't part with <u>Tarr</u> for that figure or contemplate an outright sale at all.[56]

As the first section of Lewis's *The Childermass* had just been published, Lewis felt 'particularly dejected' that his new novel was coming out in 'this atmosphere of disappointment'. Lewis had high hopes for *The Childermass*, a novel marketed as an ambitious book that would rival Joyce's *Ulysses*.[57] His bargaining over *Tarr* sheds light not only on his financial difficulties, but also on his conviction that his first novel was central to his career and, more generally, to the modernist movement. This explains why Lewis took the trouble of entirely rewriting the novel once an agreement was reached with Chatto & Windus. 'I should be sorry to have gone down to posterity as "the author of *Tarr*" in its unrevised first version', declared Lewis in *Blasting and Bombardiering*.[58]

In an effort to obtain better terms for *Tarr*, he suggested that Chatto & Windus issue a more expensive edition first – a proposal that Prentice rejected:

There would be no real market for a 7/6 reissue; such a reissue would only prevent and delay the book's chances in a cheaper form. The best course therefore is to publish at 3/6 straight away. You asked us to make you an outright offer for the English book rights. We could only publish at 3/6, we offered £150. This amounts to very nearly the sale of 10,000 copies on a 10% royalty, which (even on books that have not to be reset) is the recognised royalty on such editions, except in the case of those books that sell very/ very quickly in huge numbers. I have asked our town traveller how long he thinks it would take us to sell these 10,000 copies. He puts it at a minimum of 5 to 6 years, and on this basis and considering there will be the extra expense of setting, I do not think this is a mean price. What might happen after 5 or 6 years is a pure gamble.[59]

This letter sheds light on the publisher's cautious strategy for *Tarr*, a novel that had sold fewer than 800 copies in its first British edition. While Lytton Strachey's bestsellers *Queen Victoria* and *Eminent Victorians* had first print-ings of 10,000 copies in the Phoenix Library, *Tarr* was a more difficult and controversial novel. 'The public must be remembered', wrote Prentice, 'and with books of the originality of yours it does take time to obtain a wide public, for which alone large circulations can be expected'.[60] For Prentice, the 10,000 mark could be reached only when the public had been educated to appreciate the originality of *Tarr*'s modernist style.

Once again, Lewis rejected Prentice's offer of £150 for an outright sale or £75 as an advance on royalties. As Lewis recognised, Chatto & Windus had attributed to him 'an important place in its lists' and 'obviously taken great trouble in pushing [his] books'.[61] Yet, the offer was too low to leave him enough time to write other books. 'I must throw *Tarr* upon the market and wait till it finds a purchaser', declared Lewis – implying that Chatto & Windus was not the only publisher interested in his first novel. The fact that Prentice did increase his offer proves that Lewis was right to present *Tarr* as valuable property. The contract signed on 29 May 1928 shows that Lewis received an advance on royalties of £150, half of that amount for *Tarr* and the other half for other books Chatto & Windus would publish.[62] This arrangement limited the risks of publishing *Tarr*: if the novel sold fewer than 5,000 copies, the firm would lose less than £75 – the amount initially offered by Prentice.

Shortly after signing the agreement, Lewis announced his intention to make extensive revisions to the novel. As we have seen, he did not want to be remembered as the author of a novel that had been hastily written, and hastily put together for publication while he was away fighting in the war. Moreover, Lewis was no longer satisfied with the style of the 1918 *Tarr*, a style that John Xiros Cooper has described as profoundly violent:

Hairline fractures in the syntax of the sentences and the syntax of the succession of sentences, unconventional stops and starts, including the invention of the equal sign (=) as a new mark of punctuation, stark juxtapositions, the elimination of the usual conjunctive tissue in the context of a standard English prose, were the stylistic means he employed to carry out the assault. They were all aimed at bringing the flow of narrative continuity and the reading process itself into moments of violent arrest, into moments of crisis or undecidability.[63]

In 1928, Lewis decided to polish his antagonistic style for the larger audience that would read *Tarr* in the Phoenix Library. 'I have throughout finished what was rough and given the narrative everywhere a greater precision', he wrote in the new preface.[64]

Lewis's revisions downplayed the experimental nature of the earlier version and improved its readability. Let's take an example from chapter 1, when Tarr explains his philosophy to a fellow bohemian, Hudson. In the earlier version, Tarr's logorrhoea has the chaotic energy of *Blast*:

Sex is a monstrosity. It is the arch abortion of this filthy universe. =How 'old-fashioned!' – eh, my fashionable friend? =We are all optimists to-day, aren't we? God's in his Heaven, all's well with the world! How robust! How manly! how pleasant, and above all, how *desirable*! It's a grand place, isn't it? Full of *white* men, *strong* men, *super* men; 'great statesmen', 'great soldiers', 'great artists', 'sacred faith', 'noble pity', 'sacrifice', '*pure* art', 'abstract art', 'civilization' and stuff. =You positively, when you think of it all, feel like dropping on your knees in a gush of gratitude to God! But I'm a new sort of pessimist. =I think I am the sort that will please! =I am the Panurgic-Pessimist, drunken with the laughing gas of the Abyss. I gaze on squalor and idiocy, and the more I see it, the more I like it. =Flaubert built up his Bouvard and Pécuchet with maniacal and tireless hands. It took him ten years. That was a long draught of stodgy laughter from the gases that rise from the dung-heap? He has an appetite like an elephant for this form of mirth. But he grumbled and sighed over his food. =I take it in my arms and bury my face in it![65]

In the revised version, the double hyphen has disappeared, and Tarr's monologue has been divided into shorter, more readable bits:

'Sex is a monstrosity. Sex is a monstrosity. It's the last and ugliest piece of nonsense of a long line. I can see you raising your eyebrows. No? You should do so: I'm a pessimist –.'

'A german pessimist!'

'A pessimist. I'm a new sort of pessimist. I think I'm the sort that will go down.'

'Why not? But you must–.'

'No! I'm the panurgic-pessimist, drunken with the laughing-gas of the Abyss: I gaze upon squalor and idiocy, and the more I see them the more I like them. Flaubert built up his *Bouvard and Pécuchet* with maniacal and tireless hands, it took him ten years: that was a long draught of stodgy laughter from the gases that rise from the dung-heap.'

'Flaubert–.'

'No' (Tarr raised his flat hand, threatening Hobson's mouth) 'he had an appetite like an elephant for this form of mirth, but he grumbled and sighed over his food. I take the stuff up in my arms and bury my face in it.'[66]

There is certainly a case to be made for the 1918 version as a more *exciting* novel. But my objective here is not to judge the literary value of the text. Instead, I want to show that Lewis revised his novel for a specific audience – an audience unfamiliar with the asperities of earlier modernist forms.

If Charles Prentice had been the same kind of publisher as Alfred Harcourt, he would probably have encouraged Lewis's decision to tame his modernist style. When Harcourt, Brace and Company issued Virginia Woolf's *Orlando* and Gertrude Stein's *The Autobiography of Alice B. Toklas*, advertisements insisted that these books were written in an easily-readable style.[67] In other words, Woolf and Stein were presented as previously difficult modernist writers who could now reach a wide public. After the *Autobiography*'s success, Harcourt reluctantly agreed to take on *The Making of Americans*, but only in an abridged version. Unlike Harcourt, Prentice believed that even experimental texts could sell well. As he told Lewis:

I do not fancy you have really very much to do, that is, unless you decide to rewrite the book, which I do not think either necessary or desirable. 'Tarr already is the best novel in the English language' (Who said this?); and it is always better to go on to things new and better still.[68]

Prentice anticipated that *Tarr* would sell between 5,000 and 10,000 copies, and there was simply no point revising it. As Sections II and III of *The Childermass* were scheduled to be published later in 1928,[69] the publisher wanted Lewis to focus on his new work and avoid any delays.

Although the revisions of *Tarr* were an initiative of the author rather than his publisher, this rewriting nevertheless exemplifies the impact of the publishing format on the modernist text. Had *Tarr* been reissued in an expensive limited edition, it is not certain that Lewis would have bothered revising the novel. There would have been no point 'finish[ing] what was rough' for a small coterie of readers already familiar with his avant-garde style. The Phoenix Library, on the contrary, would reach a new readership foreign to modernist experimentations. While Arnold Bennett had described the 1918 *Tarr* as 'unreadable', the revised version was meant to be palatable to this new audience.

Ironically, *Tarr* was released at the same time as the Phoenix Library edition of Bennett's *The Grim Smile of the Five Towns*. These two books had been 'for some time out of print', as the firm told Frank Mumby of the *Times Literary Supplement*.[70] Lewis's novel was number 27 in the series, Bennett's book number 26, and Aldous Huxley's *Little Mexican and Other Stories* number 28. The fact that *Tarr* appeared alongside novels by well-known names such as Bennett and Huxley undoubtedly increased its appeal. The series made no difference between Lewis and Arnold Bennett and encouraged readers to collect all Phoenix Library books.[71]

The publication of *Tarr* was announced for November 1928, but Lewis took longer than expected to revise the novel. In late August, he wrote to his publisher: 'I am very sorry to say that it has been impossible for me during the last 3 weeks to devote myself to the correcting of the last 200 pages of Tarr, but I am now about to do so.'[72] By mid-November, Lewis had finished revising the corrected proofs, and had written a new preface. The book, published with a bright orange cover on 12 December 1928, had a first printing of 5,250 copies.[73] A second printing of 3,000 copies was ordered in February 1935, as the Phoenix Library celebrated its 100th title (Figure 3.2). Of this reprint, 1,460 copies were bound with cancel titles in July 1941 and published in the Pelham Library series at four shillings.[74] In total, the cheap edition of *Tarr* sold approximately ten times more copies than the Egoist Press edition.

ADVERTISING, DISTRIBUTING AND REVIEWING *TARR*

To sell *Tarr* to a large audience, Chatto & Windus emphasised the unique story of the book. As Plate 2 shows, the uniform red dust jacket included a wrap-around band with the following text:

> TARR, in a sense the first book of a period in England, and Mr Wyndham Lewis's first book and first work of fiction, was originally published in 1918. For some time it has been out of print and copies have been procurable only at a premium. It has now been revised, and the new version is here presented for the first time to the public.

It was highly unusual for a reprint series to include a wrap-around band, especially one that emphasised the qualities of a specific book (rather than the series as a whole). But for Chatto & Windus, *Tarr*'s publishing and textual history could be used to create a desirable product. As the firm's narrative made clear, the book had the aura of an early moment of modernism. Like other modernist landmarks first published in limited editions, the 1918 *Tarr* was 'procurable only at a premium', restricting its appeal to a small elite. The Phoenix Library promised customers that they, too, could join this elite without spending more than three shillings and six pence.

Unlike small presses, Chatto & Windus could spend large amounts on advertising. Between December 1928 and June 1929, *Tarr* was mentioned in five advertisements in the *Times Literary Supplement* alone.[75] These advertisements can be classified in three categories. The first kind, which appeared shortly after the publication of *Tarr*, focused on new Chatto & Windus titles, rather than on the Phoenix Library. 'Mr WYNDHAM LEWIS has also *completely* revised and expanded his magnificent novel', declared one advertisement. 'It is virtually a new book, of first-rate importance.'[76] In an attempt to present the reprint of *Tarr* as a new, exciting book, the firm advertised Lewis's novel alongside recent books such as Aldous Huxley's *Point Counter Point* (sold for 10s. 6d.). The second kind of advertisements started appearing in spring 1929, and focused on the Phoenix Library as a whole. In the *Times Literary Supplement* of 25 April 1929, *Tarr* was mentioned below *The Gentle Art of Cookery*. As a uniform series, the Phoenix Library did not distinguish between 'a cookery book *de luxe*' that 'combines literary lore with literary grace', and a modernist novel initially published for a small coterie (Figure 3.2). The third group of advertisements focused only on Lewis's books. For example, a full-page advertisement in Lewis's review *The Enemy* mentioned *Time & Western Man* (sold for 21s.), *The Art of Being Ruled* (18s.), *The Childermass*, Section I (8s. 6d.), *Tarr* (3s. 6d.) and *The Wild Body* (7s. 6d.).[77] As the cheapest book by Lewis on the market, the Phoenix Library edition of *Tarr* appealed to those who were interested in his work but could not afford to spend eighteen or twenty-one shillings on a book.

This advertising strategy was based first on the reputation of the firm Chatto & Windus, second on the brand name of the Phoenix Library, and third on the well-known name of the author. But the novel's specific subject was not described. Instead, Chatto & Windus followed Lewis's advice to use blurbs that praised the first edition: '*Tarr* is a thunderbolt' (*The Weekly Dispatch*) and 'Here we have the forerunner of the prose and probably of the manner that is to come' (*The New Witness*).[78] Rebecca West's review in the *Nation* also appeared on the wrap-around band shown on Plate 2: 'A beautiful and serious work of art that reminds one of Dostoievsky only because it too is inquisitive about the soul, and because it contains one of vast moral significance which is worthy to stand beside Stavrogin.' Advertising materials thus assumed that readers had already heard of *Tarr*, or at least of his author. In contrast, when Alfred Knopf issued a second edition in 1926, he advertised the book as an authentic and exciting tale on Bohemian artists in Paris. 'Many novels have been written to sentimentalize and falsify them and the Latin Quarter they have made their own', declared their advertisement. 'None before has given the truthful picture of that intense society' (Figure 3.3). Knopf's advertisement

BOORZKOS

What Are They Really Like?

The Latin-Quarter Artists

in Paris, who spend their days painting in dark studios, and their nights talking outside the cafés of Montparnasse? And occasionally one of them sets the Seine on fire with a masterpiece...

Many novels have been written to sentimentalize and falsify them and the Latin Quarter they have made their own. None before has given the truthful picture of that intense society.

T A R R

By Wyndham Lewis

$2.50 at all bookstores

Alfred A. Knopf, 730 Fifth Avenue, New York

BORZOI BOOKS

Figure 3.3 Advertisement for *Tarr* (Knopf ed.), *New York Times*, 18 July 1926, p. BR20.

invited curious readers to view *Tarr* as a quasi-sociological document on a fascinating artistic lifestyle. While Wyndham Lewis was almost unknown in the United States, he needed no introduction in Britain – which explains why Chatto & Windus's advertisements did not focus on the content of his first book.

The Phoenix Library was advertised in literary publications such as the *Times Literary Supplement*, *The Nation and Athenæum* and *The Enemy*, but also in more 'lowbrow' papers such as *John O'London's Weekly* and *Everyman*. According to Andrew Nash, these advertisements were placed by the Phoenix Book Company, which also sold the Phoenix Library and other books 'direct to the general public' 'by mail order and house-to-house visiting'.[79] In fact, advertisements for the Phoenix Library appeared in *John O'London's Weekly* before Chatto & Windus started working with the Phoenix Book Company.[80] From its creation, the Phoenix Library was marketed as a series for a lower-middle- and middle-class audience with intellectual aspirations. In *Fiction and the Reading Public*, Q. D. Leavis suggests that *John O'London's Weekly* sold 100,000 copies per week, which then 'pass through innumerable hands in the reading-rooms of public libraries'.[81] Drawing on Leavis, Jonathan Wild speculates that 'a combined weekly readership of, say, 500,000 would not appear an unreasonable assessment'.[82] For many of these readers, buying books (and especially recent books) was still a luxury. Once in the Phoenix Library, modern literature became affordable for an audience eager to acquire signs of cultural capital.

The Phoenix Library was sold to a wide public in Britain, but also in continental Europe, Japan, Canada, Australia, New Zealand and even (illegally) in the United States. In early 1928, the launch of the series was announced to major Anglophone bookshops in Paris (including Shakespeare & Company, whose owner Sylvia Beach had published Joyce's *Ulysses* six years before).[83] The small format of Phoenix Library books was well suited to the expatriate lifestyle. 'We intend to keep the series very select', wrote Harold Raymond to one bookseller in Rome. 'Their portable size should especially appeal to your clientele, many of whom I imagine "living in their boxes", or, at any rate, afraid to accumulate bulky books.'[84] The Phoenix Library was also available in Japan, where Chatto & Windus was already well established (Maruzen & Co., a bookshop in Tokyo, had one of the firm's three largest accounts outside England). Following the suggestion of a professor of English literature at the University of Tokyo, Chatto & Windus placed an advertisement for the Phoenix Library in *Studies in English Literature* (the journal of the English Literary Society of Japan) and encouraged Maruzen to stock the series.[85] It shows that the Phoenix Library targeted an increasingly international academic market. In addition to Europe and Asia, the series was well distributed in the British dominions. As Chatto & Windus told A. A. Milne, 'colonial buyers frequently insist on buying "cheaps" at half price'.[86] In Canada, therefore, the profit margin on the Phoenix Library was small. But in Australia and New Zealand, Chatto & Windus resisted the booksellers' demand for a 50 per cent discount, and sold the Phoenix Library 'at ordinary English rates, which will mean to owing to costs of freightage and duty the books will be retailed over there at 4s. 6d.'[87] In an announcement to its sales representatives in the British dominions, Chatto & Windus reminded them to push the Phoenix Library and also to pay attention to Wyndham Lewis, 'whose works are exciting very considerable attention in this country'.[88] The Phoenix Library edition of *Tarr* was therefore available in Canada (Lewis's country of birth) and the rest of the dominions.

Although Chatto & Windus did not sell the Phoenix Library in the United States, some wholesalers illegally provided the books to the trade. As Bennett Cerf (the co-owner of the Modern Library) said, 'literally hundreds of copies of their Phoenix Library books – many of them books that are copyrighted in this country – are for sale in practically every bookstore in New York'.[89] Cerf had been reminded not to sell the Modern Library edition of Proust's *Swann's Way* in Italy (a market controlled by Chatto & Windus), and he in turn asked Chatto & Windus to restrict the sale of Phoenix Library books in the USA.[90] It is likely, however, that Phoenix Library books continued to be sold in America, since it was difficult for publishers to prevent copies from leaking through their wholesalers.

The Phoenix Library edition of *Tarr* was advertised and sold to various audiences, in Britain and abroad, and it was widely reviewed – an unusual fact for a reprint edition. While advertisements for the Phoenix Library appeared at all levels (from the 'lowbrow' *John O'London's Weekly* to the 'highbrow' *Nation and Athenæum*), reviews of *Tarr* were concentrated at the upper end of the spectrum. 'The art of choosing the right thing to reprint is almost as subtle as the art of choosing the right thing to print', declared *The Sketch*. 'I am glad to see that the latest edition is Mr Wyndham Lewis's brilliant "Tarr", his first book, but, in fiction at all events, probably his best.'[91] In the *Advertiser's ABC* (1929), *The Sketch* was presented as a luxurious illustrated magazine which 'sets itself to provide cheery entertainment for the smoking-room and boudoir'.[92] Literary reviews such as *New Statesman* (that Q. D. Leavis described as 'highbrow Labour') and the new *Life & Letters* also reviewed the revised edition of *Tarr*.[93] The young critic Cyril Connolly described Lewis's novel as 'an arid and untidy little picture of even more untidy and arider people': 'It seems in every way an immature book, but worth republishing, if only to reveal how well developed even then was the author's capacity for revenging himself on his associates.'[94] It is hardly surprising that this aggressiveness did not appeal to Connolly, who belonged to a cultural elite that Lewis detested. The *Life & Letters* reviewer was more enthusiastic:

> Mr Wyndham Lewis's admirers have long been hoping for a re-issue of his excellent post-war novel, *Tarr* . . . Apparently, Mr Lewis has held it back because he felt that, as it stood, the book needed re-writing; it was written hastily, he tells us, during a period of convalescence; so the new edition has been considerably enlarged and revised. After comparing the present version with what I remember of the book in its original form, I should say that the author has done his work very well indeed. I recollect having been delighted by it at a first reading some years ago, and, on looking through it again, I was once more, and as completely, subjugated by the extraordinary satiric verve which goes to its telling, the positively

rhinoceros vigour with which the narrator tramples on the path he has set himself.

Interestingly, the reviewer was aware that the Phoenix Library would open up new markets for Lewis's novel: '*Tarr* can be recommended not only to Mr Lewis's usual public, but also to a wider public in search of entertainment rather than instruction – to every reader, that is to say, capable of appreciating true satire when he finds it.'[95] Not everybody welcomed the fact that the new *Tarr* was more readable and accessible to a large audience. In *Apes, Japes and Hitlerism: A Study and Bibliography of Wyndham Lewis*, published by a small press in 1932, John Gawsworth wrote: 'The book as it now stands possesses perhaps more literary value but one misses in it "the cussedness and rugosities of manner" that the old *Tarr* possessed.'[96] This inaugurated the long-standing dispute over the merits of the 1918 and 1928 texts.

Although Lewis's effort to tame his modernist style did not appeal to all his supporters, it helped him attract the attention of other cheap series of reprints. As early as 1925, Ezra Pound suggested Tauchnitz as a potential publisher. 'Of course Tauch. has up to the present done only reprints', wrote Pound, 'but Otto says this is not imperative. And that now that they have recovered a bit from the lyte hostilities they wd. like to do a bit-er-igh-Brow stuff. (He used much more dignified langwidge).'[97] Nothing came out of this proposal. But in November 1930, nearly two years after the publication of the revised *Tarr*, Lewis signed a contract with Tauchnitz for a cheap edition to be sold in continental Europe. He received an immediate advance of £30 for the first 8,000 copies, and the promise of £10 for each additional printing of 2,000 copies.[98] For an author used to small print runs of 1,000 to 2,500, the Tauchnitz edition was the key to a much broader market. The fact that Tauchnitz based its edition on the 1928 text highlights the importance of the Phoenix Library in the diffusion of Lewis's novel. This expanding market for *Tarr* was both *vertical* (from 'high-' to 'lowbrow') and *spatial*, since the revised text was now available in two cheap editions in Europe and in the whole British Empire. In 1948, Penguin made an offer for a paperback publication of *Tarr* – 'the novel was to be issued in an edition of not fewer than 50,000 copies, to be sold at 2s.'[99] The publisher was undoubtedly aware that the book had been a commercial success in the Phoenix Library, and wanted to sell it to the mass market. Although Penguin eventually dropped its offer, this episode shows the central role of the Phoenix Library in bringing *Tarr* to the attention of new audiences.[100]

The Phoenix Library, which had gone out of print during the Second World War, was relaunched in 1950. 'Do you remember those gay little volumes, red with a stylized phoenix in white, which stood on every sensible undergraduate's bookshelf?', asked the magazine *Time & Tide*. 'Lytton Strachey, C. E.

Montague and Aldous Huxley figured largely as their authors and most people read *Tarr* in this edition.'[101] There are two interesting points here: first, the fact that the original Phoenix Library was read by students (at the time when modernism was being institutionalised in academia) and, second, the attribution of *Tarr*'s expanding readership to the series.[102] More than two decades after the publication of the revised *Tarr*, the Phoenix Library continued to be praised for making the book available to a broader audience. By that time, however, Lewis had long dissociated himself from Chatto & Windus. He once wrote to his old friend William Rothenstein: 'it was very unwise of me to allow my books to pass into the hands of the official "Bloomsbury" publisher'.[103] The year the New Phoenix Library was launched, Lewis's autobiography *Rude Assignment* was published under the Hutchinson imprint. 'I am what is described as a "highbrow"', wrote Lewis, before deploring the gap between the cultural extremes: 'The invisible line separating the two Publics cannot be crossed with impunity by one of the Minority.'[104] The publication of *Tarr* in the Phoenix Library ('an aristocrat among pocket libraries') was one of the rare moments when Lewis did cross this line to reach all kinds of readers – the 'aristocratic audience' he desired but also the 'lowbrow' readers of *John O'London's Weekly* and *Everyman*.

NOTES

1. Lewis to Kenner, 23 November 1953, *Letters of Wyndham Lewis*, p. 552.
2. Cooper, *Modernism and the Culture of Market Society*, p. 215.
3. Klein, 'Note on the Text', p. xxxii.
4. Klein, 'Note on the Text'; O'Keeffe, ed., *Tarr: The 1918 Version*; Sturgeon, 'Wyndham Lewis's *Tarr*'.
5. Sturgeon, 'Wyndham Lewis's *Tarr*', p. 23.
6. Nash, 'Literary Culture', p. 337.
7. Nash, 'Sifting Out "Rubbish"', pp. 191, 199.
8. Lewis, *Blasting and Bombardiering*, p. 46.
9. Rainey, *Institutions of Modernism*, p. 38.
10. Lewis, *Blasting and Bombardiering*, p. 47.
11. Lewis to Captain Guy Baker, 4 January 1916, *Letters of Wyndham Lewis*, p. 74.
12. O'Keeffe, *Some Sort of Genius*, p. 189.
13. Cooper, *Modernism and the Culture of Market Society*, p. 215.
14. Meyers, *The Enemy*, p. 85.
15. Lidderdale and Nicholson, *Dear Miss Weaver*, p. 464.
16. In 1926, Knopf issued a second edition priced at $2.50. The book had previously been out of print according to Grattan, 'In the Pages of Books'.
17. Eliot, 'Tarr'.
18. The Egoist Ltd Extracts from Press Notices of *Tarr*, MS 57355, Harriet Shaw Weaver papers, British Library.
19. Edwards, *Wyndham Lewis*, p. 33.
20. Lewis did not stop writing during this period. For example, he was editing and contributing to the *Tyro* (1921–2).
21. Meyers, *The Enemy*, p. 135.
22. Nash and Knowlson, 'Charles Prentice and T. F. Powys', p. 35. For Aldington,

Prentice was 'the ideal publisher, a scholar whose advice in literary matters was of great value and a man of such gentle sweetness and charm that I came to feel the greatest affection for him', *Life for Life's Sake*, p. 353.

23. Schneller, 'Chatto & Windus'.
24. Prentice to Huxley, 3 November 1927, Letter book, CW A/119.
25. Chatto & Windus to Pinker, 2 November 1927, Letter book, CW A/119.
26. A five-shilling leather edition, 'uniform in a smooth rich crimson', was advertised in 1928 (see, for example, advertisement for the Phoenix Library, *Observer*, 29 January 1928, n.p.). A 1931 letter refers to 'the now defunct Phoenix Library leather edition'. Phoenix Book Co. to Harold Raymond, 6 March 1931, Letters from The Phoenix Book Company, CW 41/5.
27. 'Derrick, Thomas', *National Archives*, <http://www.nationalarchives.gov.uk/theartofwar/artists/derrick_thomas.htm> [accessed 27 March 2016].
28. Phoenix Library leaflet, 1928, Advertisements book, CW D/5.
29. Chatto & Windus to *TLS* Editor, 17 January 1928, Letter book, CW A/119.
30. CW to Pinker, 2 November 1927, Letter book, CW A/119.
31. Satterfield, *The World's Best Books*, p. 93.
32. Chatto & Windus to *TLS* Editor, 17 January 1928, Letter book, CW A/119.
33. Nash, 'Sifting Out "Rubbish"', p. 190.
34. Prentice to C. F. Leyel, 7 November 1928, Letter book, CW A/122.
35. Raymond to G. O. Anderson (George H. Harrap & Co.), 22 November 1928, Letter book, CW A/122.
36. Chatto & Windus to Fry, 15 December 1927, Letter book, CW A/119.
37. Stock book 9, CW B/2/20.
38. Stock book 9, CW B/2/20.
39. Hibberd, 'Monro, Harold Edward (1879–1932)', *Oxford Dictionary of National Biography*.
40. Hibberd, *Harold Monro*, p. 144.
41. Monro, 'Introduction', p. 10.
42. Owen's *Poems*, with an introduction by Edmund Blunden, appeared in the Phoenix Library in 1933. Six thousand copies of this edition were printed from June 1933 to March 1939. Stock book 9, CW B/2/20. This edition thus reached a much wider audience than the 1920 anthology of his work, ed. Sassoon. See Todman, *The Great War*, p. 162.
43. Quoted in Grant, *Harold Monro*, p. 161.
44. 'The Best Anthology', *Morning Post*, 13 December 1929, n.p.
45. Bennett, 'Thousands Argue about the Modern Novel – But the Revolutionary Poetry of To-Day is Left Out of Conversation', *Evening Standard*, 12 December 1929, n.p. Reprinted in Bennett, *The Evening Standard Years*, p. 332.
46. Richard Aldington described Bennett as 'the only English reviewer in my experience who could induce people to read the books he praised'. *Life for Life's Sake*, p. 344.
47. Prentice to Monro, 23 November 1927, Letter book, CW A/119.
48. Stock book 9, CW B/2/20.
49. Grant, *Harold Monro*, p. 162.
50. 'The two Phoenix names were coincidental.' Nash, 'Literary Culture', p. 337.
51. Phoenix Book Co. Catalogue (my emphasis), Letters from The Phoenix Book Company, 1930–1931, CW 41/5.
52. See N. N. Feltes's distinction between 'list' and 'enterprising' publishers. *Literary Capital*, pp. 25–34.
53. Nash and Knowlson, 'Charles Prentice and T. F. Powys', p. 57.

54. Bennett, 'An Artist Turned Author – Mr Wyndham Lewis', *Evening Standard*, 28 April 1927, n.p. Reprinted in Bennett, *The Evening Standard Years*, p. 44.
55. Lewis to Editor, *Evening Standard*, 6 May 1927, Box 64, Folder 93, Wyndham Lewis collection, Cornell.
56. Lewis to Prentice, 18 May 1928, Correspondence between Wyndham Lewis and Chatto & Windus, CW 144/3.
57. 'The novel will rival "Ulysses" in scale: in scope it is far wider' (*The Nation*). This blurb appeared in an advertisement for *The Childermass* (Section I), *New Statesman*, 30 June 1928, p. 395.
58. Lewis, *Blasting and Bombardiering*, p. 86.
59. Prentice to Lewis, 17 May 1928, Correspondence between Wyndham Lewis and Chatto & Windus, CW 144/3.
60. Prentice to Lewis, 17 May 1928, Correspondence between Wyndham Lewis and Chatto & Windus, CW 144/3.
61. Lewis to Prentice, 19 May 1928, *Letters of Wyndham Lewis*, p. 177.
62. Contract for the Phoenix Library edition of *Tarr*, 29 May 1928, Random House Group Archive, Rushden.
63. Cooper, *Modernism and the Culture of Market Society*, p. 218.
64. Lewis to Prentice, 17 November 1928, Correspondence between Wyndham Lewis and Chatto & Windus, CW 144/3.
65. O'Keeffe, ed., *Tarr: The 1918 Version*, pp. 26–7.
66. Lewis, *Tarr*, Phoenix Library edition, pp. 7–8.
67. See Jaillant, *Modernism*, p. 81 and 'Shucks, We've Got Glamour Girls Too!', p. 150.
68. Prentice to Lewis, 9 June 1928, Letter book, CW A/121.
69. Chatto & Windus to Mumby, 28 June 1928, Letter book, CW A/121.
70. Chatto & Windus to Mumby, 28 June 1928, Letter book, CW A/121.
71. 'They are an admirable series to collect and to go on collecting.' Advertisement for the Phoenix Library, *Observer*, 29 January 1928, n.p.
72. Lewis to Prentice, 27 August 1928, Correspondence between Wyndham Lewis and Chatto & Windus, CW 144/3.
73. Prentice to Lewis, 6 December 1928, Letter book, CW A/122; Stock book 9, CW B/2/20.
74. Stock book 9, CW B/2/20. See also Morrow and Lafourcade, *A Bibliography of the Writings of Wyndham Lewis*, p. 34; Pound, Grover and Bridson, *Wyndham Lewis: A Descriptive Bibliography*, pp. 7, 9.
75. *Times Literary Supplement*, 13 December 1928, p. 979; 31 January 1929, p. 70; 21 February 1929, p. 126; 25 April 1929, p. 334; 6 June 1929, p. 452.
76. *Times Literary Supplement*, 31 January 1929, p. 70.
77. *Enemy*, c. 1929, Advertisement book, CW D/6.
78. Lewis to Prentice, 1 December 1928, Correspondence between Wyndham Lewis and Chatto & Windus, CW 144/3.
79. Nash, 'Literary Culture', p. 337.
80. See for example, advertisement for the Phoenix Library, *John O'London's Weekly*, 17 March 1928, n.p. Chatto & Windus started working with the Phoenix Book Company in early 1931. Shortly after, the Company asked Chatto & Windus for the permission to place advertisements in *Everyman* and *John O'London Weekly* ('Do you think there would be any objection sufficient to cause you embarrassment from the trade if we do this?'). Phoenix Book Co. to Harold Raymond, 20 April 1931, Letters from The Phoenix Book Company, CW 41/5.
81. Leavis, *Fiction and the Reading Public*, pp. 20–1.

82. Wild, '"Insects in Letters"', p. 59.
83. Chatto & Windus to Galignani Library, 3 February 1928, Letter book, CW A/120 (includes the following note: 'A copy of this letter sent to Miss S. Beach, Shakespeare & Co., Paris & Messrs Brentano's, Paris').
84. Raymond to Miss Grimes (Wilson's Library), 26 January 1928, Letter book, CW A/119.
85. Chatto & Windus to Arundell del Re, 11 November 1927; Chatto & Windus to Maruzen, 11 November 1927, Letter book, CW A/119.
86. Chatto & Windus to Milne, 3 November 1927, Letter book, CW A/119.
87. Chatto & Windus to Fry, 15 December 1927, Letter book, CW A/119.
88. Chatto & Windus to G. J. Hicks & Co., 5 January 1928; Chatto & Windus to G. J. McLeod Ltd, 5 January 1928, Letter book, CW A/119.
89. Cerf to Alma Levin (Brandt & Brandt), 29 May 1929, Box 99, Random House records, Columbia.
90. Cerf to Bernice Baumgarten (Brandt & Brandt), 7 June 1929, Box 99, Random House records, Columbia.
91. *The Sketch*, 6 February 1929, n.p.
92. Quoted in Leavis, *Fiction and the Reading Public*, p. 277.
93. Leavis, *Fiction and the Reading Public*, p. 182.
94. *New Statesman*, 5 January 1929, n.p. *Tarr* was number 29 on Connolly's list of 100 key books from 1880 to 1950. *The Modern Movement*, pp. 34–5.
95. *Life & Letters*, May 1929, n.p.
96. Gawsworth, *Apes, Japes and Hitlerism*, p. 43.
97. Pound to Lewis, 2 May 1925. Reprinted in Materer, ed., *Pound/Lewis*, p. 146. The 'Otto' that Pound mentions is Curt Otto, the head of the firm.
98. Contract for the Tauchnitz edition of *Tarr*, Box 60, Folder 45, Wyndham Lewis collection, Cornell.
99. Morrow and Lafourcade, *A Bibliography of the Writings of Wyndham Lewis*, p. 36.
100. Similarly, the fact that the Modern Library reprinted Sherwood Anderson's *Winesburg, Ohio* (a book first published by the small press of Ben Huebsch) brought it to the attention of Penguin, which published a paperback edition in 1946 with a first printing of 150,000. See Jaillant, *Modernism*, p. 58.
101. *Time & Tide*, 10 February 1951, n.p.
102. F. R. Leavis was of course instrumental in the institutionalisation of modernist studies from the 1930s. See Hilliard, *English as a Vocation* and Mulhern, *The Moment of 'Scrutiny'*.
103. Lewis to Rothenstein, 30 November 1938, Box 68, Folder 52, Wyndham Lewis collection, Cornell.
104. Lewis, *Rude Assignment*, pp. 13, 18.

4

'PARASITIC PUBLISHERS'? TAUCHNITZ, ALBATROSS AND THE CONTINENTAL DIFFUSION OF ANGLOPHONE MODERNISM

In May 1933, Ezra Pound's article 'Past History' appeared in the *English Journal*, the publication of the National Council of Teachers of English. Writing for this audience of American professors, Pound reflected on James Joyce's career – at the time when the publisher Bennett Cerf was preparing to challenge the ban on *Ulysses*. In his article, Pound told a story that would become the conventional narrative on the early days of modernism. Joyce's struggles against philistine publishers, hostile censors and prudish readers eventually leads to his triumphant entry into the literary canon. As Pound put it, 'anyone who has not read these three books [*Dubliners, A Portrait of the Artist as a Young Man* and *Ulysses*] is unfit to teach literature in any high school or college.'[1] For Pound, this recognition had attracted the wrong kind of publishers:

> *The Portrait* and *Ulysses* were serialized by small honest magazines, created to aid communication of living work; after a lapse of years, these vols. arrived at such a state of acceptance that parasitic publishers issued them. The Tauchnitz which cares only for money but pretends to other aims, issued *The Portrait* and the Albatross issued *Dubliners* and *Ulysses* in continental cheap editions, indicating that the books had passed out of the exclusive circle of people who think and want to know what is being thought, and into the general mass of people who read because an author has a 'name,' etc.[2]

There are several interesting things here. First, Pound compares reprint publishers such as Tauchnitz and Albatross to parasites, who obtain nutrients at the expense of the host organism (the little magazines). This parasitic behaviour is presented as harmful, since the reprint publishers have primarily commercial motivations. Second, Pound notes that the wide diffusion of Joyce's work in cheap continental editions has led to a changing readership, from an 'exclusive circle' of autonomous readers to the 'general mass of people' attracted by an author's reputation.

By the late 1920s and early 1930s, Joyce and other modernist writers certainly had a well-known 'name'. But what Pound does not mention is that reprint publishers had in part contributed to this increasing recognisability. As we have seen in Chapter 2, the Travellers' Library in Britain and the Modern Library in the United States had made *Dubliners* available to a large audience as early as 1926. Tauchnitz published *Portrait of the Artist* in 1930 (the same year as the Travellers' Library edition of this novel). Two years later, *Dubliners* was the first title included in the Albatross Modern Continental Library. The story of the transition from 'small honest magazines' to 'parasitic publishers' leaves aside a central element: the fact that Joyce and Pound had eagerly courted publishers of cheap editions. Only when the interest of these publishers was no longer in doubt did Pound dismiss them as parasites eager to cash in on the growing popularity of modernism.

In this chapter, I want to fill the gaps in Pound's narrative, focusing particularly on the case of Tauchnitz and Albatross. In the 1930s, these two paperback publishers were instrumental in opening European markets for Anglophone modernism. Woolf's *Mrs Dalloway* and *Orlando* appeared on the Tauchnitz list in 1929, with numbers 4867 and 4866 respectively (*The Squeaker*, by the bestselling crime novelist Edgar Wallace, was number 4865 – another example of the simultaneous publication of modernism and detective fiction in the interwar period).[3] Tauchnitz also published D. H. Lawrence's *The Woman Who Rode Away* and *Sons and Lovers* in 1929, and Wyndham Lewis's revised version of *Tarr* in 1931 (see Chapter 3). When Albatross was launched in 1932, its first ten titles included Joyce's *Dubliners* (#1), Woolf's *To the Lighthouse* (#7) and Wallace's *The Man at the Carlton* (#9).

Despite their enormous impact on the diffusion of modernism, Tauchnitz and Albatross have attracted almost no interest from modernist scholars. The few sources of information come from bibliographers and book historians. In 1984, four years before the publication of his magisterial bibliography of Tauchnitz editions, William Todd declared,

> the name of Tauchnitz is now barely recognized, its mountains of ephemeral paperback books mostly gone (at least in US libraries), its 'mediating' effect completely ignored in current Anglo-American criticism, and

its considered evaluation of certain titles thus entirely lost upon the present reader.[4]

More recently, Alistair McCleery and Michele Troy have examined Tauchnitz and Albatross with a book history framework.[5] But their accounts focus more on the historical evolution of these publishing enterprises and their relationship with the Nazi state in the 1930s, than on the publication of modernism.[6] McCleery also tends to simplify the positioning of Tauchnitz. He thus presents the 1930 edition of Edna Ferber's *Cimarron* as 'the sort of middlebrow bestseller that characterized Tauchnitz at this period'.[7] Yet, Tauchnitz published *Cimarron* (#4938) in May, the same month as *Portrait of the Artist* (#4937). Like many reprint publishers, Tauchnitz (and Albatross) had a flexible editorial line – modernist texts appeared alongside crime fiction and 'middlebrow' bestsellers.

This chapter is organised chronologically, starting with Joyce's early relationship with Tauchnitz. I want to show that the transnational nature of Tauchnitz, a German publisher of Anglophone literature, particularly appealed to expatriate modernists such as Joyce. I then turn to the period from 1929 to 1932, at the time when Max Christian Wegner was manager-in-chief of Tauchnitz and attempted to modernise the company before co-founding Albatross. Wegner understood that titles by Joyce, Woolf and Lewis could appeal to a wide audience in Europe. The last section is on Albatross, a publisher that not only helped to popularise modernist texts, but was also shaped by the modernist movement. Its stylish covers and intrinsic cosmopolitanism exemplify modernism's growing influence on mainstream culture in the 1930s.

JOYCE AND TAUCHNITZ

In 1904, when James Joyce left Ireland to settle on the Continent, Tauchnitz had long dominated the European market for cheap books in English. At the time when no international copyright agreement existed, Tauchnitz offered to pay a fixed sum to authors for the right to issue their work in continental Europe and the rest of the world (with the exception of Britain and its Empire). The catalogue issued for the centenary of the firm in 1937 declares:

> Tauchnitz understood that if the true profit of his customer was derived from the pleasure of reading, the satisfaction of the publisher must depend in large measure upon paying to the author the equivalent value of the commerce the writer enables the publisher to exercise.[8]

Here, Bernhard Tauchnitz is presented as a gentleman who derived 'satisfaction' from treating authors fairly. The bibliographer Simon Nowell-Smith later confirmed this narrative: 'I have yet to discover an instance in the nineteenth century of a dissatisfied author not being won back to happy relations with

Tauchnitz and his good German heart.'[9] These accounts of the first Baron Tauchnitz's generosity and gentlemanly behaviour leave aside a central reason behind his strategy – the fact that paying authors made perfect business sense to distinguish the firm from its competitors. As McCleery points out, Tauchnitz 'used the authorized editions of these authors as its "headline" publications, but continued to produce out-of-copyright reprints of the classics of English-language literature such as Shakespeare and Austen as the mainstay of its catalogue'.[10] In other words, Tauchnitz understood that many readers preferred to buy authorised rather than pirated editions, and he skilfully exploited this preference to build a monopoly on Anglophone books in Europe. The 500th, 1,000th, and 2,000th volumes were published respectively in 1860, 1869 and 1881. By 1904, the collection already contained nearly 3,800 volumes.

As an impoverished Irishman living in Europe, Joyce heavily relied on cheap books published by the Leipzig firm. His Trieste library (now preserved at the Harry Ransom Center in Texas) includes fifty Tauchnitz reprints. Among the authors most represented are Shakespeare (eleven titles), George Moore (five titles), Joseph Conrad (four titles), Bernard Shaw (four titles), Oscar Wilde (four titles) and Rudyard Kipling (two titles). Tauchnitz thus allowed Joyce to have his own copies of older classics, as well as more recent books such as Moore's *Hail and Farewell, Vale* and Conrad's *Chance* (first published in 1914; reprinted by Tauchnitz the same year). It was of course highly unusual for reprint publishers to issue books almost simultaneously with the original edition. Since Tauchnitz did not compete with publishers in Britain and the British Empire it was in a position to rapidly offer desirable titles for a fraction of their original price.

In addition to being cheap and offering access to contemporary literature, Tauchnitz books carried a cosmopolitan aura that undoubtedly appealed to Joyce. In the late 1930s, at a time of rising international tensions, the publisher Walter Hutchinson wrote:

> There are no boundaries in literature – neither race nor creed, and books, I sometimes think, form probably the best basis for that true internationalism which it is hoped will one day be established in the world. Baron Tauchnitz, whose Centenary is to be fittingly celebrated throughout the world, was, in my opinion, one of the greatest of ambassadors, for he made available to millions of people the works of the greatest authors of all nations. Baron Tauchnitz's brilliant idea developed into an international institution and few men have left behind them in their work a more enduring memorial.[11]

Internationalism was indeed at the core of Tauchnitz's 'brand story'. The firm emphasised its German origins (through its name and place of publication), its commitment to English-language literature and its wide diffusion in continental Europe. One 1901 edition of Kipling's *Kim* (in Joyce's library in Trieste) includes a yellow sticker from the bookshop W. H. Smith in Paris, with the price in francs. Joyce belonged to a generation of writers eager to escape national boundaries. To be a modernist was, indeed, to be an expatriate. While scholars have challenged this association between modernism and internationalism, it remains a fact that many modernist writers had a complicated sense of national identity.[12] The 'bibliographic code' of Tauchnitz books, with its emphasis on multilingualism and international locations, mirrored the experience of expatriation shared by Joyce and others.

A Tauchnitz catalogue for 1914 can also be found in the Joyce collection at the Harry Ransom Center. That year, Joyce wrote to Grant Richards, who had finally agreed to publish *Dubliners* in England: 'I think you should agree to withhold the continental (Tauchnitz etc) rights for two years. This would allow me to sell the English edition even after the 120 copies which are now sold.'[13] Joyce was well aware that the simultaneous publication of *Dubliners* in a Tauchnitz edition would make it nearly impossible to sell the more expensive edition on the Continent. But he and Ezra Pound remained interested in the possibility of working with the Leipzig firm. In 1920, Joyce contacted the publisher to suggest a possible reprint edition of *A Portrait of the Artist as a Young Man*.[14] A copy was sent by Harriet Shaw Weaver in May of that year, but it was not until 1930 that Tauchnitz published the novel.

In 1925, Pound also corresponded with the firm 'as part of his campaign to make important modern works available at affordable prices'.[15] In a letter to Wyndham Lewis, Pound declared:

> Now that I have a little strength and time I am ready for any dark intrigues that might conduce to our ultimate glories. I have, as a matter of fact written both to Tauchnitz and Liveright; though dont know how useful they can be. For moral effect and to BUST the goddam strangle hold of Smiff and Son [W. H. Smith and Son, Booksellers]. I think Tauchnitz is to [be] encouraged, though there is hardly any direct payment to be got out of him . . . Dont fer Xt's sake mention that I am in touch with T. to any one. A flank move again the buggers, bastards, Squires, Geeses [Gosses] etc. of no val. unless it succks seed.[16]

In the mid-1920s, at the time when modernism was still seen as an esoteric cultural product for a small audience, Pound was eager to get the support of a major commercial enterprise such as Tauchnitz. Far from dismissing it as a 'parasitic publisher', he saw the firm as an ally in his quest to widen the market for the new literature. Tauchnitz, however, showed little interest in modernism until the late 1920s – a turning point in the history of the company. Curt Otto, who had run the publishing house for more than three decades in partnership with the Tauchnitz family, died in July 1929 and was replaced by Max

Christian Wegner. Under the leadership of the new 'Geschäftsführer' or man-ager-in-chief, Tauchnitz transformed itself into an institution of modernism.

1929–1932: MODERNISING TAUCHNITZ

Before taking up his position at Tauchnitz, Wegner had worked at Insel-Verlag, a distinguished publishing house run by his uncle Anton Kippenberg. He eventually became 'Abteilungsleiter' (departmental officer), whose respon-sibilities included the production of the Insel-Bücherei – a uniform series of reprints created in Leipzig in 1912. As Russell Edwards and David J. Hall note, 'the growth of popular education had stimulated a thirst for knowl-edge, and that was already being catered for in a highly competitive market, not least in Leipzig, long a centre of the publishing industry and the home of Tauchnitz and Reclam among others'.[17] While the latter offered cheap books in plain, paper-covered editions, the Insel-Bücherei paid particular attention to the physical format of its books. The distinctive covers consisted of 'abstract or semi-figurative patterns (resembling wallpaper) with a label, stuck on or printed, that gives author, title and series data in the same Gothic typeface in which the text of all the books is printed'.[18] The uniformity of the cover made the books easily recognisable, thus contributing to the enduring success of the series. The books were sold for fifty pfennigs – more than double the price of Reclam's Universal-Bibliothek, but only approximately six pence in British currency. Wegner's experience producing the Insel-Bücherei, wrote Die Zeit after his death, left him with a fondness for books that were both well pro-duced and affordable.[19]

When the thirty-six-year-old Wegner moved to Tauchnitz in 1929, he was faced with the task of reinvigorating a publishing house that had been flagging for several years. The literary agent Curtis Brown thus wrote in his memoirs:

> The much-beloved and respected house of Tauchnitz emerged wounded from the war. The grand days when Baron Tauchnitz used to come over and royally entertain his famous English authors were gone. And gone, too, were the days when the astute and ingratiating Dr Kurt [sic] Otto made the London rounds in succession to the Baron.[20]

The wartime problems (including the lack of paper and other primary materi-als) left the company in a vulnerable position to face the difficult conditions of the post-war period. The hyperinflation, following the introduction of the Reichsmark in 1924, was yet another blow that contributed to Tauchnitz's decline. Rising competition from English publishers' series also threatened the firm's monopoly on the continental market. Before the creation of the Travellers' Library and other three-and-six-penny libraries, Tauchnitz was the only continental publisher to offer recent English-language books for a small portion of their original price. For British and American publishers and authors, the modest rates offered by the Leipzig firm were simply better than nothing. But after 1926, there was a growing awareness that Tauchnitz books were competing with the new cheap series of modern literature (as well as with the original 7s. 6d. editions). That year, the Society of Authors recommended that at least one year should separate the publication of the original and the Tauchnitz editions.[21]

The reactions of Aldous Huxley and Richard Aldington to these propositions exemplify the growing reluctance to accept Tauchnitz's terms. Both authors had titles in Chatto & Windus's Phoenix Library, and both saw Tauchnitz as a threat rather than an opportunity. In April 1928, Huxley sent a circular explaining the changes proposed by the Society of Authors to his literary agent J. B. Pinker and Son. 'I should think the idea is good, provided enough authors agree', wrote Huxley.[22] In 1928 alone, seven Huxley titles were included in the newly-created Phoenix Library: *Antic Hay* (#3 in the series), *Along the Road* (#4), *Crome Yellow* (#11), *Those Barren Leaves* (#14), *Limbo* (#18), *Mortal Coils* (#22) and *On the Margin* (#25). Tauchnitz also published *Those Barren Leaves* the same year, thus competing directly with the Phoenix Library in continental Europe. The same situation happened with *Two or Three Graces* (Tauchnitz, 1928 and Phoenix Library, 1929) and *Brief Candles* (Tauchnitz, 1930 and Phoenix Library, 1931).

This led to growing tensions between Pinker on the one side, and Chatto & Windus on the other. For the literary agent, Tauchnitz offered an additional, if modest, source of income. Pinker seemed to have accepted Curt Otto's argument that Huxley had only a limited market in continental Europe. 'Although Mr Aldous Huxley's books, of which we have up till now published two, have not yet sold particularly well with us as I may tell you confidentially', wrote Otto in November 1928, 'I am so greatly interested personally in his works that I should like to publish *Point Counter Point* in spite of its extraordinary length'. Otto added that Tauchnitz would have to publish the book 'in two volumes, which is a particularly serious drawback in the case of such authors who are not yet popular with our public'. And he concluded: 'I do not think we should in any case recover the costs of publication for this particular book.'[23] *Point Counter Point* appeared on the Tauchnitz list in 1929 (#4872–4873). In April of that year, Charles Prentice, the senior partner at Chatto & Windus, wrote to Pinker and Son in an effort to convince them to stop selling rights to Tauchnitz so soon after the publication of the first edition:

> Our Paris traveller has just returned from Paris and reports that the publication of *Point Counter Point* in the Tauchnitz edition has put the closure on the sales of the English edition. I believe that the Society of Authors has recommended its members not to dispose of Continental library rights in their books until the English edition has had a year's

run: *Point Counter Point* has been out only six months. ... I do not know what Tauchnitz has paid for *Point Counter Point*, but for another book he has just offered us £35, which, calculated at 12 ½ % on 3s. 6d., covers only the sale of 1600 copies in the Phoenix Library. But whereas Tauchnitz makes, presumably, an out and out purchase, the Phoenix books go on paying a royalty year in, year out.[24]

For Prentice, Pinker was using an outmoded economic model to sell books on the Continent. Allowing Tauchnitz to publish a cheap edition only six months after the release of the first edition made absolutely no sense. It was more advantageous (for both the original publisher and the author) to publish the 7s. 6d. edition first, then the 3s. 6d. Phoenix Library and perhaps only after that, consider a cheaper Tauchnitz edition. While Tauchnitz offered a one-off payment, the Phoenix Library continued to pay royalties to the author, year after year. In short, Prentice was trying to convince Pinker and Son that the Phoenix Library, with its reasonable price and long print run, offered a credible alternative to Tauchnitz in Europe. In a following letter, Prentice told the literary agency: 'It is, I fancy, one of Tauchnitz's own arguments that publication in his library increases the chances of translation sales, but I cannot see that this is conclusive, especially in the case of a writer like Huxley.'[25] For Prentice, Tauchnitz could offer little to Huxley, who was already a well-known, commercially successful author.

Richard Aldington shared this growing frustration with Tauchnitz's meagre payments. In September 1929, Chatto & Windus published his novel *Death of a Hero* in a 8s. 6d. edition. Aldington lived in Paris at that time, and was well familiar with Tauchnitz books. 'Tauchnitz is bunkum', he wrote to Charles Prentice, 'I can't think why everyone doesn't see it. I can understand highbrows falling for it, but not a man of sense like Edgar Wallace.'[26] Aldington was referring to the prestige of Tauchnitz among serious writers (in an effort to debunk this image, a 1932 report of the Publishers' Association declared that 'publication in Tauchnitz is not an academic prize').[27] But of course, a bestselling crime writer such as Wallace, who should have cared more for money than for prestige, was also associated with the Leipzig firm. The opposition between the 'purists' and the 'profiteers', between the 'field of restricted production' and the 'field of large-scale production', was blurred in the case of Tauchnitz.[28]

In another letter to his publisher, Aldington dismissed the Tauchnitz collection as 'a mausoleum of unreadable works', and reiterated his opposition to them publishing his novel:

> The Tauchnitz was all very well before the War, but people travel so much nowadays that an early Tauchnitz edition is a mistake. I myself have read Huxley and Garnett and Virginia Woolf in Tauchnitz editions recently, and feel I ought to send them the royalty on their English

edition. Is it true that they pay only 50 pounds and no royalties? If so, the whole thing's absurd.[29]

On the one side, Aldington presented Tauchnitz as an exploitative publisher of unreadable texts, and on the other, he admitted reading books by Huxley, Woolf and David Garnett in this collection. This paradoxical attitude explains his bad conscience, his impression that he owed something to the authors who had been exploited by Tauchnitz. But it also tells us a lot about the ubiquity of Tauchnitz in continental Europe (even at the time when the firm was experiencing severe difficulties): 'Paris is simply smothered with *Point Counter Point*, *No Love* and *Lady into Fox*', Aldington wrote.[30] Despite his sharp criticism of the Leipzig firm, he could hardly resist Tauchnitz's offer of cheap English-language books.

Interestingly, Aldington's experience of expatriation had made him particularly aware that books (like people) were no longer limited by borders. Of course, there had always been overlaps between the continental and the British markets. In 1905, the *Longman's Magazine* declared that women were more likely than men to smuggle Tauchnitz books in England: 'Many a lady smuggles who would no more tip her ball into the better position at croquet than she would cut a throat or scuttle a ship.'[31] Bringing back Tauchnitz books was so common because it carried little risks, as the *Essex County Chronicle* observed:

> Some travellers like to smuggle things on the return journey. The oldest, most tattered Tauchnitz novel, utterly worn out and out-of-date, is carefully stowed about the person, and triumphantly produced on reaching home. Probably the custom-house officials recognise the distension of a pocket, or the suspicious look of a bundle of wraps, but they take no notice.[32]

The late 1920s and early 1930s saw an increase of these international and cultural exchanges. As the Publisher's Association pointed out in its 1932 report on Tauchnitz, 'the continental market has for many years shown a steady advance, owing both to the increasing number of British and American residents abroad, and to the increasing study of the English language by foreigners'.[33] This growing market explains the determination of British publishers to challenge Tauchnitz's monopoly.

In a letter to Aldington, Charles Prentice presented Chatto & Windus's strategy to conquer the continental market. 'Tauchnitz's terms are miserable', he wrote after giving the example of Lytton Strachey who had been persuaded that 'he will get more through his Phoenix editions circulating on the Continent than he could out of Tauchnitz'. In order to make its cheap books available in continental Europe, Chatto & Windus had stepped up its sales efforts:

> We have a man who goes specially to Paris, and also another travel-
> ler who rolls round Spain, the South of France, Italy, Switzerland,
> Germany, Holland, and Scandinavia. In spite of the rates of exchange,
> our European trade has greatly increased during the last few years. In the
> Phoenix Library I am sure the 'Hero' will be a big and constant seller.[34]

For Prentice, Tauchnitz's argument that a publication in their library would
help an author 'to dispose of his foreign rights' was hardly convincing in
the case of bestselling writers like Aldington (and Huxley). Unlike the latter,
Aldington never had any of his works included on the Tauchnitz list. The
Phoenix Library reprinted *Death of a Hero* in 1930 (one year after the first
edition) and *Medallions* in 1931, and sold these cheap editions in continental
Europe and elsewhere.

To respond to this growing competition from British publishers and to a
challenging economic context following the 1929 crash, Max Christian Wegner
implemented a series of bold changes. As McCleery observes, this included
'cutting back on the size of the backlist kept in print' and 'divorcing the editorial and marketing aspects of Tauchnitz books from their in-house production'.[35] Wegner also introduced a coloured wrap-around band to indicate the
genre of the texts published. 'It frequently happens, that readers, wishing to
make a purchase of a book hesitate to buy one by an author with whose work
they are not acquainted', declared a catalogue of 1931 publications.[36] The coloured band was thus designated to 'facilitate' the reader's choice. Red was used
for detective and humoristic tales, 'particularly suitable for travellers'; yellow
for historical novels and stories of adventure; green for love stories; and blue
for 'books of a serious character, plays, essays, psychological novels'.[37]

For example, the 1930 Tauchnitz edition of *Portrait of the Artist* included a
blue band with the following text:

> This autobiographical novel by the eminent author of *Ulysses* is an
> intimately veracious analysis of the soul of a poet. His life in a Jesuit
> college in Ireland, his sensual awakening, his fears and doubts and his
> poetic vocation are set forth with the subtlest psychological insight in
> unsurpassed purity of style.

Tauchnitz was not the first reprint series to use the subversive reputation
of *Ulysses* to market Joyce's earlier works. The Travellers' Library and the
Modern Library also presented Joyce as the well-known author of the banned
novel. Like its competitors, Tauchnitz stressed Joyce's distinctive style – stream
of consciousness – which gave access to the 'subtlest psychological insight'.
Tauchnitz might have been a latecomer in the marketing of modernism, but it
remained a reference for other publishers' series. For the centenary of the firm,
Bennett Cerf declared:

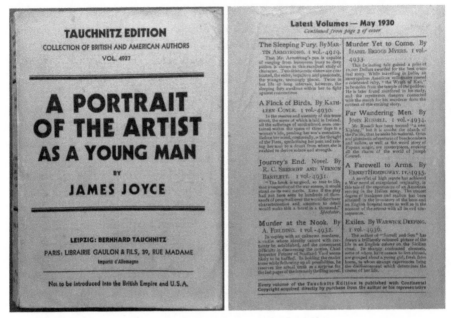

Figure 4.1 Cover and back cover of *A Portrait of the Artist as a Young Man*, Tauchnitz (1930). Note the mix of 'high', 'low' and 'middlebrow' literature on the Tauchnitz list – including titles by Ernest Hemingway, Warwick Deeping and crime fiction authors.

> The best compliment that I can pay to Tauchnitz Editions is to say that in promoting the sale of our own Modern Library series into the best-selling reprint series in the United States, we have been guided to a considerable extent by the editorial acumen and manufacturing skill shown by the directors of the House of Tauchnitz.[38]

Serious books with a blue wrap-around band were often published alongside popular fiction, including stories of crime and adventure (Figure 4.1). For example, Hugh Walpole's *Above the Dark Circus* was number 4988 on the Tauchnitz list, next to Wyndham Lewis's *Tarr* (#4989). Tauchnitz recommended Walpole's text to 'readers in search of recreation and entertainment'. But the firm was also eager to emphasise the quality of its list. 'We should like … to emphasise the fact, that the Tauchnitz Edition excludes books of an all-too superficial character', declared a catalogue. 'In publishing such books as detective novels and stories of adventure, care is taken to keep the level up to a given literary standard.'[39] In 1932, when this Tauchnitz catalogue was published, Q. D. Leavis's *Fiction and the Reading Public* presented the reading of detective fiction as an 'addiction'.[40] Tauchnitz reassured readers that only well-written texts had been selected, texts that reached the standards of classics.

In addition to modernising the Tauchnitz list and the physical aspect of the books, Wegner offered better royalties and increased the number of new titles: 'From four to six new volumes published monthly!', as the catalogue for 1931 put it.[41] His strategy met with opposition from the conservative Board. 'Baron Tauchnitz's family was not backing up his forward policy', wrote C. Kearton of Curtis Brown Ltd shortly after Wegner's dismissal.[42] The pretext was that he had published Ferber's *Cimarron* before the contracted date, thus provoking the anger of the author. Although Wegner stayed less than two years as manager-in-chief of Tauchnitz, the experience was a crucial turning point in his career. Liberated from the control of the Tauchnitz family, he was able to apply his ideas to a new publishing venture – Albatross.

ALBATROSS AND MODERNISM

'The Continental trade received the appearance of the Albatross Series in 1932 with very detached interest', later wrote John Holroyd-Reece, Wegner's partner. 'They pointed out that we were the 42nd rival of Tauchnitz in less than a hundred years.'[43] Indeed, it must have been difficult to convince the book trade – both on the Continent and elsewhere – that Albatross was a serious competitor to the long-established Tauchnitz. Approached by Curtis Brown Ltd, the representative of the American writer Joseph Hergesheimer hesitated to sell the rights of *The Limestone Tree* to the new firm: 'Your recommendation ordinarily would have my approval but Tauchnitz's reputation is such, and I think Mr Hergesheimer's satisfaction is such, that I hesitate to encourage further negotiations along this line.'[44] Yet, Albatross had several assets – starting with, as Curtis Brown Ltd observed, 'important connections and good backing'.[45]

The literary agent claimed to have introduced Holroyd-Reece and Wegner to each other, thus facilitating the birth of Albatross. The two publishers were only in their mid-thirties but already had extensive experience of the book trade. Holroyd-Reece, who came from a cosmopolitan background, was completely at ease in navigating various cultures. A natural networker who seemed to know everybody in the publishing world, he was 'equally at home in London, New York, and all the chief capitals of Europe' and spoke 'the principal languages precisely like a native', wrote Curtis Brown in his memoirs. 'That urbane and picturesque international' had dabbled in journalism – contributing to the *Westminster Gazette*, the *New Statesman*, the *Nation and Athenaeum* – before turning to publishing.[46] One 1926 letter preserved at the Harry Ransom Center shows his involvement in a Paris firm called 'A l'enseigne du Pégase' (Les éditions du pégase), which specialised in limited editions of books on fine arts and bibliography.[47] For example, the press issued a two-volume history of paper 'principalement à Troyes et aux environs depuis le XIVème siècle'.[48] In 1927, Holroyd-Reece started publishing fine books in English under the imprint Pegasus Press. Among the first titles was a facsimile of 'the earliest known block book printed in colours'.[49] The press also gained a reputation for publishing erotica.[50] When Radclyffe Hall's *The Well of Loneliness* was banned in Britain in 1928, Holroyd-Reece undertook the publication of the book in Paris.[51] The original publisher Jonathan Cape discreetly sent moulds of the type, and the Pegasus Press printed a second impression of 3,000 copies.[52] Using Cape's list of unfilled English orders, Holroyd-Reece and his colleagues then sent the book back to England.[53] The Pegasus Press should therefore be situated within the Parisian network of small modernist presses that dealt with controversial materials – including Shakespeare & Company, Edward Titus's Black Manikin Press and the Black Sun Press (also founded in 1927).

While Wegner had acquired his experience of well-produced books with a cheap series of reprints (the Insel-Bücherei), Holroyd-Reece's connections belonged to the rarefied world of the luxury editions. Publishing these books put Holroyd-Reece in contact with people who later proved central to the success of Albatross – including Sir Edmund Davis, a wealthy businessman who provided the financial support for the Pegasus Press before backing the reprint series. Holroyd-Reece also worked with Hans 'Giovanni' Mardersteig, a distinguished printer who had created his own hand press, the Officina Bodoni in Montagnola – a Swiss village near the Italian border. In 1926, the press was moved to Verona within the printing works of Arnoldo Mondadori, and remained active for half a century. During that time, as Hans Schmoller puts it, the Officina Bodoni 'acquired a fame which only a few of its great predecessors can rival'.[54] And this fame was especially long-lasting in modernist circles. In a 1983 interview for the *Paris Review*, James Laughlin, Pound's American publisher, said:

> The man from whom I learned the most about the beauty of a book was Giovanni Mardersteig of the Officina Bodoni in Verona. He was the greatest hand printer in Europe until he died a few years ago. I would visit him when I was in Italy. He did three or four superb books for me. Gide's *Theseus*, two Pound texts, and a Dylan Thomas. They were limited editions, very expensive. He showed me a little bit about how he designed books, which was very valuable in establishing a criterion.[55]

Laughlin was often critical of those who had abandoned artistic ideals to embrace the market. But Mardersteig's association with Albatross did not affect the publisher's admiration. For Laughlin, the printer remained associated with the highest level of skill in the production of beautiful, luxurious, exclusive books.

Holroyd-Reece's collaboration with Mardersteig tells us a lot about the positioning of the Pegasus Press, an imprint that targeted wealthy customers with the promise of a tasteful product. 'Craft and a sense of place are almost always part of the narrative', part of the story that luxury tells, as *The Economist* declares.[56] The aura of a book such as *Andres Brun: Calligrapher of Saragossa*, which the Officina Bodoni printed in 1928 for the Pegasus Press, stemmed from the guarantee of *savoir-faire* brought by its Italian manufacture. For the very rich, today's equivalent of buying a book printed on a hand press in Verona is perhaps to order a Brunello Cucinelli cashmere cardigan knitted in Solomeo, 'a timeless village perched on an Umbrian hilltop'.[57] In both cases, the product's story is anchored in a specific locale associated with the finest quality.

Holroyd-Reece's career – from small press to large-scale commercial enterprise – mirrors the trajectory of the modernist movement in the late 1920s and early 1930s. Having established an extensive network of contacts in the high end of the book market (from hand printers such as Mardersteig, to luxury book dealers and well-off customers), Holroyd-Reece turned towards a broader audience with modest buying power. His familiarity with the economic habitat of modernism made him particularly aware that there was an untapped market for subversive texts. Limited editions published by small presses could not, by definition, reach this wide audience – whereas a cheap series such as Albatross could. But the new series did much more than broaden the audience for modernism. Indeed, Holroyd-Reece used his contacts within modernist institutions to shape Albatross books into strikingly modern objects.

It is highly significant that the first title published by Albatross was James Joyce's *Dubliners*. As we have seen, Max Christian Wegner already had experience of publishing Joyce under the Tauchnitz imprint. But the physical appearance of Tauchnitz books was very far from the kind of modern design that had started to colonise mainstream culture. The squat format and plain cover, which had not changed significantly since the nineteenth century, formed a rather odd packaging for modernist texts such as *Portrait of the Artist*. By the time Tauchnitz added Joyce's name to its list, British publishers had already begun to promote modernist *visual* culture to a large audience (see Chapter 3). But spreading modernist visual culture did not simply mean publishing books on modern art, and educating readers to appreciate new aesthetic forms. The pervasiveness of the modernist revolution also affected the materiality of the book itself. To compete against Tauchnitz, Wegner and Holroyd-Reece thus launched a series whose physical format reflected the modernity of its content.

That they entrusted Mardersteig with the design and typography of Albatross books was not in itself surprising. After all, it was not the first time that a renowned printer associated with small presses and luxurious editions turned to projects for a broader audience. For example, in the mid-1920s, Elmer Adler of

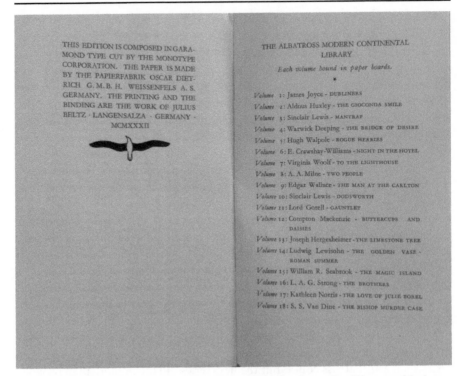

THIS EDITION IS COMPOSED IN GARA-
MOND TYPE CUT BY THE MONOTYPE
CORPORATION. THE PAPER IS MADE
BY THE PAPIERFABRIK OSCAR DIET-
RICH G. M. B. H. WEISSENFELS A. S.
GERMANY. THE PRINTING AND THE
BINDING ARE THE WORK OF JULIUS
BELTZ · LANGENSALZA · GERMANY ·
MCMXXXII

THE ALBATROSS MODERN CONTINENTAL
LIBRARY

Each volume bound in paper boards.

Volume 1: James Joyce - DUBLINERS
Volume 2: Aldous Huxley - THE GIOCONDA SMILE
Volume 3: Sinclair Lewis - MANTRAP
Volume 4: Warwick Deeping - THE BRIDGE OF DESIRE
Volume 5: Hugh Walpole - ROGUE HERRIES
Volume 6: E. Crawshay-Williams - NIGHT IN THE HOTEL
Volume 7: Virginia Woolf - TO THE LIGHTHOUSE
Volume 8: A. A. Milne - TWO PEOPLE
Volume 9: Edgar Wallace - THE MAN AT THE CARLTON
Volume 10: Sinclair Lewis - DODSWORTH
Volume 11: Lord Gorell - GAUNTLET
Volume 12: Compton Mackenzie - BUTTERCUPS AND DAISIES
Volume 13: Joseph Hergesheimer - THE LIMESTONE TREE
Volume 14: Ludwig Lewisohn - THE GOLDEN VASE - ROMAN SUMMER
Volume 15: William R. Seabrook - THE MAGIC ISLAND
Volume 16: L. A. G. Strong - THE BROTHERS
Volume 17: Kathleen Norris - THE LOVE OF JULIE BOREL
Volume 18: S. S. Van Dine - THE BISHOP MURDER CASE

Figure 4.2 Colophon and list of the first eighteen titles in the Albatross Modern Continental Library.

the Pynson Printers worked on the typography of the Modern Library, a series that shares many characteristics with Albatross. But Adler's role was somehow limited (he did not design the logo, for instance). In contrast, Mardersteig shaped many aspects of the physical format of Albatross books – starting with their size, 181 x 112 mm, 'in line with the "golden ratio" of 1.618 widely used in art and architecture'.[58] The same size then became the standard of British paperbacks after Penguin Books adopted it. At the end of Albatross books, a colophon indicated the typeface, the printer and the paper-maker (Figure 4.2). 'Though this may appear a trifle self-conscious', wrote Hans Schmoller, 'the books were so perfect in detail that an expression of the makers' pride was jus- tified'.[59] The colophon thus positioned Albatross books in the tradition of the beautiful book, in contrast to Tauchnitz's less distinguished physical format. It is also significant that Albatross often printed limited editions of its books, to be offered rather than sold. *Dubliners*, for example, was issued in a special edition of ten copies (including one for the author), 'printed upon Japanese vellum and bound in half-leather'. No other cheap series of reprints issued presentation copies in such a sumptuous format. In short, Albatross positioned itself as a luxury brand priced for a broad audience.

Mardersteig also designed the emblem of the series, a stylish, black-and-white drawing of a bird stretching its wings. Suggesting the ability to fly, to travel to various places, this ornithological image follows Chatto & Windus's Phoenix and anticipates the Penguin logo. As in the case of other reprint series, the trademark served to strengthen brand recognition. According to Holroyd-Reece, the Albatross brand became so well known in Europe that 'two of the leading Continental booksellers have asked if it were not possible to have for instance the World's Classic [sic] with an Albatross title page'.[60] On the Continent, British publishers' series were often seen as commodities among others, whereas Albatross had a unique character and promise thanks to effective branding.

The colourful covers of Albatross books also contributed to brand recognition. In an article entitled 'An English Tauchnitz', *The Times* noted the quality of the type and paper of the series, before explaining the meaning of the colours:

> A red cover means a story of adventure and crime (*Night in the Hotel*, by E. Crawshay-Williams); blue, a love story (*The Bridge of Desire*, by Warwick Deeping); green, a story of travel and foreign peoples (*Mantrap*, by Sinclair Lewis); purple, a biography or historical novel (*Rogue Herries*, by Hugh Walpole); yellow, a psychological novel, or essays (*Dubliners*, by James Joyce); and orange, a book of tales or short stories, or a humorous and satirical work (*The Gioconda Smile*, by Aldous Huxley).[61]

Albatross chose different colours to indicate the type of books, wrote *The Times*, in order 'to save the English reader trouble at a railway or other bookstall, but also to help the foreign bookseller and reader, who will thus be able to tell at a glance the nature of each volume'. The newspaper thus distinguished between various audiences for Albatross books: English travellers who lacked time and wanted to identify a book quickly before continuing their journey; and foreigners with limited English-language skills, who needed to be guided towards their preferred genre. In a 1937 memo, Holroyd-Reece wrote: '98% of the Continental booksellers to whom we sell Albatross and Tauchnitz books cannot read English'.[62] And he added that the trade, having noticed that bestsellers often appeared on the Albatross list, concluded that the series selected 'the pick of American and English literature'. Interestingly, Holroyd-Reece seemed to agree with booksellers who equated commercial success with literary quality. Like the Modern Library, Albatross relied on the perception that all the books on its list (whether 'high-', 'low-' or 'middlebrow') could be read by a wide audience.

To help non-English native speakers, Albatross books also included a description in three different languages: English, French and German. The text sometimes varied significantly, reflecting national taste and cultural expectations. In the case of *Dubliners*, the English description is very factual ('No writer during the last few years has given rise to more controversy than the author of *Ulysses*') – whereas the French description is much more philosophical, with its reference to 'Joyce's formidable appetite to express life, all life'. Joyce's style is also contrasted to that of the naturalists, who had an 'annoying pretension to prove something'. Naturalism, a movement dominated by French writers, is not mentioned in the English and German descriptions. Likewise, Woolf's style in *To the Lighthouse* is described as 'a sort of English surrealism, where dream is mixed so strangely with reality'.

Although Albatross adapted to local tastes, cosmopolitanism remained at the centre of its brand story. Indeed, the publisher targeted readers from a wide range of national backgrounds, united only by a desire to read books in English. Because this audience was spread across various countries, it had traditionally been difficult for publishers to reach it. One advantage that Albatross had over Tauchnitz was its ability to fill in orders quickly. According to Holroyd-Reece, the promise 'to supply within 24 hours to any bookseller in some 30 countries' increased the commercial appeal of authors who had limited sales in the Tauchnitz series.[63] In short, these efficient distribution methods allowed Albatross to target a wider international audience.

The physical format of Albatross books confirmed this international focus. The cover of Albatross books stated 'copyright edition', 'not to be introduced into the British Empire or the USA'. On the back cover of some editions, the price was given in three different currencies: German, French and Italian – which gives us a sense of the market for these books. *Dubliners* was thus sold for 1.80 marks, 12 francs and 9 lires. At the end of the book, the colophon indicated that it was printed in Italy. The fact that *The Times* had presented Albatross as an 'English Tauchnitz' led to an outcry among UK publishers. 'We fear that the reviewer cannot have examined the books very carefully', wrote one commentator.[64] The publisher Thornton Butterworth also invited *Times* readers to take the slogan 'Buy British Goods' seriously and turn their back on Albatross and Tauchnitz. For Butterworth, the latter 'undoubtedly cuts into the Continental sales of the British Publishers, much to the disadvantage, but greatly to the supposed kudos, of the Authors'.[65] In a context of economic depression and rising protectionism, the continental series were increasingly presented as enemies of the British good trade, rather than allies in the spread of Anglophone books and culture.

Albatross's cosmopolitanism and striking modern appearance positioned it as an important institution of modernism. The series did not escape the attention of Wyndham Lewis. Returning from a visit to Berlin in 1934, he wrote to

Stuart Gilbert: 'The Albatross editions I saw everywhere.'[66] In his autobiography *Blasting and Bombardiering*, Lewis celebrated the expansion of modern art, which had become part of everyday life – through the posters of E. M. Kauffer displayed in tube stations, for example.[67] As a visual artist himself, Lewis undoubtedly noticed that Albatross was spreading modern design 'everywhere'. The series' physical format fitted well with the modernity of the list, a list that reflects its owners' appetite for subversive modern fiction, with James Joyce and D. H. Lawrence occupying a dominant place.

The Lawrence papers at the Harry Ransom Center show Holroyd-Reece's determination to secure *Lady Chatterley's Lover* and other works for his series. In early 1932, as the first Albatross titles were being released, Holroyd-Reece contacted literary agents to express his interest in Lawrence's unpublished manuscripts. As he explained to Curtis Brown, he was prepared to buy 'for the Albatross the Continental rights in books before you sell them in England, in which case there can be no argument about the English publisher objecting to the Continental edition'.[68] This was a clever way to bypass the British publishers' growing opposition to Albatross and Tauchnitz, but it also positioned Albatross in direct competition with small presses specialising in limited editions and erotic materials. 'Of course', wrote the literary agent Laurence Pollinger, 'Holroyd Reece knows that Titus-Paris publishes an unexpurgated edition of "LADY C" in English.'[69] If Albatross were to publish such a sexually explicit text in a trade edition, it risked attracting the attention of censors and, perhaps, alienating some readers. An obvious solution would be to publish an expurgated text, as Martin Secker in England and Alfred Knopf in America had done. But this had little appeal for Holroyd-Reece, a publisher who once announced his readiness to fight the *Well of Loneliness* case 'all the way'.[70] He and Wegner wanted to publish the most daring texts, *Lady Chatterley's Lover* and *Ulysses* in unexpurgated editions, without taking unnecessary risks with censors. This had traditionally been done through the model of the limited, expensive edition – a model that the Albatross owners were determined to overthrow to reach a much broader audience.

In September 1932, Joyce wrote to Harriet Shaw Weaver about Albatross's offer to issue a continental edition of *Ulysses*:

> The Albatross Press (rival of Tauchnitz) has been bombarding me with phone calls, telegrams etc from Germany to Z'ch, Geneva and here. They want to take over Miss Beach's continental rights whether Cerf wins the US case or not. They would sell at ¼ her price but pay only half as much royalties. Of course the sales would be infinitely more numerous.[71]

Here, Joyce outlined the difference between Sylvia Beach's and Albatross's business models. Like the Travellers' Library, Albatross could not afford to pay the high royalty rates that Beach was paying to Joyce. However, by dividing the price of the Shakespeare & Company edition by four, they hoped to reach an untapped audience – and thus provide Joyce with an attractive income. This plan resembled that of Bennett Cerf of Random House, who envisaged the publication of a trade edition of *Ulysses* if he secured the right to publish the book in America.

Interestingly, Beach herself suggested cheap editions of Joyce's work: she pushed for the publication of *Portrait of the Artist* in the Travellers' Library, and of *Ulysses* in the Albatross series. Wegner found her suggestion 'excellent', and he added: 'I am quite sure that we should reach a very extensive public with our edition and a public that previous editions have never touched.'[72] This shows that Albatross explicitly targeted readers who could not afford to buy a Shakespeare & Company edition. At the time when *Ulysses* was still banned in Anglophone countries, Wegner was confident that the book had a huge market potential. And in order to obtain Joyce's approval, he was prepared to pay a high royalty rate. Albatross generally offered a rate of 5 per cent of the published price – which is what Joyce got for *Dubliners*.[73] But for *Ulysses*, the firm paid an unusually high advance of 15,000 francs – on a royalty basis of 12.5 per cent on every copy sold, with the exception of the first 6,000 copies on which a royalty of 7.5 per cent was paid.[74] 'The production cost of the first edition', explained Wegner, 'is, on account of the length of the book, extremely high'.

As a uniform series, Albatross usually published books that had approximately the same length. But since Joyce was opposed to the publication of *Ulysses* in two volumes, Wegner offered to sell only the complete work for RM 5.60 ('the price of two extra volumes in the Albatross Library'). Wegner added that they were ready to publish the book in just a few months, 'in spite of the fact that a cheap American edition may appear soon' (the Random House edition did not appear until January 1934). He concluded his letter to Beach with a reminder that Albatross had already helped Joyce reach new readers:

> As I know that Mr Joyce likes the appearance of the ALBATROSS edition whose first volume contains his *Dubliners* of which more than 4,000 copies have been sold during the first six months although two cheap English editions had been published long before, I hope that he will like the idea of including *Ulysses* in the ALBATROSS LIBRARY.[75] It seems to me that an edition which began its programme with James Joyce's first book would provide the most appropriate setting for his greatest work.[76]

The commercial success of *Dubliners* and its central position in the Albatross series undoubtedly helped convince Joyce to sign the contract for *Ulysses*. The book was published in December 1932 by the Odyssey Press, an imprint created especially for this purpose. This had at least two advantages: dissociating Albatross from associations with obscenity, and targeting an audience that was not easily shocked. It would be a mistake, however, to see the launch of the Odyssey Press as a case of 'niche marketing'. While niche marketers have a large share of a small market, the new imprint was from the start addressing a wide and heterogeneous audience – all those interested in Joyce's reputation for innovative and controversial prose. In practice, the imagined audiences of the Odyssey Press and Albatross were so close that the two names were often used interchangeably.

In the field of small presses, Sylvia Beach's enthusiasm for the cheap editions published by Albatross and the Odyssey Press seemed to have been the exception rather than the norm. The founder of the Black Manikin Press, which published an unexpurgated edition of *Lady Chatterley's Lover* in Paris, was particularly enraged. 'I have just received an abusive letter from Titus', wrote Pollinger to Frieda Lawrence, before explaining that the Albatross planned to issue a cheap edition of the book in March 1933 and was 'ready to pay exceedingly good terms, provided we can find some way of cutting out Mr Titus'.[77] The main competitors of the Odyssey Press were small presses specialising in controversial writing, rather than other commercial publishers and cheap series of reprints. The firm did not compete directly against Martin Secker, Lawrence's publisher in Britain, who also had *Lady Chatterley's Lover* on his list. As Wegner wrote to Pollinger,

> there is no doubt that as far as the contents are concerned, the expurgated Secker edition and our own are quite as different as any two books can be, and the gentle maidens who like to read Mr Secker's edition would not touch the strong meat of ours – and vice versa.[78]

In other words, Wegner and Holroyd-Reece were doing what no publisher had ever done before: marketing unbowdlerised cheap editions of *Lady Chatterley's Lover* and *Ulysses* to a broad readership.

From a business point of view, Joyce made an excellent bargain with the cheap continental edition of *Ulysses*: the 'fat advance' he received was followed by regular royalty payments. In the six years following publication, 17,600 copies were printed – a significant number for an edition that could not be sold in Britain and the United States.[79] And it is precisely the commercial success of Albatross/Odyssey books that upset Ezra Pound. Not only did he criticise the firm for profiting from Joyce's work, he also wanted 'to assassinate Holroyd-Reece for pandering to the lowest common denominator of taste' in *The Albatross Book of Living Verse*, edited by Louis Untermeyer.[80] After years spent courting large-scale publishers, Pound condemned Albatross for being too commercial, too interested in reaching a wide audience.

In fact, Albatross carefully cultivated an aura of sophistication and taste, claiming to publish the best of all genres – from modernist novels to crime fiction. The first twenty-five titles published by the firm in 1932 included yellow-covered 'psychological' texts by Joyce, Woolf and Katherine Mansfield,[81] alongside red-covered crime fiction by Edgar Wallace, S. S. Van Dine and Dashiell Hammett (Plate 3). *The Maltese Falcon* had first been published by the American publisher Alfred Knopf in 1930, and was then reprinted in the Albatross Modern Continental Library in Europe and the Modern Library in the United States (in 1932 and 1934 respectively). Like the Modern Library, Albatross did not hesitate to mix the 'high' and the 'low'. The description in the inside cover insists on the realism of *The Maltese Falcon*, a novel grounded in the author's own experience: 'As a Pinkerton detective for many years, the author has an unrivalled knowledge of the American underworld which comes to life in these pages teeming with the exploits of gangsters, rum runners and dope fiends.' In 1933, shortly after publishing Woolf's *The Waves*, Albatross launched its red-covered Crime Club series in close collaboration with the British publisher Collins. Books that had appeared in the Collins Crime Club in the United Kingdom were then issued as Albatross paperbacks on the Continent. These titles, as Michele Troy points out, were presented as 'a first-class choice' selected by 'the leading experts'.[82] Indeed, the Albatross list included the best of the 'Golden Age' of crime fiction – from Agatha Christie to Dorothy Sayers.

Despite his mistrust of Albatross and his wish to 'assassinate' Holroyd-Reece, Ezra Pound read and apparently enjoyed the Crime Club series.[83] Responding to the poet's praise for the sub-series, Holroyd-Reece wrote: 'I note with mixed feelings that the result of your buying and reading – an uncommon combination – some Albatross Crime Club titles, causes you feelings of clemency towards me.'[84] Pound's leniency did not last long. He soon wrote back, asking Holroyd-Reece to select better books for his series. The publisher replied:

> the ALBATROSS is interested in supplying the best stuff which it can market. The ALBATROSS on the whole is particularly fortunate because, so far, broadly speaking, the best stuff has, contrary to the experience of most publishers, found the best market for us.[85]

In other words, Holroyd-Reece was trying to convince Pound that Albatross was not a parasitic publisher interested only in making money. As the success of *Dubliners* and other Albatross titles had shown, quality texts could find an audience and make a profit.

By 1934, Albatross had achieved such a dominant position that it was able to buy its rival Tauchnitz. The monopolistic position of the firm meant that agents and publishers had few opportunities to negotiate for better rates. As the literary agent A. D. Peters told one writer, 'there is not much point in our standing out against them because we should have nowhere else to go'.[86] Like Tauchnitz, who had once been accused of exploiting its monopoly on continental editions to offer meagre royalties, Albatross was now criticised for imposing harsh conditions. Pressed by an author to obtain a better deal, Sonia Chapter of Curtis Brown agency wrote: 'There is no other publisher of English books on the Continent who can put up a better offer.'[87] Holroyd-Reece could triumphantly proclaim: 'Tauchnitz is dead – long live the Albatross.'[88]

Even the rise of Nazism did not threaten, at least not immediately, Albatross's success story. The firm was obviously in a precarious position: not only did it publish English-language books by authors that the Nazis reviled (such as Aldous Huxley), it also failed the test of racial purity with its Jewish director of German operations (Kurt Enoch) and Jewish financier (Sir Edmund Davis) – in addition to Holroyd-Reece, who had a Jewish father. This posed a series of difficulties, most obviously when Albatross was preparing its takeover of Tauchnitz. As Piet Schreuders points out, objections from the authorities (or fear of an intervention) led to 'an arrangement according to which the printer of Tauchnitz, Oscar Brandstetter in Leipzig, purchased the Tauchnitz Company but turned over all editorial, design and marketing activities to Albatross'.[89] However, as Michele Troy has shown, the Nazi regime was also surprisingly accommodating with Albatross – for example, by providing tax breaks and allowing the firm to sell titles by otherwise banned authors. To explain these allowances, Troy notes that Albatross's sales abroad counted as German exports and delivered foreign currency.[90] In other words, the Nazi regime saw Albatross as an important economic asset that had to be protected. This attitude changed after the invasion of France and the launch of a total war against Britain, but until 1940 Albatross could freely sell books both outside and within the Reich.[91]

Despite attempts to revive Albatross and Tauchnitz after the Second World War, the firms never returned to their former glory. In Britain, 3s. 6d. hard-back series also struggled to compete against Penguin Books and eventually they disappeared. Unlike these series, however, Albatross and Tauchnitz had always been issued in paperback format – and therefore earned a place in histories of the paperback revolution. For example, Alistair McCleery has studied Albatross's influence on Penguin – from the bird logo to the book design and the coloured covers.[92] Less noticed is the fact that Albatross served as a training ground for Kurt Enoch: fleeing the Nazi regime, he immigrated to the United States and founded the New American Library (NAL) in 1948 with Victor Weybright. Like Albatross, a firm that published both modernist texts and detective fiction (albeit under different colours), NAL mixed the 'high' and the 'low'. As I have shown elsewhere, Joyce's *A Portrait of the Artist as a Young Man* was published alongside hard-boiled fiction in this paperback series.[93] Enoch's familiarity with modernism, and confidence that difficult texts could find a market, was undoubtedly something that he learnt from his experience with the continental series. In a 1949 letter to the sales manager of Random House/the Modern Library, Enoch explained the changes in the continental publishing business that he had witnessed:

> ... at that time [i.e. before the Second World War] the publication of continental editions was practically the only means for a wider distribution of American and English books on the continent of Europe. Today, conditions are very different. The American and English reprint series are in a position to offer the European customers lists of books of much greater variety and at a much lower price than continental publishers can.[94]

Enoch then gave examples of NAL titles sold in Europe – including *Portrait of the Artist* (a title that had first appeared on the Tauchnitz list nearly two decades before). Tauchnitz, Albatross and the NAL therefore shared not only a similar paperback format but also a common ambition to find new markets for modernist texts. Pound's denunciation of 'parasitic publishers' and his proclaimed wish to kill Albatross's founder did nothing to stop a process that he had once encouraged: the transition from niche to mass market, and the conquest of new audiences for modernism.

NOTES

1. Pound, 'Past History', p. 355.
2. Pound, 'Past History', p. 351.
3. See Jaillant, *Modernism*, pp. 63–82.
4. Todd, 'A New Measure of Literary Excellence', p. 335.
5. There were also several papers on Tauchnitz and Albatross at the 2016 conference of SHARP (Society for the History of Authorship, Reading and Publishing) in Paris – including Charles Johanningsmeier, 'Exporting America via Leipzig and Paris: The Role of Tauchnitz Editions in Making American Literature Popular Among International Readers', and Alberto Gabriele, 'Beyond Tauchnitz: Brockhaus's Foreign Language Editions, Copyright Law and the Restructuring of Book Production at the End of the 19th Century' (Panel 'Studying the Foreign Literature Series', 19 July 2016).
6. See Troy, *Strange Bird: The Albatross Press and the Third Reich* (Yale University Press, forthcoming 2017).
7. McCleery, 'Tauchnitz and Albatross', p. 301.
8. *The Harvest*, p. 10.
9. Nowell-Smith, *International Copyright Law*, p. 55.
10. McCleery, 'Tauchnitz and Albatross', p. 297.
11. Quoted in British Library, *Tauchnitz-Edition*, p. 6.
12. In *Devolving English Literature*, Robert Crawford argues that 'modernism was an essentially provincial phenomenon' (p. 270). See also White, *Transatlantic Avant-Gardes* for a recent account of 'localist modernism'.
13. Joyce to Richards, 3 February 1914, James Joyce collection, UB. Joyce had agreed to take on 120 copies of the book at trade price for sale in Trieste. Scholes, 'Grant Richards to James Joyce', p. 154.
14. *Letters of James Joyce*, vol. 2, p. 464.
15. Spoo, 'Unpublished Letters', p. 543.

16. Pound to Lewis, 2 May 1925. Reprinted in Materer, ed., *Pound/Lewis*, p. 146.
17. Edwards and Hall, *'So Much Admired'*, p. 4.
18. McCleery, 'The Paperback Evolution', p. 4.
19. Trunz, 'Christian Wegner'.
20. Brown, *Contacts*, pp. 177–8.
21. McCleery, 'Tauchnitz and Albatross', p. 299.
22. Huxley to Pinker and Son, 10 April 1928, Box 6, Aldous Huxley collection, HRC.
23. Otto to Pinker and Son, 24 November 1928, Box 6, Aldous Huxley collection, HRC.
24. Prentice to F. C. Wicken (Picker and Son), 4 April 1929, Letter book, CW A/123.
25. Prentice to Wicken, 8 April 1929, Letter book, CW A/123.
26. Aldington to Prentice, 8 October 1929, Letters from Richard Aldington to Chatto & Windus, CW 48/3.
27. Publishers' Association, *Report on Tauchnitz Editions*, 1932, Correspondence with Chatto & Windus concerning The Albatross, CW 48/11.
28. McDonald, *British Literary Culture and Publishing Practice*, p. 14; Bourdieu, *The Field of Cultural Production*, p. 39.
29. Aldington to Prentice, 1 October 1929, Letters from Richard Aldington to Chatto & Windus, CW 48/3.
30. Aldington to Prentice, 1 October 1929, Letters from Richard Aldington to Chatto & Windus, CW 48/3.
31. Quoted in 'Woman and Her Critics', *Daily Telegraph – Penny Illustrated Paper and Illustrated Times*, 24 June 1905, p. 394.
32. 'The Ladies' Column', *Essex County Chronicle*, 2 September 1904, p. 3.
33. Publishers' Association, *Report on Tauchnitz Editions*, 1932, Correspondence with Chatto & Windus concerning The Albatross, CW 48/11.
34. Prentice to Aldington, 4 October 1929, Letter book, CW A/125.
35. McCleery, 'Tauchnitz and Albatross', pp. 300–1.
36. Tauchnitz, *Publications of 1931*, p. 3.
37. Tauchnitz, *Publications of 1931*, p. 2.
38. *The Harvest*, p. 72.
39. Tauchnitz, *Publications of 1931*, p. 11.
40. Leavis, *Fiction and the Reading Public*, p. 50.
41. Tauchnitz, *Publications of 1931*, p. 2.
42. C. Kearton (Curtis Brown Ltd) to Joseph Hergesheimer, 16 June 1931, Box 32, Joseph Hergesheimer collection, HRC.
43. Holroyd-Reece to Harold Raymond, 30 April 1945, Chatto & Windus correspondence concerning The Albatross editions, CW 100/16.
44. John Hemphill to Kearton, 30 June 1931, Box 45, Joseph Hergesheimer collection, HRC.
45. Kearton to Hergesheimer, 16 June 1931, Box 32, Joseph Hergesheimer collection, HRC.
46. Brown, *Contacts*, p. 178.
47. Éditions du pégase to Librairie Dorbon Aîné, 18 March 1926, Box 158, Carlton Lake collection of French manuscripts, HRC.
48. Le Clert, *Le papier*.
49. *Symbolum Apostolicum*.
50. De Grazia, *Girls Lean Back Everywhere*, p. 94. For more on expatriate Jewish publishers of English pornography in Paris, see Colligan, *A Publisher's Paradise*.
51. See Chapter 2.
52. Potter, 'Censorship and Sovereignty', p. 86.
53. De Grazia, *Girls Lean Back Everywhere*, p. 177.

54. Schmoller, *Two Titans*, p. 19.
55. Ziegfield, 'James Laughlin'.
56. 'A Rose by Many Names', *The Economist*, 13 December 2014, <http://www.ec onomist.com/news/special-report/21635759-why-luxury-so-hard-pin-down-rose-many-names> [accessed 25 March 2016].
57. 'A Rose by Many Names,' *The Economist*, 13 December 2014, <http://www.ec onomist.com/news/special-report/21635759-why-luxury-so-hard-pin-down-rose-many-names> [accessed 25 March 2016].
58. 'Albatross', *Tauchnitz Editions*, 2010, <http://www.tauchnitzeditions.com/alba tross.htm> [accessed 25 March 2016].
59. Schmoller, 'Reprints', p. 38.
60. Holroyd-Reece to Harold Raymond, 30 April 1945, Chatto & Windus corre-spondence concerning The Albatross editions, CW 100/16.
61. 'The Albatross', *The Times*, 1 March 1932, p. 10.
62. Holroyd-Reece, 'Albatross Activities in France', 14 September 1937, Box 129, William A. Bradley Literary Agency records, HRC.
63. Holroyd-Reece to Harold Raymond, 30 April 1945, Chatto & Windus corre-spondence concerning The Albatross editions, CW 100/16.
64. Note to *The Times*, c. 1932, correspondence with Chatto & Windus concerning The Albatross, CW 48/11.
65. Butterworth to W. Lints Smith, 1 March 1932, correspondence with Chatto & Windus concerning The Albatross, CW 48/11.
66. Lewis to Gilbert, 19 June 1934, Box 2, Folder 3, Stuart Gilbert papers, HRC.
67. Lewis, *Blasting and Bombardiering*, p. 254.
68. Holroyd-Reece to Curtis Brown, 15 February 1932, Box 36, D. H. Lawrence col-lection, HRC.
69. Pollinger, Memo addressed to C[urtis] B[rown], 18 February 1932, Box 36, D. H. Lawrence collection, HRC.
70. De Grazia, *Girls Lean Back Everywhere*, p. 182.
71. Joyce to Weaver, 22 September 1932, *Letters of James Joyce*, vol. 3, pp. 259–60.
72. Wegner to Beach, 6 September 1932, James Joyce collection, UB. Beach also mentioned her meeting with Wegner in her memoirs: 'I had a visit from one of the members of the Odyssey Press, and he accepted with alacrity my suggestion that he ask Joyce's consent to bring out a Continental edition.' Beach, *Shakespeare & Company*, p. 205.
73. See Contract for *Dubliners*, 16 June 1931, Box 2, James Joyce collection, HRC.
74. Contract for *Ulysses*, 12 October 1932, Box 2, James Joyce collection, HRC. For *Lady Chatterley's Lover*, the firm paid only a £100 advance on royalties amount-ing to 10 per cent on the first 30,000 copies sold, and 12 per cent thereafter. See Contract for *Lady Chatterley's Lover*, 25 January 1933, Box 40, D. H. Lawrence collection, HRC.
75. The 'two cheap English editions' are the Travellers' Library and the Modern Library editions of *Dubliners*, both published in 1926.
76. Wegner to Beach, 6 September 1932, James Joyce collection, UB.
77. Pollinger to Frieda Lawrence, 15 November 1932, Box 37, D. H. Lawrence collec-tion, HRC.
78. Wegner to Pollinger, 20 June 1934, Box 39, D. H. Lawrence collection, HRC.
79. Sonia Hambourg to Sylvia Beach, 11 January 1939, James Joyce collection, UB.
80. Troy, 'Behind the Scenes', p. 205.
81. A 1946 letter to the Society of Authors declared that 'the Albatross has taken an especial interest in the works of Katherine Mansfield, particularly in view of the very close association which existed between her and us at a time when her works

were not so widely known as they are at the present time'. Albatross to Society of Authors, 26 September 1946, Box 2, Katherine Mansfield collection, HRC. Albatross published *The Garden Party* in 1932 (#22), Mansfield's *Journal* (1933) (#52), her letters (1934) (#209), *Doll's House* (1934) (#225) and *Bliss* (1935) (#283).

82. Troy, 'Behind the Scenes', p. 205.
83. See Holroyd-Reece to Pound, 18 September 1933, Box 23, Folder 997, Ezra Pound papers, American Literature collection, Beineke Rare Book and Manuscript Library, Yale University.
84. Holroyd-Reece to Pound, 11 January 1934, Box 23, Folder 997, Ezra Pound papers, Yale University.
85. Holroyd-Reece to Pound, 4 March 1934, Box 23, Folder 997, Ezra Pound papers, Yale University.
86. Peters to L. A. G. Strong, 10 October 1934, Box 112, A. D. Peters collection, HRC.
87. Chapter to John Hemphill, 18 December 1934, Box 44, Joseph Hergesheimer collection, HRC.
88. Holroyd-Reece to F. E. Loewenstein, 16 September 1949, Box 55, George Bernard Shaw collection, HRC.
89. Schreuders, *The Book of Paperbacks*, p. 8.
90. Troy, 'Books, Swords and Readers', p. 60.
91. Archival documents show that Albatross continued to operate until the mid-1940 in Paris. AJ/40 701, Archives allemandes de la Seconde Guerre mondiale, Archives nationales, Paris.
92. McCleery, 'The Paperback Evolution'.
93. See Jaillant, *Modernism*, p. 80.
94. Enoch to Emanuel Harper, 6 June 1949, Box 253, Random House records, Columbia Rare Book and Manuscript Library, New York.

5

'CLASSICS BEHIND PLATE GLASS': THE HOGARTH PRESS AND THE UNIFORM EDITION OF THE WORKS OF VIRGINIA WOOLF

On Monday, 30 September 1929, readers of the *Aberdeen Press and Journal* came across a short article entitled 'Virginia Woolf "Collected"'. The Hogarth Press had just started publishing a 'charming' Uniform Edition at five shillings a volume. 'Of pocket size, tastefully produced in green, and clearly printed, this edition is a model of what such reprints should be', declared the newspaper. Readers were encouraged to buy *Jacob's Room* and *Mrs Dalloway*, which had their place among the 'leading fiction of our day', as well as *The Common Reader*, a book with passages 'of great beauty and insight'.[1]

The Uniform Edition was a new step in Woolf's campaign to reach ordinary readers – including readers based in Aberdeen and other cities far from the literary centres of southern England. As we have seen in Chapter 1, Woolf was already a well-known writer in the late 1920s, a writer whose name could boost the sales of titles in cheap series of reprints. She was also determined to expand her readership on both sides of the Atlantic. But there was one hurdle on the way to a greater audience: the price and availability of her own books. The Hogarth Press had given Woolf exceptional creative freedom ('I'm the only woman in England free to write what I like', she declared in 1925. 'The others must be thinking of series & editors').[2] But it had also tied her – at least initially – to the sphere of small presses with limited market opportunities.[3] Between 1919 and 1923, books were available by subscription: 'A' subscribers received all publications in exchange for a deposit of £1; 'B' subscribers ordered and paid for only specific works.[4] When *Jacob's Room* was first published in 1922, its audience was restricted to a relatively small readership already familiar with Woolf and her press. Three years later, *Mrs Dalloway* had a first printing of 2,000 copies and sold for seven shillings and six pence.[5] By 1929, both novels were out of print. The Uniform Edition gave new life to Woolf's titles: they were now advertised in major newspapers and available in bookstores for a reasonable price. As J. H. Willis puts it, the Uniform Edition 'marked one more stage in the evolution of the Hogarth Press into a commercial publishing house'.[6] Most importantly, the books were sold as part of a complete edition – thus positioning Woolf as a canonical author whose work deserved to be collected and preserved.

Virginia Woolf was not the only writer to understand the importance of a 'Collected Edition'.[7] Ford Madox Ford kept asking his numerous publishers, in Britain and in the United States, to issue such an edition.[8] In 1922, his literary agent James Pinker died in the midst of negotiations with the American branch of Macmillan. Ford then wrote to Edgar Jepson:

> You see, I have written four or three – I am not sure which – books that ought to be 'classics' and from which I ought to draw a comfortable if small provision for my approaching old age. They are all out of print and unlikely to be re-published[9]

No collected edition of Ford's work appeared during his lifetime.[10]

Unlike Ford, Woolf did not have to rely on publishers to reprint her work. She could also market her books exactly as she wished. In short, the Hogarth Press allowed her to control all aspects of the 'Virginia Woolf brand', a brand that became associated with commercial success, international prestige and canonicity. As Willis argues, 'to put a living novelist's works into a standard edition is to make a claim for the permanence and importance of the writer's work, to establish a canon, to suggest the classic'.[11] In her late forties, armed with a long list of publications and achievements, Woolf made the bold decision to enter the literary canon, a canon that had hitherto been dominated by male writers.

Collected editions and series of classics share many common points, including the claim to include only texts of lasting value. A collected edition (i.e. a comprehensive edition of the writings of a specific author) is generally uniform – all the books have the same physical format. Collected editions can also be included in a uniform series of classics: for example, from 1928, Chatto & Windus included its backlist of Aldous Huxley's books in the Phoenix Library. The Uniform Edition published by the Hogarth Press competed against this kind of three-and-six-penny libraries and contributed to the expansion of the market for modernism.

The story of the Hogarth Press cannot be reduced to its origins as a hobby for Virginia Woolf or to its traditional image as a 'highbrow' publishing enterprise. As Elizabeth Willson Gordon, Helen Southworth and others have shown, the press published all kinds of 'popular' and 'middlebrow' texts, as well as educational books, political tracts, children's literature, and self-help manuals. This increased interest in the Hogarth Press as a commercial enterprise has led to the creation of the Modernist Archives Publishing Project. However, the Uniform Edition has so far been largely neglected.[12] More work remains to be done in the press archive, which contains a wealth of quantitative information (for example in the notebooks that Leonard Woolf used for accounting). As Simon Eliot puts it, 'when studying book history one is never very far away from money or, at least, if one is doing it properly one *should* never be far away from money'.[13] In this chapter, I use a mix of quantitative and qualitative information to argue that the Uniform Edition contributed to Virginia Woolf's leading reputation in the 1930s – both in Britain and in the United States. While other modernists depended on publishers to market them as important writers, Woolf used her own press to canonise herself.

CONTEXT

For Elizabeth Willson Gordon, the Uniform Edition finds its origins in the success of the pamphlet series that the Hogarth Press launched from the mid-1920s.[14] The Hogarth Essays, a series created in 1924, was followed by the Hogarth Lectures on Literature (1927–34) and the Hogarth Living Poets (1928–37). Leonard Woolf later wrote that the pamphlets showed the Press,

> how valuable from the business point of view a series is to a publisher. If one gets a series started successfully with good books, it makes it possible subsequently to publish in the series successfully other books which, if published on their own, however good they might be, would almost certainly have made a substantial loss.[15]

By the late 1920s, the Hogarth Press was flourishing thanks in part to the growing demand for Virginia's work. The printing figures of her novels show an upward trend. While *Jacob's Room* had a first printing of 1,200, this rose to 3,000 for *To the Lighthouse* and 5,080 for *Orlando*.[16] As late as 1924, Woolf had earned just £37 from her books.[17] With the success of *To the Lighthouse*, *Orlando* and *A Room of One's Own*, her annual income increased significantly. As John Young points out, '1929 was Woolf's second-most profitable year as an author, earning her nearly £3000'.[18] Thanks to Woolf's bestselling titles as well as other strong sellers, the Hogarth Press was making unprecedented profits. Net profits jumped more than threefold in 1928–9 (Figure 5.1). The growth continued until 1930–1, with a profit peak at around £2,433 (the equivalent of £1,018,000 in 2015).[19] No longer an amateurish enterprise, the Hogarth Press was now a major publishing house with a list of appealing titles and an aggressive marketing strategy.

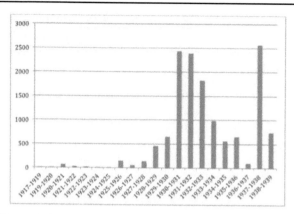

Figure 5.1 Hogarth Press net profits (£). Profit and Loss Summaries Book, MS 2750/A/11, HP. In his autobiography *Downhill All the Way*, Leonard Woolf gives gross income figures for the press from 1924 to 1939 (p. 142).

The Uniform Edition originated in this context of expansion, and in turn contributed to increased profits. In December 1928, two months after the publication of *Orlando*, Leonard Woolf contacted Gerald Duckworth, who had issued Virginia's two first novels. 'We are thinking of publishing a **cheap edition** of Virginia's books next year', wrote Leonard, 'and we should very much like, if that were possible, to make it eventually a complete edition'. He asked to buy the rights to *The Voyage Out* and *Night and Day* and added: 'Without those, of course, our edition would be incomplete.'[20]

This insistence on the *completeness* of the Uniform Edition tells us a lot about the Woolfs' project. Their ambition was not only to reach a wider audience with a cheaper price, but also to present Virginia as a major writer whose entire work deserved to be collected. Leonard Woolf was able to strike a deal with Duckworth – he bought the remaining stock and paid a fixed sum for the rights. *The Voyage Out* was published as a Uniform Edition in September 1929, and *Night and Day* in November 1930.

At the time when the three-and-six-penny libraries were enjoying noteworthy success, why did the Woolfs decide to sell the Uniform Edition for five shillings? This decision is all the more surprising given that after 1920, Duckworth sold the second impression of *Night and Day* for three shillings and six pence. So why did the Hogarth Press publish a higher priced reprint *after* Duckworth's cheap edition? The price structure of the Uniform Edition was in fact suggested by Jonathan Cape. In April 1929, he asked Leonard Woolf for permission to include *The Common Reader* in the Travellers' Library. 'I think the book would find another public in that Series', wrote Cape.[21] Indeed, the original edition sold for twelve shillings and six pence – more than three times the price of Travellers' Library books. Rejecting this offer, Leonard explained that the Hogarth Press already planned to publish a 3s. 6d. edition of Virginia's titles in the autumn.[22] Cape then offered advice 'as a friendly colleague', suggesting a price of five shillings for two main reasons:

> If you publish at three and sixpence you will come into competition with all the other pocket libraries such as The Travellers Library. Every publisher now publishes or has announced a three and sixpenny Series similar to The Travellers Library. The Travellers Library however, perhaps because it was early in the field, and because fresh titles are being added regularly, holds its own. I am informed that most of the other three and six-penny Series are very much less in demand.

The second reason was that more popular publishers were also offering books at three shillings and six pence with an ordinary format (not a pocket format). Cape gave the example of 'Hodder, Cassell, Collins, and in fact almost every publisher'.[23] He concluded his letter by making an offer to the Woolfs, suggesting a five-shilling collected edition published under a joint imprint. Cape did not explain what he would bring to the table. Presumably, he thought that his firm had a lot more experience publishing cheap series. What is certain is that he approached the Hogarth Press with a very entrepreneurial attitude: he clearly wanted to have his firm associated with Virginia Woolf – a well-known, bestselling writer. Leonard Woolf declined the offer of a joint imprint, but he kept Cape's idea to price the Uniform Edition at five shillings, thus choosing a more upmarket positioning than the Travellers' Library and the Phoenix Library.[24]

PRODUCING AND ADVERTISING THE UNIFORM EDITION

The physical format of the Uniform Edition shows a meticulous attention to detail. In her bibliography of Virginia Woolf, B. J. Kirkpatrick points out the subtle variations of colours, from the 'jade-green cloth boards' to the 'pale peacock-blue dust-jacket printed in navy-blue', and the use of gold letters on the spine.[25] This high quality of production differentiated the Uniform Edition from 'the usual type of cheap edition', as the *Cambridge Review* declared. 'The printing and binding are of the best, and they make a delightful addition to any library.'[26] This review was then reproduced on advertisements, thus reinforcing the impression of consensus over the attractive appearance of the books.

The colophon of the Hogarth Press (a wolf's head designed by Vanessa Bell) adorned dust jackets, contributing to this distinguished physical format. As Edward Bishop notes: 'While the Vanessa Bell dust jackets with their hand-drawn designs . . . preserve the link with the avant-garde, the jade-green cloth boards with the gold lettering on the spine assert Woolf's entry into the literary establishment.'[27] In 1928, E. M. Kauffer had designed the press's new

Figure 5.2 Advertisement for the Hogarth Press (with E. M. Kauffer's colophon), *Sunday Times*, 2 December 1934, p. 12. By permission of Penguin Random House UK.

logo, which appeared on many advertisements for the Uniform Edition. An American expatriate, Kauffer crossed the boundary between art and commerce. He had been associated with the Omega Workshop and the Vorticists, and later became famous for his London Underground posters. Like the Modern Library (which commissioned dust jackets to Kauffer), the Hogarth Press was positioning itself as an institution that made the new literature, but also the new art available to a larger audience.[28] In 1934, for example, one advertisement featured Kauffer's logo and a modern design where the titles of the books formed a 'V' for Virginia (Figure 5.2).

The name of the author was also used as a selling point, appearing in bold type on dust jackets and advertisements. The first announcement in the magazine of the book trade *Publisher & Bookseller* covered half a page, with 'VIRGINIA WOOLF' printed in large font above 'Cheap Uniform Edition'. Booksellers were encouraged to stock an edition that looked good on the shelves and could fit in a pocket: 'The books are attractively produced and of a small and convenient size.' Since *'Jacob's Room* and *Mrs Dalloway* have been out of print for some time', a strong demand for these titles was expected.[29] By 1929, then, the Hogarth Press had access to a nationwide distribution network, which ensured easy access to books by its star authors.

The publication of the Uniform Edition was often announced alongside *A Room of One's Own*, a short book issued in October 1929. In December, the Hogarth Press was already promoting it as 'an established bestseller, now 3rd impression' (there was a fourth impression later that month). Advertisements insisted on the wide appeal of the book, which would be of interest to men as well as women. 'No woman who loves art, or scholarship, or science, no woman who is bounded by the four walls of a house, can afford to miss this treasure of a book, with its insight and grace', declared a blurb from *Country Life*. 'No man of any sort can afford to miss it either. It is not a feminist tract, it is wit and art, truth and beauty.'[30] With its audience of aspirational readers attracted to the lifestyle of the British upper class, *Country Life* carried an aura of distinction that fitted well with the image that the Hogarth Press wanted to project. The emphasis of the Hogarth press was on taste, but also on cheapness. At five shillings, the original edition of *A Room of One's Own* had the same price as the older titles included in the Uniform Edition. A blurb from *The Sketch* described Woolf's 'brilliant books' published in the collected edition as 'bargains'.[31] Like *Country Life*, *The Sketch* cultivated an upper-class image (Q. D. Leavis put it in the same category as other 'luxurious shilling illustrated news magazines' such as *Tatler* and *Sphere*).[32] Reading Woolf titles was presented as a way to join the cultural elite, without spending too much money.

The Uniform Edition was advertised alongside *A Room of One's Own*, but also C. H. B. Kitchin's murder mystery *Death of My Aunt* (1929). Born in 1895, Kitchin read classics at Oxford and, after serving in France during the First World War, was called to the bar in 1924. The Hogarth Press had already published two Kitchin titles – *Streamers Waving* (1925) and *Mr Balcony* (1927). Both of them failed to make a profit.[33] In today's publishing world, Kitchin would probably have been dropped from the list. But the Hogarth Press persevered, and *Death of My Aunt* became one of its bestselling titles.[34]

In the late 1920s, literary modernism and detective fiction were often issued by the same publishers and advertised in the same periodicals. The Oxford World's Classics series reprinted Wilkie Collins's *The Moonstone*, with an introduction by T. S. Eliot that described the book as 'the first, the longest, and the best of modern English detective novels' (see Chapter 1). Similarly, the Hogarth Press advertised *Death of My Aunt* and the Woolf titles as quality literature endorsed by the most prominent critics. An advertisement in *The Times* included a blurb from Arnold Bennett: 'It is that rare thing – a detective story which I have read with pleasure.'[35] It was not the first time that the press had quoted Bennett, despite Virginia Woolf's criticism of his work. For *Orlando*, the following blurb appeared on advertisements: 'You cannot keep your end up at a London dinner party in these weeks unless you have read Mrs Virginia Woolf's *Orlando*.'[36] As John Young points out, 'Woolf the author famously uses Bennett as a foil for her diagnosis of Edwardian fiction', but 'Woolf the publisher capitalizes on his praise to market' her books.[37] Bennett's endorsement contributed to the success of Kitchin's novel: *The Times* advertisement announced that, following publication on 26 September 1929, a second printing had been ordered on 9 October and a third on 5 November. These precise details aimed at convincing readers that *Death of My Aunt* was indeed a bestseller – 'the season's detective story', as advertisements proclaimed.[38]

The Hogarth Press not only advertised Woolf's and Kitchin's books side by side, it also explicitly drew parallels between these two authors. A table comparing *A Room of One's Own* and *Death of My Aunt* gathered the main characteristics and selling points of both books, including their price, the number of printings and the opinions of reviewers (Figure 5.3). The repetition of 'it is' followed by similar statements ('a detective story, and a very good one'; 'a

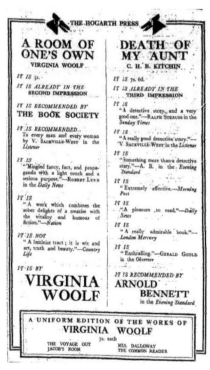

Figure 5.3 Advertisement for the Hogarth Press, *The Times*, 22 November 1929, p. 20. By permission of Penguin Random House UK.

really good detective story'; 'something more than a detective story') gave a playful tone to the advertisement. Far from presenting itself as a 'highbrow' publisher of difficult books, the Hogarth Press projected a more relaxed image. *A Room of One's Own* was thus described as witty and entertaining, with a serious purpose ('A work which combines the sober delights of a treatise with the vitality and humour of fiction', as the blurb from the *Nation* declared). The Press insisted, tongue-in-cheek, that Woolf's essay was not intended to a small readership of feminists: 'it is recommended to every man and every woman by V. Sackville-West in the *Listener*'. The endorsement of the newly established Book Society was another sign that *A Room of One's Own* had a wide popular appeal.[39] At the bottom of the advertisement, Virginia Woolf's and Arnold Bennett's names appeared side by side, highlighting the prominence of both writers while also establishing a hierarchy. The larger font used for Woolf, the repetition of her name and the reference to the Uniform Edition conveyed the impression of permanent literary quality – while Bennett remained associated with an ephemeral periodical, the *Evening Standard*.

These advertisements do not fit well with the narrative on the 'Battle of the Brows' – which Melissa Sullivan defines as 'a period of great tensions over culture hierarchies, disparagement of popular writers by more elite authors and critics, and challenges to the cultural dominance of intellectual or 'highbrow' authors by more popular authors and the mainstream reading public'.[40] For Sullivan and Sophie Blanch, 'the height of the tensions over cultural divides' can be situated 'from the late 1920s through the early 1930s'.[41] If the boundary between the High and the Low was so rigid, why would the Hogarth Press advertise Woolf and detective fiction side by side? Why would it present Arnold Bennett as a 'consecrated' writer with the authority to recommend books?[42] And why would it proudly display an endorsement by a 'middlebrow' institution such as the Book Society? This shows that the Battle of the Brows was less fierce than Q. D. Leavis could lead us to believe (she described the success of the Book Society as evidence that 'a middlebrow standard of values has been set up' and encouraged 'an armed and conscious minority' to resist).[43] In Leavis's account, Woolf is presented as an archetypal 'highbrow' writer – a writer of 'what is considered by the critical minority to be the significant work in fiction'.[44] Woolf herself later dismissed the 'middlebrow' cultural sphere, in a letter to the *New Statesman* that she wrote but never sent.[45]

Yet, Woolf's positioning in the literary field was characterised by hybridity rather than radical separation from lower cultural forms. In their introduction to the special issue of *Modernist Cultures* on the 'middlebrow', Sullivan and Blanch note that,

> Woolf's actual participation in middlebrow culture, including serving as a featured author for the Book-of-the-Month club with *Flush* (1933)

and publishing middlebrow writers such as E. M. Delafield through the Hogarth Press, indicates a more nuanced understanding of and involvement in that sphere.[46]

This comment appears in an endnote, as if it had only minor interest. Many scholars are still reluctant to consider Woolf anything other than an arch-'highbrow' who published difficult texts under her own imprint. Nicola Wilson thus notes 'a lingering persistence in criticism on the Hogarth Press that sees it as a small, coterie publishing house existing throughout its history as somehow outside of the concerns of the literary marketplace'.[47]

In fact, Woolf – as author and publisher – fully exploited the commercial opportunities offered by the 'middlebrow' cultural sphere. In his autobiography, Leonard Woolf explains the difference between their publishing enterprise and presses that specialised in luxury and limited editions:

> We did not want the Press to become one of those (admirable in their way) 'private' or semi-private Presses the object of which is finely produced books, books which are meant not to be read, but to be looked at. We were interested primarily in the immaterial inside of a book, what the author had to say and how he said it; we had drifted into the business with the idea of publishing things which the commercial publisher could not or would not publish. We wanted our books to 'look nice' and we had our own views of what nice looks in a book would be, but neither of us was interested in fine printing and fine binding. We also disliked the refinement and preciosity which are too often a kind of fungoid growth which culture breeds upon art and literature; they are not unknown in Britain and are often to be found in cultivated Americans.[48]

For Leonard and his wife, the Kelmscott Press, the Nonesuch Press and other 'private' presses were anti-models, obsessed with the physical format of the book to the detriment of the content. With the Hogarth Press, the Woolfs wanted to reach an audience far beyond 'cultivated' collectors. Not only did the press advertise Virginia as a bestselling writer, it also actively sought after reviews from a wide range of periodicals across the 'brow' spectrum and across the country.

READING AND REVIEWING THE UNIFORM EDITION

Woolf's celebrity was not confined to literary communities in privileged parts of England. 'Mrs Woolf is among the very foremost of living British writers', declared the Dundee *Evening Telegraph*, 'no other woman of our day approaches her'. To justify this hyperbolic claim, the newspaper added:

> Anyone who doubts the wisdom of speaking of her 'genius' has only to pick up any of the four volumes of her early works just reissued

by the Hogarth Press: these novels, and the one volume of criticism *The Common Reader* are books of wonderful loveliness, subtlety, and individuality.[49]

Readers in Dundee were encouraged to familiarise themselves with this great author, whose work was now available in cheap form. '*Mrs Dalloway* is a masterpiece', added the same newspaper one month later.[50]

Far from positioning Woolf in a 'highbrow' category, newspapers reviewed her work alongside other reprints. The Dundee *Courier* thus announced the publication of cheap editions of *To the Lighthouse* and *Anna Lombard*, a 'heady romance' by Victoria Cross (the pen-name of Annie Sophie Cory). When the novel was first published in 1901 it caused a sensation for its daring portrayal of a New Woman. 'The heroine is a pagan wanton who might have luxuriated in ancient Rome', noted the *Courier*.[51] Set in the British Indian Empire, the plot was subversive at many levels: not only does Anna claim a right to sexual freedom, she also chooses a lover among her Muslim servants. 'This is a novel emphatically not for the young person', declared one reviewer.[52] Nearly thirty years later, the publisher Werner Laurie issued a 39th edition, priced at three shillings and six pence. The *Courier* then described *To the Lighthouse* (first published in 1927) as 'brilliant, but in a mood and manner very different':

> That this tour de force, not yet three years old, should appear in a uniform edition of its author's productions implies the existence of a considerable critical community, appreciating not so much a story as the style in which it is presented.

Not only was Woolf's readership large enough to justify a new edition of the novel, it was also knowledgeable and appreciative of the author's experimental style. This 'considerable critical community' justified the Hogarth Press's decision to market Woolf as a canonical writer.

Like the Dundee *Courier*, many newspapers saw Woolf as sufficiently distinguished to warrant the publication of a Uniform Edition. For the *New Statesman*, 'Mrs Woolf has reached a stage at which her reader deserves to be able to look back and review the path by which she has come.'[53] Likewise, *Time and Tide* declared: 'Whether to judge her as great or as little, one must read her, and the Hogarth Press has prepared an admirably printed and bound edition, without which no library of modern literature would be complete.'[54] Here, the emphasis was on quality and durability: the well-produced Uniform Edition offered a lasting physical format to texts with permanent literary value.

SELLING THE UNIFORM EDITION

In the early 1930s, the Hogarth Press continued to add new titles to the Uniform Edition shortly after their first publication. In autumn 1933, the *Yorkshire Post* announced that '*Orlando* – that queer blend of history, biography, and fantasy – and *The Waves* – that difficult subjective novel – can now be had in this form at five shillings each.'[55] Woolf's anti-conformism had become a selling point, as the publication of *Flush* shows. This playful account of the life of Elizabeth Browning's dog was published in October 1933 with ten images, before being issued the following month with three illustrations.[56] Why did the Hogarth Press decide to release the Uniform Edition so soon after the first edition? And if five shillings was the right price for this short book, why did the Woolfs first publish the book at 7s. 6d.?

In her article on the Book Society, Nicola Wilson offers a fascinating account of the publishing history of *Flush*. The Hogarth Press had initially intended to publish the book in the cheap Uniform Edition and in a signed, limited edition at fifteen shillings. But the Book Society made a series of suggestions in order for *Flush* to be considered as a possible 'choice'. The book had to be initially published at 7s. 6d. 'so that it could be sold to its members at the same rate as its other "choice" books'. To justify the higher price, additional illustrations were added. Not only were 'the publishing and printing schedules of the Hogarth Press' altered, 'the production and form of the work of Virginia Woolf herself was directly impacted upon, and indeed changed, to meet the demands and expectations of the middlebrow, book-buying public'.[57] This reminds us of *Tarr*, which Wyndham Lewis entirely rewrote to appeal to Phoenix Library readers.

Flush, *Orlando* and *The Waves* were not the last titles to join the Uniform Edition, but the 1933 additions mark a high point in the history of the collected edition. After that year, new additions were few and far in between (the press added *The Common Reader*, second series, *The Years* and *Three Guineas* in 1935, 1940 and 1943 respectively). More importantly, the 1933 additions shaped the identity of the Uniform Edition as a collection of bestsellers and less accessible books. In a letter to her friend Hugh Walpole, Woolf wrote that '*Flush* is only a joke—done by way of a lark when I had finished *The Waves*: but it's too long—got out of hand—and not worth the trouble.'[58] Yet, she put a lot of effort into revising *Flush* and published it in the same physical format as *The Waves*. Far from seeing her popular texts as a threat to her reputation, Woolf invited readers to collect *all* her books in a 'permanent edition' as she called it.[59] Readers who might have discovered her work with *Flush* or *Orlando* were encouraged to read her other titles, available for only five shillings. In the United States, the Modern Library adopted a similar strategy with Gertrude Stein, reprinting *Three Lives* in September 1933 (the month when Harcourt Brace published *The Autobiography of Alice B. Toklas*).[60] The Hogarth Press and the Modern Library did not separate popular and difficult books by Woolf and Stein; instead, they used bestsellers to 'hook' readers and introduce them to less accessible books.

The Uniform Edition gave a new life to out-of-print titles that had reached only a limited audience when they were first published. In 1915, Duckworth issued *The Voyage Out* with a first printing of 2,000 copies. No further copies were printed until fourteen years later, when the Uniform Edition appeared with a first printing of 3,200 copies – an increase of 60 per cent compared to the first print run. Most importantly, the book was reprinted several times after that – there was another printing of 3,200 copies in 1933 and the book was available in the Uniform Edition until the 1970s.[61] In short, *The Voyage Out* became a long seller – available over several decades.

Jacob's Room and *Mrs Dalloway* also enjoyed a renewal of interest following their inclusion in the Uniform Edition. In 1922, there were forty active 'A subscribers' who received a copy of *Jacob's Room* with a slip signed by Woolf. Seven years later, the Hogarth Press targeted a completely different audience with its cheap edition, issued in a first printing of 3,100.[62] Profits soon exceeded previous earnings. By 1937, the Uniform Edition of *Jacob's Room* had made a total profit of around £137 – twice the amount earned by the 7s. 6d. edition (Figure 5.4).[63] *Mrs Dalloway* was also a commercial success in the

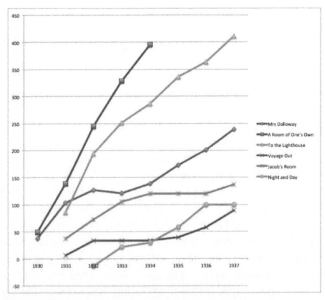

Figure 5.4 Profit and loss accumulations, Uniform Edition of Virginia Woolf's work (£). Profit and Loss Summaries Book, MS 2750/A/11, HP.

collected edition, eventually topping the profit made by the original edition; 6,435 copies of the cheap edition were printed in the first four years after publication – more than twice the total print run of the 1925 first edition.[64]

The Uniform Edition also amplified the success of titles that had already reached a large audience. When *To the Lighthouse* was first issued, the first printing of 3,000 copies was soon followed by a second and third printing of 1,000 and 1,500 copies.[65] For the Uniform Edition, Kirkpatrick indicates a total of 6,800 copies printed between 1930 and 1932, and a further printing of 1,500 in 1941.[66] There might have been further printings, since profit figures show a large gap between first and reprint edition. In 1937, the Uniform Edition had made a total profit of around £411 – against approximately £157 for the first edition.[67] Along with *To the Lighthouse*, *A Room of One's Own* was one of the most profitable titles in the collected edition. The first edition had been particularly successful, with five printings in 1929 and 1930 reaching a total of 14,650 copies.[68] With the Uniform Edition, *A Room of One's Own* was positioned as a classic rather than an ephemeral bestseller.

The only title that initially made a loss in the Uniform Edition was *Night and Day* (Figure 5.4). As we have seen, the book was already available for three shillings and six pence *before* it was published in the Uniform Edition. This made it difficult to sell it for five shillings, but in the long term, it earned a modest profit and was even reprinted in 1938. The total print run reached 6,010 in the first ten years after publication in the Uniform Edition – compared with 3,000 copies for the first edition published by Duckworth.[69]

IMPACT OF THE UNIFORM EDITION

Among the cheap collections that made modernism available to a large audience, the Uniform Edition remained a modest enterprise. The Modern Library sold 61,000 copies of the edition of *Mrs Dalloway* between 1928 and 1948, probably much more than the sales of the Hogarth Press edition.[70] And when Everyman's Library included *To the Lighthouse* in 1938, the first printing reached 10,000 copies, followed by further printings during and immediately after the war. If we turn to paperbacks, the limited scope of the Uniform Edition becomes even clearer. In 1942, for example, Penguin issued a 9d. edition of *Orlando* with a first printing of 75,000 copies.[71]

Yet, the Uniform Edition was an important enterprise for several reasons. Not only did it make out-of-print titles available in cheap format, it also gave Woolf total control over her brand. Think of other modernist writers in the 1920s and 1930s: how many of them fully controlled the way their works were published and marketed? James Joyce's entry in the literary canon was facilitated by cheap editions of *Dubliners* and *A Portrait of the Artist as a Young Man*, published by the Modern Library and the Travellers' Library. But Joyce had no say over the pricing strategy, the physical format or even the introductions selected for his books. This is significant, because these editions stayed in print for decades and were used by numerous students and scholars. For Gertrude Stein, the difficulty to attract publishers and the lack of control over the publication process were sources of intense frustration. As early as 1916, she hoped that a publisher would issue her work in a cheap series. 'Alas about every three months I get sad', she wrote to her friend Carl Van Vechten. 'I make so much absorbing literature with such attractive titles and even if I could be as popular as Jenny Lind where oh where is the man to publish me in series. . . . He can do me as cheaply and as simply as he likes but I would so like to be done.'[72] In 1930, perhaps inspired by Woolf's example, Stein set up her own imprint – the Plain Edition. But it remained a tiny enterprise, and Stein had to wait until commercial publishers became interested in her work to finally reach a wide market. Among her modernist peers, Woolf was therefore in the unique position to directly shape the literary canon – not as an author, but as a publisher.

In particular, the Uniform Edition enabled her to regain control over earlier titles published by Gerald Duckworth. In 1918, she wrote: 'His commercial view of every possible subject depressed me, especially when I thought of my novel destined to be pawed & snored over by him.'[73] As Bishop notes, 'the reference to having her works "pawed over" obviously links publishing to the sexual abuse she had endured'.[74] Setting up her own firm gave Woolf the opportunity to free herself from her abusive half-brother. With the Uniform Edition, she also had her say on the text that readers would encounter over the long term. For *The Voyage Out*, she chose to reprint the first edition, rather the version published by George H. Doran Company in the United States (and reissued by Duckworth in 1920 and again in 1927). As Young points out, this has been a source of confusion among scholars: why would Woolf cast aside the version that she had so carefully revised for American readers? 'By restoring *Voyage*'s original text for Hogarth's 1929 publication', Young claims, 'Woolf casts aside the Duckworth imprint from her first novel and remakes it on her own terms, as the opening volume in Hogarth's "Collected Edition" of her works'.[75]

The Uniform Edition not only allowed Woolf to control her own canon in the United Kingdom, it also triggered the publication of a similar edition in the United States. In 1931, Harcourt Brace announced to the book trade the publication of five novels by Woolf 'in a new inexpensive edition, convenient size, uniform binding, stamped in gold, to be published January 22, $1.35 each'. The *Publishers' Weekly* advertisement included a drawing of Woolf's profile and two blurbs that presented her as a talented, renowned writer. While the *Yale Review* insisted on Woolf's Englishness ('The most distinguished English woman of letters'), the *Forum* drew a parallel with the American literary scene: 'With Willa Cather, she is one of the two most gifted women writers today.'[76]

With this edition, Harcourt Brace was capitalising on Woolf's existing fame in America. In 1929, the *Daily Mail* described Woolf as 'a particular favourite with the American collector' who enjoyed the 'delightful first edition of her fanciful *Orlando*'.[77] By 1931, many readers had heard of Woolf, but few were familiar with her earlier works – which had first appeared in small print runs. In 1926, Harcourt Brace's edition of *The Voyage Out* had a first printing of only 1,000 copies and sold for $2.50. Five years later, there was a re-impression of 2,100 copies as the Uniform Edition – the same print run used for other titles in the collection, *Night and Day*, *Jacob's Room* and *Mrs Dalloway*.[78] Whereas early Harcourt issues of *Mrs Dalloway* had featured Vanessa Bell's dust jacket artwork, the Uniform issue elected a blue-on-cream design consistent with other titles in the edition (Plate 4). Moving away from the avant-garde, the new dust jacket gave a more classic aura to the edition.

Unlike the Hogarth Press, Harcourt Brace did not include more popular books (*Orlando*, *A Room of One's Own* and *Flush*) in its Uniform Edition. Presumably, Harcourt feared that a cheaper edition would endanger the sales of the first edition. Moreover, Woolf's American publisher made little effort to advertise the Uniform Edition. Readers were much more likely to encounter *Mrs Dalloway* or *To the Lighthouse* in the 95-cent Modern Library edition than in the $1.35 Uniform Edition. The American Uniform Edition struggled to find a market – in part because of the existing competition of cheap classics series.

It is precisely because the Hogarth Press rejected offers from reprint series that its own Uniform Edition prospered. In 1931, Chatto & Windus approached Woolf to suggest including a few of her books in the Phoenix Library:

> We realise that your firm publishes your works in a uniform edition at 5/-, and we will not pretend to think that publication of some of them in a series at a cheaper price would be wholly without effect on the sales of your edition. At the same time we should hope that the majority of the sales in the Phoenix Library would be additional, and that inclusion in the series would help to extend your already wide public of readers, since several booksellers tell us that the Phoenix Library sells better than any of the other thin-paper 3/6 series.

Chatto & Windus also offered to remunerate Woolf not only as an author but also as a publisher – since they would need to use the plates of the Hogarth Press.[79] Despite her high regard for Chatto & Windus, Woolf was not interested: 'the Hogarth Press 5/ edition is at present selling very well, and I feel that to bring out some of the books at 3/6 with another publisher would be likely to cause some confusion and I doubt that you would find it profitable'.[80] And she added that she had already rejected the same offer twice from other publishers.

However, Woolf made an exception with Everyman's Library. In 1937, J. M. Dent's editorial department approached her, asking for a few comments on Dorothy Richardson's *Pilgrimage*.[81] Unlike Woolf, Richardson had little control over the publication process, and she had to wait until the end of her life to see her work appear in a collected edition.[82] The fact that Dent was ready to reissue Richardson's works (in partnership with Cresset) seemed to have favourably impressed Woolf. She promised to buy the proposed edition and, at around that time, sold the reprint rights to her novel *To the Lighthouse*. In May 1938, the editorial department contacted her again:

> Now that the printers have finished setting the text of *To the Lighthouse* for the Everyman's Library edition – may I ask if you would be so good as to write a very short introductory note for it? This has been done by most of the few living writers who have recently been represented in Everyman's Library, and I am sending to you copies of books by Walter de la Mare, Aldous Huxley and Frank Swinnerton so that you can see what they have done.[83]

The interesting thing here is the reference to 'the few living writers' who had joined Everyman's Library, a series that traditionally specialised in non-copyrighted works. In the late 1930s, Dent was broadening the scope of its series towards modern classics. Woolf was an obvious candidate for inclusion: her own Uniform Edition had been in print for nearly a decade, and she had already collaborated with the Oxford World's Classics – a series nearly as conservative as Everyman's Library. However, she refused to write the introduction to the new edition of *To the Lighthouse*, which later appeared with a preface by D. M. Hoare. By the late 1930s, Woolf probably felt she no longer had to agree to such requests, since her reputation was already well established on both sides of the Atlantic.

In her letter on the 'middlebrow' collected in *The Death of the Moth*, Woolf wrote: 'I dislike bound volumes of the classics behind plate glass.'[84] Series of classics operate on the assumption that readers need a selection of the best texts – an idea that Woolf found deeply problematic. And yet, thanks to her own 'permanent edition', Woolf's texts became 'classics'. The Hogarth Press manufactured books with a lasting physical format, and encouraged readers to collect all of Woolf's titles. The achievements of the Uniform Edition were threefold. First, it reached a large audience of common readers in Britain and elsewhere. As Willis points out, by 1929 the Woolfs had made arrangements for distribution in Canada, and by 1936 they had agents in Australia, New Zealand, and South Africa.[85] Second, the Uniform Edition encouraged Harcourt Brace to issue a similar edition in the United States. Third, these editions on both sides of the Atlantic positioned Woolf as a canonical writer whose work deserved to be 'collected'.

After the Second World War, new reprints continued to make Woolf's works available to readers. On 22 March 1951, the *Listener* featured an advertisement for Chatto & Windus's New Phoenix Library: *Mrs Dalloway* was number 2 on the list and sold for five shillings. On the same page, the Hogarth Press announced the publication of *The Years* in the Uniform Edition.[86] These publications show the dynamism of the market for Woolf titles, more than two decades after the launch of the Uniform Edition.

NOTES

1. 'Virginia Woolf "Collected"', *Aberdeen Press and Journal*, 30 September 1929, p. 4.
2. *Diary of Virginia Woolf*, vol. 3, p. 43.
3. Before the creation of the Hogarth Press, Woolf's *Night and Day* and *The Voyage Out* were published by Duckworth, a mid-range publishing firm.
4. 'The Hogarth Press', *Modernist Archives Publishing Project*, <http://www.modernistarchives.com/business/hogarth-press> [accessed 28 March 2016].
5. Kirkpatrick and Clarke, *A Bibliography of Virginia Woolf*, p. 38.
6. Willis, *Leonard and Virginia Woolf as Publishers*, p. 155.
7. *Diary of Virginia Woolf*, vol. 3, p. 225.
8. Ford particularly admired Henry James's New York Edition, published by Scribner. Attridge, '"We Will Listen to None But Specialists": Ford, The Rise of Specialization, and *The English Review*', p. 30. For more on the New York Edition, see David McWhirter's edited volume, *Henry James's New York Edition: The Construction of Authorship*.
9. Ford to Jepson, 15 August 1922, *Letters of Ford Madox Ford*, p. 143.
10. See Lise Jaillant, 'Ford Madox Ford and Book History', in *The Routledge Research Companion to Ford Madox Ford*, edited by Laura Colombino, Sara Haslam and Seamus O'Malley (Routledge, forthcoming).
11. Willis, *Leonard and Virginia Woolf as Publishers*, p. 156.
12. To the best of my knowledge, there is only one essay (by John Young) on the Uniform Edition. See also Willis, *Leonard and Virginia Woolf as Publishers*; Kirkpatrick and Clarke, *A Bibliography of Virginia Woolf*.
13. Eliot, 'What Price Poetry?', p. 425.
14. Willson Gordon, 'Under the Imprint of the Hogarth Press', p. 135.
15. L. Woolf, *Downhill All the Way*, pp. 162–3.
16. Kirkpatrick and Clarke, *A Bibliography of Virginia Woolf*, pp. 27, 48, 61.
17. L. Woolf, *Downhill All the Way*, p. 63.
18. Young, 'Canonicity', p. 237. Young also notes that 'by 1929, Hogarth had expanded significantly from its original husband-and-wife team to seven employees'. 'Murdering an Aunt or Two', p. 188.
19. In 2015, the economic power value of an income of £2,433 is £1,018,000. The economic power 'measures the amount of income or wealth relative to the total output of the economy'. Officer and Williamson, 'Five Ways to Compute the Relative Value of a UK Pound Amount'.
20. L. Woolf to Duckworth, 10 December 1928, MS 2750/546, HP (my emphasis).
21. Cape to L. Woolf, 12 April 1929, File *The Common Reader*, MS 2750/552, HP.
22. L. Woolf to Cape, 13 April 1929, File *The Common Reader*, MS 2750/552, HP.
23. Cape to L. Woolf, 17 April 1929, MS 2750/546, HP.
24. L. Woolf to Cape, 22 April 1929, MS 2750/546, HP.
25. Kirkpatrick and Clarke, *A Bibliography of Virginia Woolf*, p. 7.
26. Quoted in Advertisement for the Hogarth Press, *Saturday Review of Politics, Literature, Science and Art*, 26 October 1929, p. 489.
27. Bishop, 'From Typography to *Time*', p. 58.
28. See Jaillant, *Modernism*, p. 48.

29. Advertisement for the Hogarth Press, *Publisher & Bookseller*, 4 October 1929, p. 622.
30. Advertisement for the Hogarth Press, *Observer*, 8 December 1929, p. 8.
31. Advertisement for the Hogarth Press, *Times Literary Supplement*, 5 December 1929, p. 1033.
32. Leavis, *Fiction and the Reading Public*, p. 11.
33. *Streamers Waving* sold only sixty copies the first month and thirty-six the second month after publication. These figures increased only slightly for *Mr Balcony* (137 copies sold before publication, thirty-nine the first month and seventy-one the second month). Profit and loss summaries book, MS 2750/A/11, HP.
34. See Gillespie, 'Virginia Woolf, the Hogarth Press, and the Detective Novel'.
35. Advertisement for the Hogarth Press, *The Times*, 8 November 1929, p. 20.
36. Advertisement for the Hogarth Press, *Times Literary Supplement*, 15 November 1928, p. 856.
37. Young, 'Murdering an Aunt or Two', p. 187.
38. Advertisement for the Hogarth Press, *Sunday Times*, 10 November 1929, p. 12.
39. 'The Book Society was established in 1929 by Walpole, who agreed to set up a selection committee and act as its chairman, and the novelist Arnold Bennett. Modeled on the American Book-of-the-Month club (established 1927), it was the first book club to operate in Britain – it would be followed by the Book Guild (1930), the Left Book Club (1936), and the Readers Union (1937) – and it achieved a membership and stature that made publishers, libraries, bookshops, and readers sit up and take notice.' Wilson, 'Virginia Woolf', p. 244.
40. Sullivan, 'A Middlebrow Dame Commander', p. 168.
41. Sullivan and Blanch, 'Introduction', p. 16, n. 2.
42. Bourdieu, *The Field of Cultural Production*, p. 42.
43. Leavis, *Fiction and the Reading Public*, pp. 24, 270.
44. Leavis, *Fiction and the Reading Public*, p. 5.
45. This letter was later published under the title 'Middlebrow' in *The Death of the Moth*.
46. Sullivan and Blanch, 'Introduction', p. 16, n. 4.
47. Wilson, 'Virginia Woolf', p. 238.
48. L. Woolf, *Downhill All the Way*, pp. 79–80.
49. 'Outstanding New Books', *Evening Telegraph and Post* [Dundee], 25 October 1929, p. 11.
50. 'Outstanding Xmas Books', *Evening Telegraph and Post* [Dundee], 29 November 1929, p. 10.
51. 'Novels Re-Issued', *Courier and Advertiser* [Dundee], 20 February 1930, p. 10.
52. 'George Eliot', *Courier and Argus* [Dundee], 10 April 1901, p. 6.
53. 'The Novels of Virginia Woolf', *New Statesman*, 9 November 1929, p. 162.
54. Review of the Uniform Edition of the Works of Virginia Woolf, *Time and Tide*, 18 October 1929, p. 1252.
55. 'Virginia Woolf', *Yorkshire Post*, 2 October 1933, p. 6.
56. 'These were the frontispiece featuring the photograph of the Woolfs' dog, Pinker, on their bed, and paintings of Miss Mitford and Mrs Browning from the National Portrait Gallery.' Wilson, 'Virginia Woolf', p. 254.
57. Wilson, 'Virginia Woolf', p. 255.
58. Woolf to Walpole, 15 April 1933, *Letters of Virginia Woolf*, vol. 5, p. 177.
59. Woolf to Vanessa Bell, 25 June 1929, *Letters of Virginia Woolf*, vol. 4, p. 68. Announcing the publication of the Uniform Edition of *The Years*, the 1940 catalogue reads: 'The original edition of *The Years*, Mrs Woolf's most recent and most popular novel, was published in 1937. All those who collect the attractive uniform

edition will want to add this latest volume to their set.' Quoted in Willson Gordon, 'Under the Imprint of the Hogarth Press', p. 177.
60. See Jaillant, 'Shucks, We've Got Glamour Girls Too!'.
61. Kirkpatrick and Clarke, *A Bibliography of Virginia Woolf*, pp. 3, 8.
62. Kirkpatrick and Clarke, *A Bibliography of Virginia Woolf*, pp. 27, 29.
63. Profit and loss summaries book, MS 2750/A/11, HP.
64. Kirkpatrick and Clarke, *A Bibliography of Virginia Woolf*, pp. 38, 40.
65. Kirkpatrick and Clarke, *A Bibliography of Virginia Woolf*, p. 48.
66. Kirkpatrick and Clarke, *A Bibliography of Virginia Woolf*, pp. 49–50.
67. Profit and loss summaries book, MS 2750/A/11, HP.
68. Kirkpatrick and Clarke, *A Bibliography of Virginia Woolf*, p. 71.
69. Kirkpatrick and Clarke, *A Bibliography of Virginia Woolf*, pp. 19–20. Leonard Woolf notes that 'nine years after it was published Duckworth had sold only 2,238 copies of *Night and Day*'. L. Woolf, *Downhill All the Way*, p. 17.
70. See Jaillant, *Modernism*, pp. 83–102.
71. Kirkpatrick and Clarke, *A Bibliography of Virginia Woolf*, pp. 40, 50, 64.
72. Stein to Van Vechten, 18 April 1916. Reprinted in Burns, ed., *Letters of Gertrude Stein and Carl Van Vechten*, p. 53.
73. *Diary of Virginia Woolf*, vol. 1, p. 129.
74. Bishop, 'From Typography to *Time*', p. 50.
75. Young, 'Canonicity', p. 239.
76. Advertisement for Harcourt Brace, *Publishers' Weekly*, 10 January 1931, p. 192.
77. Bullock, 'American Boom in English Authors'.
78. Kirkpatrick and Clarke, *A Bibliography of Virginia Woolf*, pp. 7, 21, 29, 39. Harcourt's Uniform Edition of *To the Lighthouse* had a first printing of 1,000 copies. Kirkpatrick and Clarke, *A Bibliography of Virginia Woolf*, p. 49.
79. Chatto & Windus to Woolf, 22 December 1931, Letter book, CW A/135.
80. Woolf wrote in the same letter: 'After the Hogarth Press, I would rather have my work published by your firm than by any other.' Woolf to Chatto & Windus, 30 December 1931, File Chatto & Windus letters 1926–1931, CW 46/12.
81. J. M. Dent (Editorial Department) to Virginia Woolf, 30 November 1937, JMD.
82. Rebecca Bowler notes: 'In 1934, Richardson's friend S. S. Koteliansky wrote to her and asked what would persuade her to change publishers. Duckworth, he claimed, wasn't doing enough to promote the successive volumes of *Pilgrimage*. Richardson replied that what she really wanted, what would really get her lifework the attention she felt it merited, was a collected edition. [Koteliansky] took her at her word, and got her a contract with Dent & Cresset' ('Dorothy M. Richardson Deserves the Recognition She is Finally Receiving'). See also Bowler, 'Publishing Pilgrimage' on the Dorothy Richardson Online Exhibition website, which features digital copies of these letters.
83. J. M. Dent (Editorial Department) to Woolf, 31 May 1938, JMD.
84. Woolf, *The Death of the Moth*, p. 116.
85. Willis, *Leonard and Virginia Woolf as Publishers*, p. 392.
86. Advertisements for Chatto & Windus and the Hogarth Press, *Listener*, 22 March 1951, p. 466.

CONCLUSION

The three-and-six-penny libraries and other quality reprint series reached their peak in the mid-1930s. By 1934, the Travellers' Library had more than 200 titles on its list. The Phoenix Library included desirable books such as *Brave New World* (the fourteenth title by Aldous Huxley in this series). Albatross had energised a continental market long dominated by Tauchnitz. But after the rise came the fall. First, there was the growing competition of the Penguin paperbacks, launched in 1935. Then, the Second World War created major disruptions. Not only was it was difficult to obtain paper to print books, it also became impossible to distribute Anglophone texts on the Continent (including in German-occupied France). Albatross was forced to close its office in Paris. Successful series simply disappeared from circulation: Albatross, but also Tauchnitz, the Travellers' Library and the Phoenix Library. Series with a more modest scope – such as the two-shilling Dolphin Books, published by Chatto & Windus – were also discontinued.[1]

For a brief moment after the war, publishers tried to revive their old collections. Albatross and Tauchnitz resumed production, but it soon became clear that both enterprises were in serious trouble. As Alistair McCleery points out, 'the Tauchnitz name and any residual rights were sold off in July 1950' and 'nothing much more was ever published under the Tauchnitz imprint'.[2] Albatross did not survive much longer, due to mismanagement and difficulties brought by the war (including the loss of many contracts). Moreover, in a context of intense competition in the reprint market, British publishers increasingly refused to sell rights for continental editions. In a letter to Arnoldo Mondadori (the printer of Albatross titles), Harold Raymond of Chatto & Windus wrote:

> What I might call the Heinemann, Cape or Chatto type of author, is generally translated into several European languages and has considerable sale in the European capitals, and a cheap edition of an author's work appearing on the Continent a year or so before the issue of the first cloth-bound reprint of a book naturally had a severe effect on its sales.[3]

In 1950, Chatto & Windus decided to launch the New Phoenix Library – and Jonathan Cape did the same thing with the New Travellers' Library. Both were commercial failures. The new series lasted approximately two years, and were then discontinued. This is surprising for two main reasons. First, the academic study of modernism was by then on the rise (think of the influence of F. R. Leavis and *Scrutiny*, for example). There was presumably a growing educational market for books such as *Dubliners* available in cheap format.[4] Second, in the United States the Modern Library series was more popular than ever. Gordon Neavill has shown that the sales of the regular Modern Library were multiplied by five between 1940 and 1948, despite the competition of paperback series.[5] From 1948, Joyce's *A Portrait of the Artist as a Young Man* was available in a Signet paperback edition with a rather lurid cover and in the Modern Library series, which targeted a different readership. While mass-market paperbacks could be found in news-stands, the Modern Library was sold in bookshops to an audience of middle-class readers (including many students). Paperbacks were meant to be read and thrown away, whereas Modern Library books were kept on the shelf. This different positioning allowed the Modern Library to prosper, reaching a high point in the late 1940s and early 1950s.

Like the Modern Library, the New Phoenix Library and the New Travellers' Library had many strong selling points that could have ensured their commercial success. At five shillings or less, they were affordable for students and their instructors.[6] Before the war, quality reprint series already targeted the educational market. In a letter to Allen Lane of Penguin, Harold Raymond justified his refusal to allow a paperback edition of a Huxley book: 'a great portion of the sales of our Phoenix Library lie in the educational field and . . . your edition would badly cut across ours in that direction'.[7] This existing experience of the educational market was an asset at a time when higher education was booming: the number of students taking first degrees in the United Kingdom increased fourfold between 1920 and 1950.[8]

As in the pre-war period, the two British series were presented as distinguished series of quality literature. One of the first advertisements for the New Travellers' Library declared:

Now the series has been revived, among them some old favourites and many new. In a pleasing, portable format and at the lowest price which modern conditions permit, they will brighten the eyes of discriminating purchasers. At least ten volumes will be issued this year, and four of them are now available.[9]

Those 'discriminating' readers were encouraged to read titles such as *A Portrait of the Artist as a Young Man* (a few months later, *Dubliners* was added to the list). Several titles by Hemingway were also reprinted in the New Travellers' Library. The dust jacket for *Selected Stories* announced: 'In the new series many of the old titles will be re-issued and at the same time new ones will continually be added, maintaining the reputation for literary quality combined with catholicity which the Travellers' Library has long enjoyed.' The focus was on the quality of the list, but also on the range of titles available.

The same could be said of the New Phoenix Library, whose first titles included Aldous Huxley's *After Many a Summer*, Virginia Woolf's *Mrs Dalloway* and Jan Struther's *Mrs Miniver* (a bestselling novel that has been described as 'middlebrow').[10] Chatto & Windus was in a particularly strong position after the war, with some of the biggest names in modern literature on its list. After acquiring the Hogarth Press, the firm now had the rights to Woolf's titles (nearly twenty years after first asking for permission to reprint them in the Phoenix Library). The first printing of *Mrs Dalloway* in the New Phoenix Library reached 7,500 copies, a significant number for a novel that had once been described as experimental and difficult.[11] And some of the authors that the firm had championed in the interwar period now achieved wide recognition, including William Faulkner. *Soldiers' Pay* joined the New Phoenix Library in 1951, followed by *Pylon*. Chatto & Windus also insisted on the refined physical format of its books, thus echoing its interwar marketing strategy. An advertisement in the *Bookseller* referred to the cyclical rebirth of the phoenix, a particularly elegant bird:

> Back again! The New Phoenix Library. . . . After ten years of enforced absence the Phoenix reappears dressed in handsome new plumage. Bound in blue cloth, blocked in gold with a panel matching the crimson of the jacket, the New Phoenix Library is ready to take the place of its famous predecessor as one of the most popular and distinctive reprint series.[12]

Another advertisement included a blurb from *Current Literature*: 'Strikingly handsome volumes. Where else but in the bookshop can one find such value for money?'[13] The reference to bookshops underlines the difference between the New Phoenix Library and ephemeral paperbacks sold by newsagents.

How did journalists react to the relaunch of the two series? *John O'London's Weekly*, a popular magazine, declared:

What a pleasure it is to welcome back the pocket editions! Between the wars nearly every leading firm had its reprint series and the best of them set a high standard. There was the Travellers' Library, for instance, which reflected great credit on the taste and discrimination of its publisher (Jonathan Cape).[14]

Here, the reference to taste highlights once again the audience for publishers' series, an aspirational readership that wanted to appear educated and refined. Six months later, the same magazine declared: 'the new Phoenix Library ... gave us such pleasure and profit before the war' and added that the books were available 'in a format which makes them a bargain at this price'.[15] Like the *John O'London's Weekly*, many periodicals referred to the nostalgic value of series so strongly associated with the pre-war period. The *Peeblesshire News* wrote: 'it is most encouraging to note the reappearance of the low priced "libraries" which were so popular before the war, bringing as they did to the reading public well-known books at a reasonable price'.[16] At the time when the series were revived, British people still suffered from the consequences of the war (food rationing did not end until 1954, for example). The Phoenix Library and Travellers' Library brands were strongly associated with a period that retrospectively seemed easier and more pleasurable.

So how can we explain the failed revival of these two series? There are at least three reasons: high production costs, competition from paperbacks and changing readership. Rising production costs created instability in the reprint market. Not only did publishers ask customers to pay more than three shillings and six pence, they also offered a lower royalty rate to authors. One year before the launch of the New Phoenix Library, Harold Raymond wrote to T. F. Powys, the author of *Mr Weston's Good Wine*:

> The pre-war price of the series was 3/6d and we used to pay you a 10% royalty. We now propose to price the new series at 5/-, and I wish I could pay you the same rate, but I am afraid I cannot – or not quite. The best terms we can offer are 5d. per copy on ordinary sales and half that amount where we are obliged to give booksellers a discount of 50% or more. Our trouble is that manufacturing cost are now two-and-a-half times what they were before the war, yet we dare not on a series like this increase the price in anything like that proportion. I shall hope, however, that at 5/- the series will sell appreciably more than it did in pre-war days at 3/6d.[17]

The publisher's hope for increased sales should be read in a context of revolutionary changes in the book trade. Indeed, buying books had become much more common than in the pre-war period. 'It is a comforting thought that the nation is spending three times as much on books now as it did before the war', wrote Raymond to Julian Huxley.[18] The firm anticipated a larger sale than the pre-war Phoenix enjoyed, but also 'a possible decrease in the price of paper'.[19] However, as production costs continued to increase, Chatto & Windus wrote to authors in March 1951 to inform them that 'recent increases in manufacturing costs . . . and particularly the 30% rise in the cost of paper, compel us to increase the published price to 6/-.'.[20] This relatively high selling price undermined the positioning of quality series, which could no longer be presented as 'bargains'.

Competition from paperbacks was another major issue. In the United States, the format of the Modern Library was radically different from that of paperbacks, sold with lurid covers and sensational blurbs. In contrast, the British market was dominated by stylish Penguin books, which could be sold to all kinds of readers. In 1938, Harold Raymond had warned the trade of the dangers of paperbacks for other reprint series. Although sixpenny paper covered books already existed before the First World War, the paperbacks of the 1930s differed from their predecessors in four respects. As Raymond put it:

> They are far better produced; their average standard of literary quality is higher; they consist of more recent publications, and indeed some of the titles appear in Penguins for the first time; and finally, they are a greater bargain both because of a post-War sixpence is of less value than a pre-War one, and because book prices as a whole have advanced since the War.

Paperbacks also reached a much wider audience thanks to new distribution channels: 'Woolworths, the village shop, the small tobacconist, and the slot-machine'.[21] To convince publishers to sell reprint rights, Allen Lane often insisted that the market for Penguins was totally different from existing book markets. 'I should think that I should be safe in saying that 90% of our total sales are to people who would not in the normal way buy the titles', Lane once wrote to Raymond.[22]

But the Chatto & Windus editor was not convinced that paperbacks only targeted those who shied away from bookshops. After selling several of its Phoenix Library titles to Lane, Raymond started worrying about the consequences of this 'Penguinisation'. In spring 1937, he reported:

> Up to March 31st [1937], the date on which we take stock, only two titles had been in the Penguins for as long as nine months, namely *Crome Yellow* and *Death of a Hero*. *Crome Yellow* shows a 20% drop compared with the previous year sales, whereas *Those Barren Leaves* shows only a 13% drop, and *Antic Hay* a drop of 2%. *Death of a Hero* shows a 40% drop; on the other hand *The Colonel's Daughter* shows an almost exactly similar decrease.[23]

For Raymond, evidence showed that existing book buyers turned away from hardcover reprint series. 'One never goes into the house of a book-conscious person without seeing Penguins', he declared in 1938. 'Many booksellers report that the sales of three-and-six penny, half-crown, and florin reprints have shown a disastrous decrease during the last few years.'[24] This had serious consequences for authors, as the royalty rate for paperbacks (4 per cent) was lower than for original 7s. 6d. editions (20 to 25 per cent) and 3s. 6d. reprints (10 per cent). Of course, authors could expect a much larger sale in paperbacks, but their overall income would still decrease if readers turned away from more expensive editions. 'I estimate that four-fifths of an author's earnings are on average drawn from the sales of his books at the initial publishing price and only one-fifth from subsequent cheap editions', Raymond wrote.[25] If readers preferred to wait for the release of a sixpence paperback edition, authors would lose a significant part of their income.

Raymond was right to fear the 'revolutionary effect' of paperbacks on the book trade.[26] The growing popularity of Penguins increased the size of the book-buying public, but it also pushed prices down. In 1949, Raymond told the literary agent A. D. Peters: 'New books as a whole are underpriced.' And he added: 'we are working on a frighteningly narrow margin of profit'.[27] To compete with paperbacks, other reprint series had to operate with a large profit margin to compensate for their lower sales. This is what happened with Modern Library books, which were four times more expensive than early US paperbacks.[28] In the case of the New Phoenix Library, the rising price tag (from the pre-war price of 3s. 6d. to 5s. and then 6s.) could not compensate for high production costs on the one hand and modest sales on the other. This was particularly problematic when a title had been available for a long time in a paperback format before being included in the New Phoenix Library, as in the case of Mr Weston's Good Wine (Plate 5). The hardback edition of Powys's novel was relatively expensive compared to paperbacks, and the positioning of the series was not distinct enough – in terms of cover design, for example.

Another problem was that the Phoenix Library and Travellers' Library had been out of print for nearly ten years and the readership had changed. People who bought three-and-six-penny series in the 1930s wanted to create their own libraries and display their books to admiring visitors. But following the paperback revolution, buying contemporary books was no longer unusual. The decline of hardback series was particularly brutal in Britain. Even in America, the Modern Library started declining in the late 1950s and 1960s, and was eventually discontinued in the early 1970s. Donald Klopfer, who had bought the Modern Library with Bennett Cerf in 1925, talked about this changing market in an oral history interview:

> There's the Modern Library over on those shelves, over there, and it's almost finished, being phased out, because of paperbacks – perfectly sound, just as it should be. I regret it, because I love it. After all, it's my baby. But the so-called egghead paperback has put us out of business. . . . Because the fashion has changed, that's all. Young people aren't interested in cloth bound books.[29]

Paperbacks had become so attractive that many readers systematically preferred them to hardback reprint series. But as we have seen in Chapter 2, Allen Lane was often reluctant to 'Penguinise' difficult modernist texts – a major difference with his US competitors.

So how did British readers encounter modernism in the 1950s, at the time when modernist studies was on the rise? These texts were still available in more expensive editions sold for 7s. 6d. – a price that had not changed since the interwar period – whereas the price of the former three-and-six-penny libraries had increased. In 1952, for example, Jonathan Cape printed 5,000 copies of *A Portrait of the Artist as a Young Man* in the 7s. 6d. edition.[30] Cape then associated with Penguin to publish paperback editions of *Dubliners* in 1956 and *Portrait of the Artist* in 1960. In this market, there was simply no place for the New Travellers' Library and similar reprint series.

The hardback series were too much associated with the pre-war period, a time when the mere fact of buying books signalled taste and education. Few series survived the changing conditions post war. In an article on Everyman's Library, Gayle Feldman notes that 'the glory days at Dent gave way to desuetude, not simply by way of the paperback revolution, but as a function of the consolidating trends of the book industry itself'.[31] Indeed, the company was sold to Weidenfeld & Nicolson in 1987. The series that did survive (such as the Oxford World's Classics) evolved towards quality paperbacks, on the model of the American 'egghead paperback' pioneered by Anchor, Vintage and others.[32]

However, hardcover series did not completely disappear. In 1982, the Library of America began reprinting works of American literature in uniform, relatively inexpensive hardcover editions. And in the early 1990s, the relaunch of Everyman's Library and the Modern Library attracted a great deal of interest. The publisher David Campbell, who collaborated with Knopf to resurrect Everyman's Library, mentioned the French series Pléiade as a model.[33] The revived series was advertised as 'the most extensive and distinguished hardcover library of great works of literature'. Like early-twentieth-century series that had mixed modernism and detective fiction, the new Everyman's Library offered a wide choice of texts: 'from Wilkie Collins' classic (and unsurpassed) thriller *The Woman in White* to Virginia Woolf's seminal short novel *To the Lighthouse*'. With full-cloth bindings, gold stamping, silk ribbon holders and decorated endpapers, the physical format of the series created 'an aura – a *bookish* look – at once old-timey and contemporary, that pleases the reader and lends an air to the bookshelf'.[34] Here, the reference to 'aura' suggests a quasi-religious experience triggered by the beautiful aspect of the books. 'Reading one, you could imagine yourself in a paneled library with a marble fireplace and leather armchairs', declared the *Wall Street Journal* thus emphasising the association with class and taste that already characterised the early Everyman's Library.[35] For the centenary of the series in 2006, Knopf's publicity director Nicholas Latimer reported that Amazon 'received a number of orders for the entire set of the "Everyman Essentials": the 100 books in the series that we put together to help people build an instant library of classics'.[36] This appetite for instant culture highlights the continuing relevance of reprint series and other 'middlebrow' institutions with roots in the early twentieth century.

NOTES

1. Dolphin Books published Samuel Beckett's *Proust* in 1931. The series included fourteen titles in the mid-1930s.
2. McCleery, 'Tauchnitz and Albatross', p. 313.
3. Raymond to Mondadori, 5 September 1947, Correspondence between Albatross Ltd and Chatto & Windus, CW 106/29.
4. See, for example, the rising number of theses on James Joyce after the Second World War, including George Bradbury, 'James Joyce's *Dubliners*' (BA thesis, Liverpool University, 1950) and A. Walton Litz, 'The Evolution of James Joyce's Style and Technique from 1918 to 1932' (DPhil. thesis, University of Oxford, 1954).
5. Neavill, 'Publishing in Wartime', p. 588.
6. The New Travellers' Library was initially priced at 4s. 6d.
7. Raymond to Lane, 16 March 1937, File Penguin Books, CW 73/16.
8. Bolton, *Education*, p. 20.
9. Advertisement for the New Travellers' Library, *Times Literary Supplement*, 17 March 1950, p. 162.
10. Beauman, *A Very Great Profession*, p. 173.
11. Index Cards, CW. This was part of an impression of 10,000 copies printed in July 1949. 'Two thousand five hundred were issued as the Uniform Edition in jade-green paper boards in 1950, and 7500 in the New Phoenix Library.' Kirkpatrick and Clarke, *A Bibliography of Virginia Woolf*, p. 41. On Woolf's image in the 1920s: 'Mrs Woolf's art is such that there is the greatest difficulty in separating external events from mental impressions and suggestions, yet there is an unaccountable fascination about the recital of these queer, incongruous threads of life which now run parallel, now intersect, now part company forever.' 'Virginia Woolf Novel', *Aberdeen Press and Journal*, 18 May 1925, p. 3.
12. Advertisement for the New Phoenix Library, *Bookseller*, 29 July 1950, Advertisement Book, CW D/12.
13. Advertisement for the New Phoenix Library, *Manchester Guardian*, 29 September 1950, p. 4.
14. *John O'London's Weekly*, 31 March 1950, Newspaper Cuttings, CW C/93.
15. *John O'London's Weekly*, 15 September 1950, Newspaper Cuttings, CW C/93.
16. *Peeblesshire News*, 5 January 1951, Newspaper Cuttings, CW C/93.
17. Raymond to Powys, 7 April 1949, Box 19, Folder 7, Theodore Francis Powys collection, HRC.

18. Raymond to J. Huxley, 1 April 1949, Letter book, CW A/248.
19. Raymond to W. P. Watt, 7 April 1949, Letter book, CW A/248.
20. Raymond to Sylvia Townsend Warner, 19 March 1951, File Chatto & Windus letters 1950–1951: New Phoenix Library, CW 121/2.
21. Raymond, *Publishing and Bookselling*, p. 23.
22. Lane to Raymond, 5 May 1937, File Penguin Books, CW 73/16.
23. Raymond to Lane, 23 April 1937, File Penguin Books, CW 73/16.
24. Raymond, *Publishing and Bookselling*, p. 24.
25. Raymond, *Publishing and Bookselling*, p. 25.
26. Raymond, *Publishing and Bookselling*, p. 23.
27. Raymond to Peters, 11 April 1949, Letter book, CW A/248.
28. Jaillant, *Modernism*, p. 79.
29. Reminiscences of Donald Klopfer, 1975, pp. 22–3, Oral History Research Office collection, Columbia University Library.
30. Production ledger, JC.
31. Feldman, 'Everyman, Knopf Will Go with Thee'.
32. Satterfield, *The World's Best Books*, pp. 161–3.
33. Feldman, 'Everyman, Knopf Will Go with Thee'.
34. Advertisement for Everyman's Library, *New York Times*, 22 November 1992, p. BR17.
35. Gamerman, 'Publishing'.
36. Quoted in Nolan, 'The Continuing Saga of Everyman's Library'.

Plate 1 Dust jacket, *A Portrait of the Artist as a Young Man*, Travellers' Library (left: c. 1930; right: c. 1934). By permission of Penguin Random House UK.

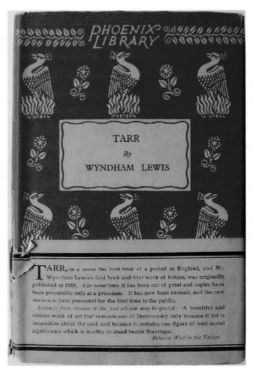

Plate 2 Dust jacket of *Tarr*, Phoenix Library (1928), with wrap-around band. By permission of Penguin Random House UK.

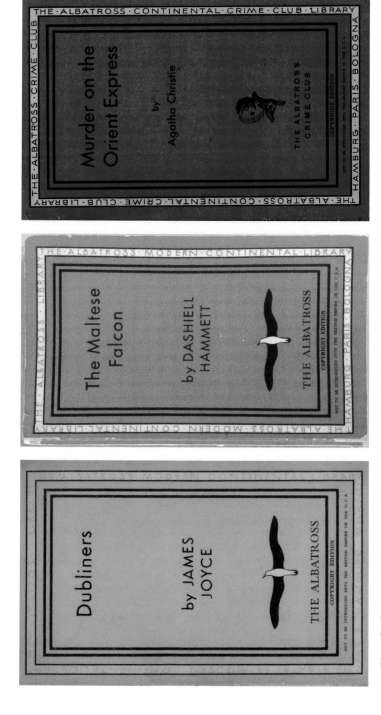

Plate 3 Covers of Albatross editions of James Joyce's *Dubliners* (1932), Dashiell Hammett's *The Maltese Falcon* (1932) and Agatha Christie's *Murder on the Orient Express* (1934). Note the different logo for the Albatross Crime Club series.

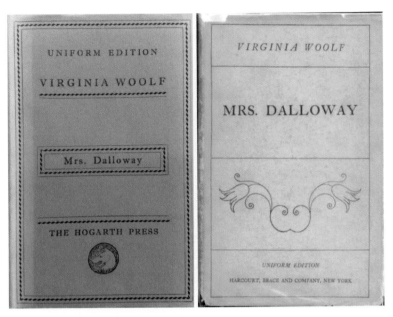

Plate 4 Dust jackets, *Mrs Dalloway*, Uniform Edition (left: Hogarth Press; right: Harcourt Brace). By permission of Penguin Random House UK.

Plate 5 T. F. Powys's *Mr Weston's Good Wine* (left: Penguin [1937]; right: New Phoenix Library [1950]). By permission of Penguin Books Ltd and of Penguin Random House UK.

REFERENCES

Aldington, Richard, *Life for Life's Sake: A Book of Reminiscences* (New York: Viking Press, 1941).

Altick, Richard, 'From Aldine to Everyman: Cheap Reprint Series of the English Classics 1830–1906', *Studies in Bibliography*, 11 (1958), 3–24.

Anderson, Patricia, and Jonathan Rose (eds), *British Literary Publishing Houses, 1820–1880* (Detroit: Gale Research, 1991), Dictionary of Literary Biography, vol. 106, *Literature Resource Center* [accessed online 2 January 2014].

Anderson, Sherwood, *Horses and Men* (London: Jonathan Cape [Travellers' Library], 1927).

Andes, George M., *A Descriptive Bibliography of the Modern Library, 1917–1970* (Boston: Boston Book Annex, 1989).

Ardis, Ann, 'Modernist Print Culture', *American Literary History*, 27.4 (2015), 813–19.

Armstrong, Tim, *Modernism, Technology, and the Body: A Cultural Study* (Cambridge: Cambridge University Press, 1998).

Arnold, Matthew, *Culture and Anarchy: An Essay in Political and Social Criticism* (London: Smith, Elder & Co., 1869).

Attridge, John, '"We Will Listen to None But Specialists": Ford, The Rise of Specialization, and *The English Review*', in *Ford Madox Ford: Literary Networks and Cultural Transformations*, ed. Andrzej Gąsiorek and Daniel Moore (Amsterdam: Rodopi, 2008), pp. 29–41. International Ford Madox Ford Studies 7.

Barnes, Djuna, *Nightwood* (London: Faber & Faber, 1979).

Beach, Sylvia, *Shakespeare & Company*, 2nd edn (Lincoln: University of Nebraska Press, 1991).

Beasley, Rebecca, 'On Not Knowing Russian: The Translations of Virginia Woolf and S. S. Kotelianskii', *Modern Language Review*, 108.1 (2013), 1–29.

Beauman, Nicola, *A Very Great Profession: The Woman's Novel 1914–39* (London: Virago, 1983).

Bennett, Arnold, *The Evening Standard Years: 'Books and Persons' 1926–1931*, ed. Andrew Mylett (London: Chatto & Windus, 1974).

Birchall, John, 'The World's Classics: A Library within a Library', *Books in Wernicke*, 11 March 2012, <http://booksinwernicke.blogspot.ca/2012/03/world-classics-library-within-library.html> [accessed 23 October 2016].

Bishop, Edward, 'From Typography to *Time*: Producing Virginia Woolf', in *Virginia Woolf: Texts and Contexts: Selected Papers from the Fifth Annual Conference on Virginia Woolf, Otterbein College, Westerville, Ohio, June 15–18, 1995*, ed. Beth Daugherty and Eileen Barrett (New York: Pace University Press, 1996), pp. 50–63.

Blunden, Edmund, 'World's Classics', *Times Literary Supplement*, 25 May 1946, p. 247.

Bolton, Paul, *Education: Historical Statistics* (London: House of Commons Library, 2012).

Bonn, Thomas L., 'American Mass-Market Paperbacks', in *Collectible Books: Some New Paths*, ed. Jean Peters (New York: R. R. Bowker, 1979), pp. 118–51.

Bornstein, George, *Material Modernism: The Politics of the Page* (Cambridge: Cambridge University Press, 2001).

Bourdieu, Pierre, *The Field of Cultural Production: Essays on Art and Literature*, trans. Randal Johnson (New York: Columbia University Press, 1993).

Bowler, Rebecca, 'Dorothy M. Richardson Deserves the Recognition She is Finally Receiving', *The Guardian*, 15 May 2015, <https://www.theguardian.com/books/booksblog/2015/may/15/dorothy-m-richardson-deserves-recognition-finally-receiving> [accessed 23 October 2016].

——, 'Publishing Pilgrimage', *Dorothy Richardson – An Online Exhibition*, 2016, <http://dorothyrichardsonexhibition.org/pilgrimage.htm> [accessed 23 October 2016].

Bradshaw, David, and Rachel Potter (eds), *Prudes on the Prowl: Fiction and Obscenity in England, 1850 to the Present Day* (Oxford: Oxford University Press, 2013).

British Library, *Tauchnitz-Edition*, ed. William B. Todd (London: National Heritage Memorial Fund, KulturStiftung der Länder, 1992).

Brooker, Peter, and Andrew Thacker (eds), *The Oxford Critical and Cultural History of Modernist Magazines*, 3 vols (New York: Oxford University Press, 2009–2013).

Brown, Curtis, *Contacts* (London: Cassell, 1935).

Brown, Erica, *Comedy and the Feminine Middlebrow Novel: Elizabeth von Arnim and Elizabeth Taylor* (London: Pickering & Chatto, 2013).

Bruccoli, Matthew, *Raymond Chandler: A Descriptive Bibliography* (Pittsburgh: University of Pittsburgh Press, 1979).

Bullock, W. F., 'American Boom in English Authors', *Daily Mail*, Atlantic edition, 27 January 1929, p. 4.

Burns, Edward (ed.), *The Letters of Gertrude Stein and Carl Van Vechten, 1913–1946* (New York: Columbia University Press, 2013).

Chinitz, David, *T. S. Eliot and the Cultural Divide* (Chicago: University of Chicago Press, 2003).

Collier, Patrick, *Modern Print Artifacts: Textual Materiality and Literary Value in British Print Culture, 1890–1930s* (Edinburgh: Edinburgh University Press, 2016).

——, 'What is Modern Periodical Studies?', *Journal of Modern Periodical Studies*, 6.2 (2015), 92–111.

Colligan, Colette, *A Publisher's Paradise: Expatriate Literary Culture in Paris, 1890–1960* (Amherst: University of Massachusetts Press, 2014).

Collins, V. H. (ed.), *Ghosts and Marvels* (London: Oxford University Press [World's Classics], 1924).

——, (ed.), *More Ghosts and Marvels* (London: Oxford University Press [World's Classics], 1927).

Collins, Wilkie, *The Moonstone* (London: Oxford University Press [World's Classics], 1928).

Connolly, Cyril, *The Modern Movement. One Hundred Key Books from England, France and America 1880–1950* (London: André Deutsch; Hamish Hamilton, 1965).

Cooper, John Xiros, *Modernism and the Culture of Market Society* (Cambridge: Cambridge University Press, 2004).

Crawford, Robert, *Devolving English Literature* (New York: Oxford University Press, 1992).

Crime and Detection, Second Series (London: Oxford University Press [World's Classics], 1930).

Daugherty, Beth, 'The Transatlantic Virginia Woolf: Essaying an American Audience', *Virginia Woolf Miscellany*, 76 (2009), 9–11.

De Grazia, Edward, *Girls Lean Back Everywhere: The Law of Obscenity and the Assault on Genius* (London: Constable, 1992).

Dent, J. M., *The House of Dent, 1888–1938* (London: J. M. Dent, 1938).

Dickens, Elizabeth, '"Permanent Books": The Reviewing and Advertising of Books in the *Nation and Athenaeum*', *Journal of Modern Periodical Studies*, 2.2 (2011), 165–84.

Earle, David M., 'Pulp Magazines and the Popular Press', in *The Oxford Critical and Cultural History of Modernist Magazines*, ed. Brooker and Thacker, vol. 2, pp. 197–215.

——, *Re-Covering Modernism: Pulps, Paperbacks, and the Prejudice of Form* (Farnham: Ashgate, 2009).

Edwards, Paul, *Wyndham Lewis: Portraits* (London: National Portrait Gallery, 2008).

Edwards, Russell, and David J. Hall, *'So Much Admired': With Checklists of the Illustrated Volumes of Die Insel-Bücherei and the King Penguin Series* (Edinburgh: Salvia Books, 1998).

Eliot, Simon, 'What Price Poetry? Selling Wordsworth, Tennyson, and Longfellow in Nineteenth- and Early Twentieth-Century Britain', *Papers of the Bibliographical Society of America*, 100.4 (2006), 425–45.

Eliot, T. S., 'Introduction', *The Moonstone, by Wilkie Collins* (London: Oxford University Press [World's Classics], 1928), pp. v–xii.

——, 'Introduction', *Nightwood, by Djuna Barnes* (London: Faber & Faber, 1979), pp. 1–7.

——, 'Tarr', *The Egoist*, September 1918, p. 106.

——, *The Letters of T. S. Eliot*, ed. Valerie Eliot, vol. 1 (London: Faber & Faber, 1988), 4 vols.

——, *The Letters of T. S. Eliot*, ed. Valerie Eliot and John Haffenden, vol. 3 (London: Faber & Faber, 2012), 4 vols.

——, *The Waste Land and Other Poems* (London: Faber & Faber, 1999).

——, 'Wilkie Collins and Dickens', *Times Literary Supplement*, 4 August 1927, pp. 525–6.

Evans, Matthew, 'Guru-in-Chief', *The Guardian*, 6 June 2009, <https://www.theguardian.com/books/2009/jun/06/t-s-eliot-faber-matthew-evans> [accessed 23 October 2016].

Feather, John, *A History of British Publishing* (London: Routledge, 1988).

Feldman, Gayle, 'Everyman, Knopf Will Go with Thee . . . in Major Fall Relaunch', *Publishers' Weekly*, 7 June 1991, p. 25.

Feltes, N. N., *Literary Capital and the Late Victorian Novel* (Madison: University of Wisconsin Press, 1993).

——, *Modes of Production of Victorian Novels* (Chicago: University of Chicago Press, 1986).

Finkelstein, David, and Alistair McCleery, *An Introduction to Book History*, 2nd edn (London: Routledge, 2013).

Flanders, Amy, 'The Press in London, 1896–1970', in *The History of Oxford University Press*, ed. Ian Gadd, Simon Eliot and Wm. Roger Louis, vol. 3 (Oxford: Oxford University Press), pp. 136–88.

Ford, Ford Madox, *Letters of Ford Madox Ford*, ed. Richard M. Ludwig (Princeton: Princeton University Press, 1965).

Forster, E. M., *Aspects of the Novel* (London: Edward Arnold & Co., 1944).

Friskney, Janet, *New Canadian Library: The Ross-McClelland Years, 1952–1978* (Toronto: University of Toronto Press, 2007).

Gadd, Ian, Simon Eliot, and Wm. Roger Louis (eds), *The History of Oxford University Press*, 3 vols (Oxford: Oxford University Press, 2013).

Gamerman, Amy, 'Publishing: Highbrow Books Make a Comeback', *Wall Street Journal*, 26 September 1991, p. A17.

Garnett, David, 'D. H. Lawrence,' *Observer*, 26 March 1950, p. 8.

Gawsworth, John, *Apes, Japes and Hitlerism: A Study and Bibliography of Wyndham Lewis* (London: Unicorn Press, 1932).

Gillespie, Diane F., 'Virginia Woolf, the Hogarth Press, and the Detective Novel', *South Carolina Review*, 35.2 (2003), 36–48.

Grant, Joy, *Harold Monro and the Poetry Bookshop* (London: Routledge & Kegan Paul, 1967).

Grattan, C. Hartley, 'In the Pages of Books', Review of *Tarr*, by Wyndham Lewis, *Evening Independent* [St Petersburg, Florida], 14 August 1926, p. 3.

Griest, Guinevere L., *Mudie's Circulating Library and the Victorian Novel* (Bloomington: Indiana University Press, 1970).

Hall, Theodore, 'No End of Books', *Washington Post*, 10 March 1934, p. 9.

Hammill, Faye, Paul Hjartarson, and Hannah McGregor, 'Introducing Magazines And/ as Media: The Aesthetics and Politics of Serial Form', *English Studies in Canada*, 41.1 (2015), 1–18.

Hammill, Faye, and Karen Leick, 'Modernism and the Quality Magazines', in *The Oxford Critical and Cultural History of Modernist Magazines*, ed. Brooker and Thacker, vol. 2, pp. 176–96.

Hammill, Faye, and Michelle Smith, 'About the Project: Magazines, Travel and Middlebrow Culture in Canada 1925–1960', *Middlebrowcanada*, 2011, <http://www.middlebrowcanada.org/AbouttheProject/tabid/398/language/en-GB/Default.aspx> [accessed 23 October 2016].

——, *Magazines, Travel, and Middlebrow Culture: Canadian Periodicals in English and French, 1925–1960* (Liverpool: Liverpool University Press, 2015).

Hammond, Mary, *Reading, Publishing and the Formation of Literary Taste in England, 1880–1914* (Aldershot: Ashgate, 2006).

Haycraft, Howard, *Murder For Pleasure: The Life And Times Of The Detective Story* (London: Peter Davies, 1942).

——, (ed.), *The Art of the Mystery Story: A Collection of Critical Essays* (New York: Simon & Schuster, 1946).

Hibberd, Dominic, *Harold Monro: Poet of the New Age* (Basingstoke: Palgrave, 2001).

——, 'Monro, Harold Edward (1879–1932)', *Oxford Dictionary of National Biography*, 2004 [accessed online 3 January 2014].

Hilliard, Christopher, *English as a Vocation: The Scrutiny Movement* (Oxford: Oxford University Press, 2012).

——, 'The Twopenny Library: The Book Trade, Working-Class Readers, and "Middlebrow" Novels in Britain, 1930–42', *Twentieth Century British History*, 25.2 (2014), 199–220.

Horder, Mervyn, 'Grant Richards: Portent & Legend', *London Magazine*, April/May 1991, pp. 36–46.

Housman, Laurence, 'What Books for Travellers?', *Now & Then*, 20 (1926), 7–9.

Howard, Michael S., *Jonathan Cape, Publisher* (London: Cape, 1971).

Howsam, Leslie, 'Sustained Literary Ventures: The Series in Victorian Book Publishing', *Publishing History*, 31 (1992), 5–26.

Humble, Nicola, *The Feminine Middlebrow Novel, 1920s to 1950s: Class, Domesticity, and Bohemianism* (Oxford: Oxford University Press, 2001).

Jaillant, Lise, *Modernism, Middlebrow and the Literary Canon: The Modern Library Series, 1917–1955* (London: Routledge, 2014).

——, 'Sapper, Hodder & Stoughton, and the Popular Literature of the Great War', *Book History*, 14 (2011), 137–66.

——, 'Shucks, We've Got Glamour Girls Too! Gertrude Stein, Bennett Cerf and the Culture of Celebrity', *Journal of Modern Literature*, 39.1 (2015), 149–69.

Jones, Phyllis (ed.), *English Critical Essays – Twentieth Century* (London: Oxford University Press [World's Classics] 1933).

Joyce, James, *Dubliners* (New York: Modern Library, 1926).

——, *Dubliners* (London: Jonathan Cape [Travellers' Library], 1926).

——, *Letters of James Joyce*, ed. Stuart Gilbert, vol. 1 (New York: Viking Press, 1957), 3 vols.

——, *Letters of James Joyce*, ed. Richard Ellmann, vol. 2 and 3 (London: Faber & Faber, 1966), 3 vols.

Kammen, Michael G., *The Lively Arts: Gilbert Seldes and the Transformation of Cultural Criticism in the United States* (New York: Oxford University Press, 1996).

Kaufmann, Michael, 'A Modernism of One's Own: Virginia Woolf's *TLS* Reviews and Eliotic Modernism', in *Virginia Woolf and the Essay*, ed. Beth C. Rosenberg and Jeanne Dubino (New York: St. Martin's Press, 1997), pp. 137–55.

Kay, S. Lloyd, 'On the Selling of Books', *Publisher & Bookseller*, 5 July 1929, p. 18.

Keating, P. J., *The Haunted Study: A Social History of the English Novel 1875–1914* (London: Fontana, 1991).

King, Julia, and Laila Miletic-Vejzovic (eds), 'The Library of Leonard and Virginia Woolf', <http://ntserver1.wsulibs.wsu.edu/masc/onlinebooks/woolflibrary/woolflibraryonline.htm> [accessed 23 October 2016].

Kirkpatrick, B. J., and Stuart N. Clarke, *A Bibliography of Virginia Woolf*, 4th edn (Oxford: Clarendon Press, 1997).

Klein, Scott W., 'Note on the Text', *Tarr, by Wyndham Lewis* (Oxford: Oxford University Press [World's Classics], 2010), pp. xxx–xxxiii.

Kluger, Richard, and Phyllis Kluger, *The Paper: The Life and Death of the New York Herald Tribune* (New York: Knopf, 1986).

Krygier, J. B., 'Modern Library and Everyman's Library Simulacra?', *Makingmaps*, 20 March 2006, <http://makingmaps.owu.edu/simulacra/simulacra.html> [accessed 23 October 2016].

Lawrence, D. H., *The Letters of D. H. Lawrence*, ed. James T. Boulton and Lindeth Vasey, vol. 5 (Cambridge: Cambridge University Press, 1989).

——, *Twilight in Italy* (London: Jonathan Cape [Travellers' Library], 1926).

Lawrence, D. H, and Martin Secker, *Letters from D. H. Lawrence to Martin Secker 1911–1930* (Buckingham: Martin Secker, 1970).

Leavis, Q. D., *Fiction and the Reading Public* [1932] (London: Chatto & Windus, 1939).

Le Clert, Louis, *Le papier, recherches et notes pour servir à l'histoire du papier, principalement à Troyes et aux environs depuis le XIVe siècle*, 2 vols (Paris: A l'enseigne du Pégase, 1926).

Leick, Karen, 'Popular Modernism: Little Magazines and the American Daily Press', *PMLA: Publications of the Modern Language Association of America*, 123.1 (2008), 125–39.

Lewis, Wyndham, *Blasting and Bombardiering* (London: Calder & Boyars, 1967).

——, *Rude Assignment: A Narrative of My Career Up-to-Date* (London: Hutchinson, 1950).

——, *Tarr* (London: Chatto & Windus [Phoenix Library], 1928).

——, *Tarr: The 1918 Version*, ed. Paul O'Keeffe (Santa Rosa, CA: Black Sparrow Press, 1990).

——, *The Letters of Wyndham Lewis*, ed. W. K. Rose (London: Methuen, 1963).

Lidderdale, Jane, and Mary Nicholson, *Dear Miss Weaver: Harriet Shaw Weaver 1876–1961* (London: Faber & Faber, 1970).

Loukopoulou, Eleni, 'Joyce's Progress through London: Conquering the English Publishing Market', *James Joyce Quarterly*, 48.4 (2011), 683–710.

McCleery, Alistair, 'Tauchnitz and Albatross: A "Community of Interests" in English-Language Paperback Publishing, 1934–51', *Library: The Transactions of the Bibliographical Society*, 7.3 (2006), 297–316.

——, 'The Paperback Evolution: Tauchnitz, Albatross and Penguin', in *Judging a Book by Its Cover: Fans, Publishers, Designers, and the Marketing of Fiction*, ed. Nicole Matthews and Nickianne Moody (Aldershot: Ashgate, 2007), pp. 3–17.

McDonald, Gail, *Learning to Be Modern: Pound, Eliot, and the American University* (Oxford: Clarendon Press, 1993).

McDonald, Peter D., *British Literary Culture and Publishing Practice, 1880–1914* (Cambridge: Cambridge University Press, 1997).

McDowall, Arthur Sydney, 'Mrs Woolf and Sterne', *Times Literary Supplement*, 10 January 1929, p. 25.

McGann, Jerome J., *Black Riders: The Visible Language of Modernism* (Princeton: Princeton University Press, 1993).

——, *The Textual Condition* (Princeton: Princeton University Press, 1991).

MacKenzie, Raymond N., 'Penguin Books', in *British Literary Publishing Houses, 1881–1965*, ed. Rose and Anderson.

McWhirter, David (ed.), *Henry James's New York Edition: The Construction of Authorship* (Stanford: Stanford University Press, 1995).

Mao, Douglas, and Rebecca L. Walkowitz, 'The New Modernist Studies', *PMLA: Publications of the Modern Language Association of America*, 123.3 (2008), 737–48.

Materer, Timothy (ed.), *Pound/Lewis: The Letters of Ezra Pound and Wyndham Lewis* (New York: New Directions, 1985).

Maw, Martin, 'Milford, Sir Humphrey Sumner (1877–1952)', *Oxford Dictionary of National Biography*, 2004 [accessed online 1 October 2012].

Meyers, Jeffrey, *The Enemy: A Biography of Wyndham Lewis* (London: Routledge & Kegan Paul, 1980).

Milford, Humphrey (ed.), *Selected Modern English Essays* (London: Oxford University Press [World's Classics], 1925).

——, (ed.), *Selected Modern English Essays, Second Series* (London: Oxford University Press [World's Classics], 1932).

Monro, Harold, 'Introduction', *Twentieth Century Poetry: An Anthology* (London: Chatto & Windus [Phoenix Library], 1929), pp. 7–11.

Morpurgo, J. E., *Allen Lane, King Penguin: A Biography* (London: Hutchinson, 1979).

Morris, A. J. A., 'Edwards, John Passmore (1823–1911)', *Oxford Dictionary of National Biography*, 2004 [accessed online 30 July 2016].

Morrow, Bradford, and Bernard Lafourcade, *A Bibliography of the Writings of Wyndham Lewis* (Santa Barbara: Black Sparrow Press, 1978).

Mulhern, Francis, *The Moment of 'Scrutiny'* (London: NLB, 1979).

Mullin, Katherine, 'Poison More Deadly than Prussic Acid: Defining Obscenity after the 1857 Obscene Publications Act (1850–1885)', in *Prudes on the Prowl*, ed. Bradshaw and Potter, pp. 11–29.

Mumby, Frank A., 'Books that Count', *Manchester Courier*, 6 February 1914, p. 13.

——, *Publishing and Bookselling: A History from the Earliest Times to the Present Day*, 4th edn (London: Jonathan Cape, 1956).

Nash, Andrew, 'Literary Culture and Literary Publishing in Inter-War Britain: A View from Chatto & Windus', in *Literary Cultures and the Material Book*, ed. Simon Eliot, Andrew Nash, and I. R. Willison (London: British Library, 2007), pp. 323–42.

——, 'Sifting Out "Rubbish" in the Literature of the Twenties and Thirties: Chatto & Windus and the Phoenix Library', in *The Culture of the Publisher's Series*, ed. Spiers, vol. 1, pp. 188–201.

Nash, Andrew, and James Knowlson, 'Charles Prentice and T. F. Powys: A Publisher's Influence', *Powys Journal*, 12 (2002), 35–66.

Neavill, Gordon B., 'Publishing in Wartime: The Modern Library Series during the Second World War', *Library Trends*, 55.3 (2007), 583–96.

Nicolson, Harold, 'These Pocket Editions', *Fortnightly Review*, April 1932, pp. 521–4.

Nolan, Tom, 'The Continuing Saga of Everyman's Library', *Wall Street Journal*, 9 January 2007, <http://www.wsj.com/articles/SB116830737614170889> [accessed 23 October 2016].

Nowell-Smith, Simon, *International Copyright Law and the Publisher in the Reign of Queen Victoria* (Oxford: Clarendon Press, 1968).

Officer, Lawrence H., and Samuel H. Williamson, 'Five Ways to Compute the Relative Value of a UK Pound Amount, 1270 to Present', *MeasuringWorth*, 2016, <https://www.measuringworth.com/> [accessed 23 October 2016].

O'Keeffe, Paul, *Some Sort of Genius: A Life of Wyndham Lewis* (London: Jonathan Cape, 2000).

Olivero, Isabelle, *L'invention de la collection: de la diffusion de la littérature et des savoirs à la formation du citoyen au XIXe siècle* (Paris: Éditions de l'Imec; Éditions de la Maison des Sciences de l'Homme, 1999).

Omnium, Jacob, 'Under Cover', *Bookseller*, April 1926, p. 14.

Ormerod, David, John Cyril Smith, and Brian Hogan, *Smith and Hogan's Criminal Law* (Oxford: Oxford University Press, 2011).

Pinto, Peter, 'We Have Been Reading Lately', *Canadian Jewish Chronicle*, 8 June 1928, p. 6.

Pirie-Gordon, Harry, 'Detectives', *Times Literary Supplement*, 12 August 1926, pp. 529–30.

——, 'Detectives in Fiction', *Living Age*, 18 September 1926, pp. 638–43.

Pollnitz, Christopher, 'The Censorship and Transmission of D. H. Lawrence's "Pansies": The Home Office and the "Foul-Mouthed Fellow"', *Journal of Modern Literature*, 28.3 (2005), pp. 44–71.

Potter, Rachel, 'Censorship and Sovereignty (1916–1929)', in *Prudes on the Prowl*, ed. Bradshaw and Potter, pp. 71–89.

——, 'Introduction', in *Prudes on the Prowl*, ed. Bradshaw and Potter, pp. 1–10.

——, *Obscene Modernism: Literary Censorship and Experiment, 1900–1940* (Oxford: Oxford University Press, 2013).

Pound, Ezra, 'Past History', *English Journal*, 22.5 (1933), pp. 349–58.

Pound, Omar S., Philip Grover, and D. G. Bridson, *Wyndham Lewis: A Descriptive Bibliography* (Folkestone: Dawson, 1978).

Radway, Janice, *A Feeling for Books: The Book-of-the-Month Club, Literary Taste, and Middle-Class Desire* (Chapel Hill: University of North Carolina Press, 1997).

Rainey, Lawrence, *Institutions of Modernism: Literary Elites and Public Culture* (New Haven: Yale University Press, 1998).

Ramsden, J. H., 'Correspondence: The Bookseller as Censor', *Bookseller*, November 1926, p. 87.

Raymond, Harold, *Publishing and Bookselling: A Survey of Post-War Developments and Present-Day Problems* (London: J. M. Dent, 1938).

Rose, Jonathan, 'J. M. Dent and Sons; J. M. Dent and Company', in *British Literary Publishing Houses, 1881–1965*, ed. Rose and Anderson.

——, 'Jonathan Cape Limited; Jonathan Cape', in *British Literary Publishing Houses, 1881–1965*, ed. Rose and Anderson.

——, *The Intellectual Life of the British Working Classes* (New Haven: Yale University Press, 2001).

Rose, Jonathan, and Patricia Anderson (eds), *British Literary Publishing Houses, 1881–1965* (Detroit: Gale Research, 1991), Dictionary of Literary Biography, vol. 112, *Literature Resource Center* [accessed online 16 May 2014].

Rota, Cyril Bertram, 'Mrs Woolf's Writings', *Times Literary Supplement*, 20 December 1957, p. 780.

Rubin, Joan Shelley, *The Making of Middlebrow Culture* (Chapel Hill: University of North Carolina Press, 1992).

Rudd, John, 'The Poisoning of Youth', *English Review*, February 1926, pp. 216–21.

Sagar, Keith M., and James T. Boulton (eds), 'Introduction', *The Letters of D. H. Lawrence*, vol. 7 (Cambridge: Cambridge University Press, 2002), pp. 1–15.

Satterfield, Jay, *The World's Best Books: Taste, Culture, and the Modern Library* (Amherst: University of Massachusetts Press, 2002).

Schmoller, Hans, 'Reprints: Aldine and After', *The Penrose Annual*, 47 (1953), 35–8.

——, *Two Titans, Mardersteig and Tschichold: A Study in Contrasts* (New York: Typophiles, 1990).

Schneller, Beverly, 'Chatto & Windus; John Camden Hotten', in *British Literary Publishing Houses, 1820–1880*, ed. Anderson and Rose.

Scholes, Robert, 'Grant Richards to James Joyce', *Studies in Bibliography*, 16 (1963), 139–60.

Schreuders, Piet, *The Book of Paperbacks: a Visual History of the Paperback*, trans. Josh Pachter (London: Virgin Books, 1981).

Seldes, Gilbert, 'Extra Good Ones', *Dial*, June 1928, pp. 519–21.

——, 'Mr Eliot's Favourite', *Dial*, November 1928, pp. 437–40.

Sigel, Lisa Z., 'Censorship in Inter-War Britain: Obscenity, Spectacle, and the Workings of the Liberal State', *Journal of Social History*, 45.1 (2011), 61–83.

Sims, George, 'Grant Richards: Publisher', *Antiquarian Book Monthly Review*, January 1989, pp. 14–27.

Slocum, John J., and Herbert Cahoon, *A Bibliography of James Joyce, 1882–1941* (London: Rupert Hart-Davis, 1953).

Sloper, L. A., 'Bookman's Holiday: We Love the Modernists', *Christian Science Monitor*, 20 June 1931, p. 10.

Southworth, Helen (ed.), *Leonard and Virginia Woolf: The Hogarth Press and the Networks of Modernism* (Edinburgh: Edinburgh University Press, 2010).

Spiers, John (ed.), *The Culture of the Publisher's Series*, 2 vols (Basingstoke: Palgrave Macmillan, 2011).

Spoo, Robert, 'Unpublished Letters of Ezra Pound to James, Nora, and Stanislaus Joyce', *James Joyce Quarterly*, 32 (1995), 533–81.

Sterne, Laurence, *Sentimental Journey* (London: Oxford University Press [World's Classics], 1928).

Sturgeon, Stephen, 'Wyndham Lewis's *Tarr*: A Critical Edition' (PhD dissertation, Boston University, 2007).

Suarez, S. J., Michael F., 'Book History from Descriptive Bibliographies', in *The Cambridge Companion to the History of the Book*, ed. Leslie Howsam (Cambridge: Cambridge University Press, 2015), pp. 199–218.

Sullivan, Melissa, 'A Middlebrow Dame Commander: Rose Macaulay, the "Intellectual Aristocracy," and *The Towers of Trebizond*', *Yearbook of English Studies*, 42 (2012), 168–85.

Sullivan, Melissa, and Sophie Blanch, 'Introduction: The Middlebrow – Within or Without Modernism', *Modernist Cultures*, 6.1 (2011), 1–17.

Sutcliffe, Peter H., *The Oxford University Press: An Informal History* (Oxford: Clarendon Press, 1978).

Sutherland, John, 'Introduction', *The Moonstone, by Wilkie Collins* (Oxford: Oxford University Press [World's Classics], 2008), pp. vii–xxix.

Symbolum Apostolicum, a Facsimile after the Unique Copy in the Vienna National Library of the Earliest Known Block Book Printed in Colours (Paris: The Pegasus Press, 1927).

Tauchnitz Edition Collection of British and American Authors, *Publications of 1931* (Leipzig: Tauchnitz, 1932).

Taylor, Henry Archibald, *Jix, Viscount Brentford* (London: Stanley Paul & Co., 1933).

The Harvest, Being the Record of One Hundred Years of Publishing, 1837–1937 (Leipzig: Tauchnitz, 1937).

Thompson, F. M. L., 'Hicks, William Joynson-', *Oxford Dictionary of National Biography*, 2004, [accessed online 28 May 2014].

Todd, William B., 'A New Measure of Literary Excellence: The Tauchnitz International Editions 1841–1943', *Papers of the Bibliographical Society of America*, 78 (1984), 333–40.

——, 'Firma Tauchnitz: A Further Investigation', *Publishing History*, 2 (1977), 7–26.

Todd, William B., and Ann Bowden, *Tauchnitz International Editions in English, 1841–1955: A Bibliographical History* (New York: Bibliographical Society of America, 1988).

Todman, Daniel, *The Great War: Myth and Memory* (London: Hambledon and London, 2005).

Troy, Michele K. 'Behind the Scenes at the Albatross Press: A Modern Press for Modern Times', in *The Culture of the Publisher's Series*, ed. Spiers, vol. 1, pp. 202–18.

——, 'Books, Swords and Readers: The Albatross Press and the Third Reich', in *Angles on the English-Speaking World – Moveable Type, Mobile Nations: Interactions in Transnational Book History*, ed. Simon Frost and Robert W. Rix (Copenhagen: Museum Tusculanum Press – University of Copenhagen, 2010), pp. 55–72.

——, *Strange Bird: The Albatross Press and the Third Reich* (New Haven: Yale University Press, forthcoming 2017).

Trunz, Erich, 'Christian Wegner', *Die Zeit*, 22 January 1965, <http://www.zeit.de/1965/04/christian-wegner> [accessed 23 October 2016].

Tyler, Lisa, 'Cultural Conversations: Woolf's 1927 Review of Hemingway', *Journal of Modern Periodical Studies*, 6.1 (2015), 44–59.

Ward, A. C. (ed.), *A Book of American Verse* (London: Oxford University Press [World's Classics], 1935).

Wells, H. G., *Ann Veronica, a Modern Love Story* (New York: Harper & Brothers, 1909).

——, *Tono-Bungay* (London: Macmillan, 1909).

White, Eric B., *Transatlantic Avant-Gardes: Little Magazines and Localist Modernism* (Edinburgh: Edinburgh University Press, 2013).

Wild, Jonathan, ' "Insects in Letters": *John O'London's Weekly* and the New Reading Public', *Literature & History*, 15.2 (2006), 50–62.

Willis, J. H., *Leonard and Virginia Woolf as Publishers: The Hogarth Press, 1917–41* (Charlottesville: University Press of Virginia, 1992).

Willson Gordon, Elizabeth, 'Under the Imprint of the Hogarth Press: Material Texts and Virginia Woolf's Corporate Identity' (PhD dissertation, University of Alberta, 2007).

Wilson, Nicola, 'Boots Book-Lovers' Library and the Novel: The Impact of a Circulating Library Market on Twentieth-Century Fiction', *Information & Culture: A Journal of History*, 49.4 (2014), 427–49.

——, 'Circulating Morals (1900–1915)', in *Prudes on the Prowl*, ed. Bradshaw and Potter, pp. 52–70.

——, 'Virginia Woolf, Hugh Walpole, the Hogarth Press, and the Book Society', *ELH*, 79.1 (2012), 237–60.

Winterton, E., 'Circulating Libraries: A Paper Read before The Society of Bookmen', *Bookseller*, March 1926, pp. 61–3.

Woolf, Leonard, *Downhill All the Way: An Autobiography of the Years 1919–1939* (London: Hogarth Press, 1967).

Woolf, Virginia, 'Introduction', *Sentimental Journey, by Laurence Sterne* (London: Oxford University Press [World's Classics], 1928), pp. v–xvii.

——, 'Journeys in Spain', *Times Literary Supplement*, 26 May 1905, p. 167.

——, 'Modern Novels', *Times Literary Supplement*, 10 April 1919, p. 189.

——, 'Sterne', Review of *The Life and Times of Laurence Sterne*, by Wilbur L. Cross, *Times Literary Supplement*, 12 August 1909, p. 289.

——, *The Common Reader* (London: Hogarth Press, 1925).

——, *The Death of the Moth and Other Essays* (London: Hogarth Press, 1942).

——, *The Diary of Virginia Woolf 1915–1919*, ed. Anne Olivier Bell, vol. 1 (London: Hogarth Press, 1977).

——, *The Diary of Virginia Woolf 1925–1930*, ed. Anne Olivier Bell and Andrew McNeillie, vol. 3 (London: Hogarth Press, 1980).

——, *The Essays of Virginia Woolf*, ed. Andrew McNeillie and Stuart N. Clarke, 6 vols (London: Hogarth Press, 1986–2011).

——, *The Letters of Virginia Woolf*, ed. Nigel Nicolson and Joanne Trautmann, 6 vols (New York: Harcourt Brace, 1975–1980).

——, 'Tolstoy's *The Cossacks*', *Times Literary Supplement*, 1 February 1917, p. 55.

Wrong, E. M. (ed.), *Crime and Detection* (London: Oxford University Press [World's Classics], 1926).

Young, John, 'Canonicity and Commercialization in Woolf's Uniform Edition', in *Virginia Woolf: Turning the Centuries: Selected Papers from the Ninth Annual Conference on Virginia Woolf – University of Delaware, June 10–13, 1999*, ed.

Ann Ardis and Bonnie Kime Scott (New York: Pace University Press, 2000), pp. 236–43.

——, '"Murdering an Aunt or Two": Textual Practice and Narrative Form in Virginia Woolf's Metropolitan Market', in *Virginia Woolf and the Literary Marketplace*, ed. Jeanne Dubino (New York: Palgrave Macmillan, 2010), pp. 181–95.

Ziegfield, Richard, 'James Laughlin, The Art of Publishing No. 1, Part 1', *Paris Review*, Fall 1983, <http://www.theparisreview.org/interviews/3039/the-art-of-publishing-no-1-part-1-james-laughlin> [accessed 23 October 2016].

INDEX

Above the Dark Circus (Walpole, Hugh), 104

academia *see* university system

Adam's Breed (Hall, Radcliffe), 58

Adler, Elmer, 108

Aesop, 54
  The Satyr and the Traveller, 54

After Many a Summer (Huxley, Aldous), 142

Aiken, Conrad, 33

Albatross, 1, 4, 19, 60, 94–6, 105–16, 140–1
  bestsellers, 109, 112–14
  colophon, 108–10
  copyright and negotiations with original
    publishers, 60, 110–12, 141
  covers, 109–10, 114–15
  detective fiction and Crime Club series,
    95–6, 109, 113–15
  distribution, 110
  end of the series, 140–1
  influence on Penguin, 108–9, 115
  modern physical format, 96, 107,
    110–11
  obscenity and censorship, 107,
    111–13
  origins, 106–7
  presentation copies, 108–9
  relationship with small presses, 106,
    111–13
  royalties, 111–15

The Albatross Book of Living Verse
  (Untermeyer, Louis), 113

Aldington, Richard, 74, 77, 80, 100–3
  The Colonel's Daughter, 144
  Death of a Hero, 80, 101, 103, 144
  Medallions, 103

Allen, Grant, 24–5

Along the Road (Huxley, Aldous), 100

'Alpha of the Plough' [Gardiner, Alfred
  George], 16
  Pebbles on the Shore, 16

Altick, Richard, 6–7, 25

Anchor [paperbacks], 146

Ann Veronica (Wells, H. G.), 15–17

Anna Livia Plurabelle (Joyce, James), 60

Anna Lombard (Cross, Victoria), 130

Antic Hay (Huxley, Aldous), 100, 144

*Apes, Japes and Hitlerism: A Study and
  Bibliography of Wyndham Lewis*
  (Gawsworth, John), 89

archives, 3–4

Ardis, Ann, 1–2

Armadale (Collins, Wilkie), 32, 42

Armstrong, Tim, 34

Arnold, Matthew, 12